DATE DUE

JAN 16 '69			
MAR 29 '69			
MAR 14 '70			
JUL 10 '70			
OCT 19 '70			
MAR 27 '7			
AUG 1 3 '73			
GAYLORD			PRINTED IN U.S.A.

TEACHING ENGLISH
IN ELEMENTARY AND JUNIOR HIGH SCHOOLS

TEACHING ENGLISH IN ELEMENTARY AND JUNIOR HIGH SCHOOLS

A MANUAL OF METHOD

BY

PAUL KLAPPER, Ph. D.

PROFESSOR OF EDUCATION IN THE COLLEGE OF THE CITY OF NEW YORK;
AUTHOR OF "PRINCIPLES OF EDUCATIONAL PRACTICE," "TEACHING
CHILDREN TO READ," "THE TEACHING
OF ARITHMETIC," ETC.

NEW YORK

D. APPLETON AND COMPANY

COPYRIGHT, 1915, 1925, BY
D. APPLETON AND COMPANY

372.6
K66t

PRINTED IN THE UNITED STATES OF AMERICA

PREFACE

Teaching English in Elementary and Junior High Schools is not a perfunctory revision of an older text, but rather a carefully planned development of it undertaken to meet new educational needs and to include approved practices of the last decade. The aim throughout is to present methods of teaching English that train pupils in effective thinking, and stir them to fullest self-expression.

The first half of the book treats composition as an exercise in self-expression, which is the aim of every device that is suggested, and of every method that is evolved. Chapters I, II, III, IV and VIII show clearly that this aim is consistently carried out.

The discussion of the selection of composition subjects, the teaching of the organization of ideas, the consideration of methods of correcting compositions, and the teaching of grammar are rich in suggestions for teaching pupils to think. The art of composing is synonymous with the art of thinking. Self-expression that is not conditioned by rigorous and disciplined thinking produces mental flabbiness. Rigorous thinking that does not prompt self-expression is never a social force. It is the earnest endeavor of this text to indicate to teachers of English the means at their command for the development of that kind of self-expression that rests on a firm foundation of adequate thought.

A second aim of this book is to evolve a text in which educational theory and classroom practice are intimately and vitally related. Too long has pedagogical theory held aloof from actual teaching procedure. Theory without application is sterile. The presentation of mere teaching practices without the basis of sound theory is empty form that weakens teaching ability. The reader is referred to the treatment of the following vital subjects for illustration of this aim: gradation, motivation, project, the

v

correction of composition, functional grammar, the teaching of memory selections, drills in spelling, the selection of the model in composition, the spelling list, etc. Here will be found numerous detailed teaching suggestions and specific teaching procedures; and underlying each of these suggestions and procedures are sound psychological or educational principles clearly set forth. The teacher must not imitate blindly a suggested practice, but must master the fundamental principles that govern all classroom technique.

A third aim is to present specifically and concretely various means of making English alive. Such subjects as how to vitalize composition (Chap. VIII), projects (pages 168, 260), problems (pages 6, 11), communal themes in composition (pages 282, 168), the rooting of grammar in language needs (pages 306, 90), give ample evidence of the earnestness with which the author sought to meet this phase of his problem.

A fourth aim of this book is to give oral composition the place it must occupy in a progressive school course in English. Chapter IV does more than stress oral forms of composition. It sets forth a detailed method of teaching oral composition in a discussion replete with classroom illustrations. The teacher is not left to resolve a host of doubts—is oral composition a lesson in phonetics? is it an invitation to make audible the haphazard thoughts that flit through the mind? A definite technique and a considerable list of practical classroom practices not only give the teacher a definite mode of introducing the work, but also direct her imagination to new situations that open up a host of social subjects that invite free, full and vigorous self-expression.

The current movement for objective devices for measuring school achievement is given its proper emphasis in the volume. Chapter IX, "How to Measure Progress in Composition," sets forth, in detail, and with adequate illustrations, the scales that have been devised for the measurement of composition ability. Each important scale is critically evaluated in the light of revealing experience. Those unskilled in the use of these scales are given definite methods of procedure in order to develop expertness with these standard measurements. And finally, there is suggested a simple means of making a diagnostic evaluation of pupils' performance in composition.

In the chapters on Spelling, Increasing Vocabulary, Dictation and Grammar, the reader is given a summary of the educational tests thus far devised for measuring pupil progress in spelling, in formal English, and in grammatical usage. The illustrations, together with the critical analyses of these scales, give the teacher a reasonably comprehensive survey of what has been accomplished in this field of educational enterprise. A mode of making independent critical evaluations is suggested.

The book is planned to serve as a manual of method for teachers of the first nine years of the common school course. It discusses as fully and as specifically as it can the work of the elementary and the junior high-school grades.

The author begs to acknowledge his indebtedness to the many publishers who have generously given permission to reproduce graded specimens of educational tests that are here discussed. Specific acknowledgment is made in the appropriate places. Without this generous response to our request for their consent to quote fully and freely, much of the effectiveness of the presentation would have been lost. To them the author is as much indebted as he is to the many teachers who have experimented with various methods suggested by him and who have given encouragement and suggestion born of actual experience.

P. K.

CONTENTS

PREFACE v

PART I

THE EXPRESSIONAL ASPECT OF COMPOSITION

CHAPTER I

INTRODUCTORY CONSIDERATION

	PAGE
Composition a Natural Exercise	1
Composing Is Thinking	3
The Spirit in Composition Teaching	4
The Teaching Problems in Composition	6

CHAPTER II

INFORMAL COMPOSITION IN THE FIRST FOUR YEARS

ORAL CONVERSATION AND REPRODUCTION LESSONS . . . 10
   The Method Governed by the Basic Difficulties 10

ORAL WORK IN THE PRIMARY GRADES 12
   Conversation and Reproduction Lessons 12
   Opportunities for Oral Language Lesson 21

CHAPTER III

FORMAL COMPOSITION IN THE FIRST FOUR YEARS

The Need of Formal Language Drills 23
Memorization and Recitation 24
Learning the Necessary Language Facts 25
The Systematic Correction of Common Errors of Speech 32
Language Games and Pictures 36
Development of Efficiency in Early Language Work Is Slow and Difficult 37

WRITTEN WORK IN THE PRIMARY GRADES 40
   Its Minor Position 40
   The Transition from Oral to Written Composition . . 41

ix

CONTENTS

CHAPTER IV

COMPOSITION IN THE GRAMMAR GRADES

	PAGE
THE SELECTION OF A PROPER SUBJECT	45
The Method-whole in Composition	45
The Preparatory Period	46
THE SELECTION OF THE SUBJECT	47
The Sources of Subject-matter	47
ORAL COMPOSITION	65
Written Composition Must Be Subordinated	65
How to Emphasize Oral Composition	66
The Conduct of Oral Composition Lessons	69

CHAPTER V

COMPOSITION IN THE GRAMMAR GRADES
(*Continued*)

HOW SECURE ORGANIZATION AND SEQUENCE: THE OUTLINE	71
The Tendency to Ramble	71
The Principle of Organization Taught by the Outline	72
Values of the Outline	74
The Drill to Insure Mastery of the Outline	75
Cautions in Developing Outlines	78
How to Secure Variety in the Outlines	79
How Closely Shall the Outline Be Followed?	82
Limit the Scope of a Composition Subject	85
Supplementary Means of Developing Power of Organization	86

CHAPTER VI

COMPOSITION IN THE GRAMMAR GRADES
(*Continued*)

EXPRESSIONAL LIMITATIONS: THE MODEL	88
Group Teaching	89
The Outline	90
The Intimacy of Grammar and Composition	90
THE MODEL	92
Basic Principle of Teaching Language Through a Model	92
The Selection of the Model	93
General Treatment of the Model	101
How Closely Shall the Model Be Followed?	113
Should the Model Precede or Follow the Composition?	114
How to Prevent Slavish Imitation of the Model	116

CONTENTS

CHAPTER VII

THE CORRECTION OF WRITTEN COMPOSITIONS

	PAGE
The Period of Written Composition	125
THE PERIOD OF CORRECTION	129
Objects of Correction	129
The Time for Correction	130
Incorrect Method	130
The Method of Correcting Written Work	132
Seeming Limitations of the Method	134
Eliminating Individual Errors	134
Form vs. Content Correction	138
How Shall the Class Work Be Kept?	138
The Rewriting of Corrected Compositions	139

CHAPTER VIII

VITALIZING ORAL AND WRITTEN COMPOSITION

Introduction	141
Greater Emphasis on Letters	141
The Correspondence Should Treat of Actual Affairs of Real Life	142
The Correspondence Itself Should Be Real	143
The Class Journal with Its Board of Editors Elected or Selected	144
Use Debatable Topics	145
Aim at Variety of Form and Content	146
The Composition Project	168
The Teacher	171

CHAPTER IX

HOW TO MEASURE PROGRESS IN COMPOSITION

The Prevailing Method of Judging Ability in Composition	174
The Analyzed Judgment of the Teacher as a Basis for Rating Compositions	177
THE MEASUREMENT OF COMPOSITION ABILITY	181
The Hillegas Scale for Measuring Composition	181
Thorndike Extension of the Hillegas Scale	185
Trabue's Nassau County Supplement to the Hillegas Scale	188
Ballou's Harvard-Newton Scale	189
Breed and Frostic Scale	190
The Willing Scale	199
Van Wagenen's Composition Scale	200
The Lewis Scales	201
The Hudelson Scales	212
The Maximal and Typical Composition Scales	217

CONTENTS

	PAGE
Classification of Composition Scales	221
Outstanding Need of Scale for Oral Composition	221
How to Use a Composition Scale	221
The Educational Significance of Standard Scales	224
Instructional Value of Composition Scales	224
Supervisory Values of Composition Scales	228
Conclusions	231

PART II
THE FORMAL ASPECT OF COMPOSITION

CHAPTER X
THE TEACHING OF SPELLING

Expressional vs. Formal Aspect of Composition	232
Spelling Usually Tested, Not Taught	232
Objects of the Teaching of Spelling	233
Principles Guiding the Selection of Spelling Words	234
Source of Spelling Words	236
Grading Spelling Lists	239
The Grouping of Spelling Words	241
The Preliminary Testing of Words	242
Media of Presenting Spelling Words	244
Method of Teaching Spelling	250
Procedure in Teaching Words	250
Independent Study of Spelling	256
The Test in Spelling	257
Record of Misspelled Words	259
Enriching the Spelling List	259
Spelling Projects	260
Evaluating a Spelling Book	261

SCALES FOR MEASURING SPELLING ABILITY 262

The Ayres Scale and Buckingham Extension	262
Ashbaugh's Iowa Scales	263
Monroe's Timed Sentence Spelling Test	263
Morrison-McCall Spelling Scales	267
Values of Standard Spelling Lists	268

CHAPTER XI
THE MEANING AND USE OF NEW WORDS

THE ENRICHMENT OF VOCABULARY 271

Shall There Be Formal Instruction in the Meaning and Use of New Words?	271
Selection of the "Meaning and Use" List	272
Methods of Teaching Meaning of New Words	273
How Make the Use of New Words Habitual	276

CONTENTS

Definitions 278
The Supplementary Means of Increasing Vocabulary . . 280
Developing Mastery of the Dictionary Habit and The Dictionary Habit 283
Language Power and Intelligence 284

CHAPTER XII

DICTATION: TEACHING THE FORMAL ASPECT OF COMPOSITION

Objects of Dictation Lessons 285
The Choice of the Selection to Be Dictated 286
Procedure in the Dictation Lesson 288
The Unprepared Dictation 292

CHAPTER XIII

MEMORY GEMS: MEMORIZATION AND RECITATION

Value of Memory Gems 294
The Selection of the Memory Gem 295
Motivating the Memory Gems 296
Procedure in Memorizing Literary Gems 297
Retention Through Thought Rather than Through Memory Appeal 301
Aids to Memorization 302
The Recitation 302

CHAPTER XIV

THE VALUES OF FORMAL GRAMMAR

The Disputed Place of Grammar in the Modern Curriculum 305
Grammar a Discredited Subject 306
Values of Grammar 309
What to Emphasize in Language Teaching; Scientific Investigation 314
Charters' Diagnostic Language Test 315
Wilson's Language Error Test 316

CHAPTER XV

PRINCIPLES GOVERNING THE TEACHING OF GRAMMAR

Begin with the Sentence 319
Make the Work as Concrete and Practical as Possible 320
Shall the Method in Grammar Be Inductive or Deductive? 322
By Avoiding Stereotyped Definitions and Set Formulæ

CONTENTS

	PAGE
We are Saved from Another Erroneous Form of Teaching Grammar	329
The Application Step Is the Final Justification of Grammar and Must Be Accorded the Most Important Place in the Lesson	331
Function Should Be Made Focal in All Grammatical Analysis	333
Do Not Analyze for the Sake of Analysis	334
"False Syntax" Must Be Emphasized, for It Is an Effective Means of Applying the Facts of Grammar	335
Great Care Must Be Exercised in the Organization of Tests	336
Proper Reviews Are Essential for Successful Work in Grammar	342
The Textbook Must Be Used Frequently in the Teaching of Grammar	343
Careful Gradation is a Potent Factor in Removing Difficulties of Comprehension in Grammar	344
All Grammatical Forms and Functions Must Be Taught in the Same Association in Which They Will Be Used in Natural Speech	346
Summary: Place of Grammar in the Elementary Curriculum	349
INDEX	351

TEACHING ENGLISH
IN ELEMENTARY AND
JUNIOR HIGH SCHOOLS

TEACHING ENGLISH IN ELEMENTARY AND JUNIOR HIGH SCHOOLS

PART I

THE EXPRESSIONAL ASPECT OF COMPOSITION

CHAPTER I

INTRODUCTORY CONSIDERATION

Composition a Natural Exercise.—Composition is that exercise in which ideas are ordered in a rational sequence and then expressed in accordance with recognized standards of form. This broad conception of the term composition shows at once how varied the art of composing may be, for there are as many kinds of composition as there are forms of expression. He who is dramatizing an action that grips him, making a pictorial representation of a scene that thrills him, or translating in symbols of musical notation a melody or sentiment that charms him, is engaged in the art of composition as truly as if he were employing language, written or oral, to express this action or scene or sentiment. In each of these forms of art an individual must group his ideas in rational sequence and give expression to them in strict accord with standard forms. This study concerns itself with one phase only of the general art of composition, for it confines itself to verbal composition.

This theoretical definition has a very practical bearing on the work of the elementary school-teacher because it shows clearly how simple and natural is the art of composition. It strips composition of the mystery and of the stiff and forbidding formalism which usually accompany it. Children must be shown that they are constantly composing, that they have been constantly composing and that they will continue to compose as long as they participate in rational communication. Composition must be shown to them to be as necessary an activity as talking or walking. The child must be led to recognize that he has "composition ability" of no mean degree. Teachers, too, must realize that most children are not deficient in the art of composition. As we listen to a narrative of a ten-year-old lad who is giving his friend a verbal picture of the athletic game he saw, or to a description by his little sister, half his age, of the particular doll that has caught her fancy, we become convinced that the art of composition is not foreign to the child. In the formal classroom lesson the life of the informal narrative and the charm of the child's description are ruthlessly crushed by the formidable technical laws of grammar and rhetoric which are imposed upon children. How to transfer this native ability to compose, so manifest in informal

INTRODUCTORY CONSIDERATION

intercourse, to the formal language lessons, is the problem, the solution of which shall occupy the succeeding chapters.

Composing Is Thinking.—Composition gives the child a training in thinking. A well graded course in composition is a means of developing clear and sequential thought. But the thought activities of the pupil are developed in composition only as the pupil consistently expresses *himself*. Mental development through self expression is the very essence of the educative process.

Let us plan a business letter ordering goods. The pupils must image the whole situation clearly. What information must be sent to insure accurate and prompt filling of an order? A few well-directed questions elicited the following from a class examining catalogues and advertising pages of magazines:

1. *The specifications:* kind, color, size, grade, quantity, price of goods.
2. *Shipment:* (a) how? express? mail? freight? (b) to whom? to dealer directly or to his customer?
3. *Charge or payment:* (a) to be charged? (b) payment sent, if so, in what form, check or money order?
4. *Additional data.*

Clearly, such a lesson, even on so matter-of-fact a subject, directs imagination, teaches organization of ideas, emphasizes the significance of accurate use of words and leads to a richer understanding of a business situation. Since thinking is directing the flow of consciousness to a satisfying or a socially significant conclusion, a composition lesson is a means of teaching children to think.

The Spirit in Composition Teaching.—The failure or the success of a composition lesson is determined to a greater extent than in almost any other school subject, by the spirit in which the recitation is conceived and carried out. In order to insure the proper atmosphere and spirit *rapport* between pupils and teacher two general cautions must constantly be kept in mind.

1. *The Play Spirit Must Pervade the Composition Period.*—Composition is too often an unwelcome period to the child. It completely overwhelms him with technicalities and empty formalism. He is asked to write on topics that are far indeed from his sphere of life; there is little that he cares to say about them. If by chance the topic is one concerning which he feels an urgency to express himself, he finds that all pleasure of self-expression is lost, for he must be careful of his penmanship; he must spell words in accordance with a tradition that seems to obey no phonetic law; his verbs must show agreement with subjects; he must bear in mind punctuation, capitalization, the thousand annoying concerns and cares that make composition a burden in his school life. Composition is an art and, like all art, is conceived in the spirit of play and is designed to give intense pleasure. The composition of the classroom must be as attractive as any other art and as natural as play.

2. *Technique Must Be Subordinated to Expression.*—The second word of caution reminds the teacher that in a composition exercise, form must be subordinated to content. In the formal lesson the child

INTRODUCTORY CONSIDERATION

must be no more conscious of the laws of paragraphing, of sentence structure or of punctuation than he is conscious of these in the informal speech of his daily life. The child should learn the laws of sequence, coherence, narration and description as he learns the laws of an athletic game. In baseball, the child gives all attention to the playing, not to the science of the game; in the actual progress of the game the rules are mere incidentals. No boy has ever deliberately memorized the regulations governing various athletic activities; yet what a mastery of them he has developed! The science of the game and the niceties of form which the child acquires are unconscious results of constant playing for the sake of the game itself rather than for its technique. So, too, the laws of unity, development, suspension, ease, force — the whole series of rhetorical laws which constitute the literary technique so pretentiously imposed upon the child—should be learned through actual expression rather than through formal teaching. A composition lesson, conceived in any but this informal spirit, and conducted with a rigor and a formalism altogether too frequent in class instruction, must inevitably produce the stilted and lifeless effects which the average school child turns out. In the light of these two cautions which are sounded in the initial step in the study of methods of teaching composition, we cannot be too severe in our condemnation of the pedagogy which the educational system of one of our leading cities offered to its teachers in its manual. Although it is not part of the current manual of that city, its spirit still animates much of the work in elementary composition.

When any topic such as sugar, nickel, circulation of the blood or the indestructibility of matter has been as fully treated in a conversational lesson and review as may be thought expedient, the exercise in composition should immediately follow. This should be a class exercise. Care should be taken that the pupils do not make them so long as to prevent proper correction. To insure a proper variety of thought and expression it is necessary that the oral lesson which formed the basis of the composition should be so selected as to give a considerable number of interesting points or items. If injuriously frequent repetition and review are avoided the several pupils will recall different groups of items and all undue sameness will be prevented. When identical phrases or sentences are frequently found in the exercises they are unquestionable evidence of bad methods, both in the oral lessons and in the teaching of composition.

The Teaching Problems in Composition.—In the teaching of composition there is a threefold aim which must be achieved. We must now turn to each member of this triple problem to consider its importance and scope in class teaching.

The first aim in the teaching of composition is to stimulate a thought basis for expression. As the formal composition lesson begins, the sources of expression seem to dry up, and the children seem to have no problem in their lives that demands expression, no urgency that craves solution, no personal preference that prompts intercourse and an attempt at convincing others. This seeming dearth

INTRODUCTORY CONSIDERATION

of material worthy of expression does not present a very difficult teaching problem. A little thought and sympathetic insight into child life soon reveal a great number of topics that especially appeal to the imagination of growing children, to their love of story, of action, of biography. The child's emotions and interests are intense even if they are short-lived; his likes and dislikes are many though ever changing. The sympathetic and resourceful teacher therefore need never lack an appropriate subject for children's compositions.

The second problem is to teach our children the laws of expression, the standards of language. The child must learn and obey the rules prescribed by legitimate usage, by grammar, and rhetoric. Here, too, we have a comparatively simple pedagogical task. A little patience and skill will enable a teacher to teach any law of grammar or rhetoric appropriate to the age and capabilities of the children. If the first lesson does not bring comprehension, a second or a third period of graded and properly presented exercises will serve this end.

The third aim of composition teaching is to inculcate in the pupil the habit of employing in the expression of his ideas those laws and principles of composition that have been taught him. This is the most vital problem, for it is the crux in composition teaching. Any seventh-year pupil can be taught that double negatives are wrong, that a participle alone cannot be a predicate, but not every child can be readily trained to avoid "ain't got no," "I seen," or "he done"—expressions that have the force of years of constant use back of them.

Habit is the result of constant drill through regular and frequent repetitions. Class teaching is today so hampered by its inherent limitations that this drill in sufficient repetitions in composition lessons is almost impossible. Composition has a science and an art side. The science of composition the child can readily learn but the art of composition he acquires only after long, conscientious and laborious practice. It must also be remembered that the incorrect forms that are characteristic of the speech of children have already been habituated and, in many cases, are further strengthened by the influences of home and street. The teacher must realize the colossal task that confronts him in composition teaching in all cosmopolitan cities and towns. Teachers must learn to feel that they are teachers of composition first and foremost, that an error in English is primary, that inaccuracies in facts of history, geography or arithmetic may, and should, be subordinated to correctness of speech. Teachers in the departmental system who are responsible for only one or two subjects must bear this particular dictum in mind. The departmental teacher who teaches English must communicate with his colleagues, tell them the specific forms of speech that are being taught and thus secure their coöperation by asking them to constantly correct the speech of children in all subjects. Unless teachers consciously emphasize the application of the lessons of the English period in all lessons, it would be better to eliminate the formal teaching of language.

SUGGESTED READING[1]

CARPENTER, BAKER and SCOTT. The Teaching of English, pp. 75-81. Longmans, Green & Co.

HOSIC, JAMES F. The Elementary School Course in English, Introduction. University of Chicago Press.

LEONARD, STERLING A. English Composition as a Social Problem. Houghton, Mifflin Co.

PARKER, SAMUEL C. Types of Elementary Teaching and Learning, chap. XII. Ginn and Co.

RAPEER, L. W. How to Teach Elementary School Subjects. Chaps. IV and V by Hosic and McKinney. Charles Scribner's Sons.

---

[1] The bibliographies at the end of each chapter are not exhaustive. The aim is, rather, to suggest such reading as will amplify and elaborate the various phases of the subject treated in each chapter. Where the publisher is not mentioned, the reader will find the book or the reference listed at the end of a previous chapter.

CHAPTER II

INFORMAL COMPOSITION IN THE FIRST FOUR YEARS

ORAL CONVERSATION AND REPRODUCTION LESSONS

The Method Governed by the Basic Difficulties.—Before planning her method of presentation in a specific subject, a teacher must comprehend clearly the basic problems which confront her. The method she finally evolves must be such as is designed to meet these specific difficulties. The primary grade teacher feels herself completely overwhelmed by a host of puzzling conditions which the children create when the formal work in composition is begun. When finally systematized and simplified, these difficulties group themselves under three heads. What, then, are the basic difficulties which children present to the teacher of primary composition?

The initial problem is found in the fact that these children seem to have nothing to say in the dignified composition period. The noisy, active, talkative child is now a social vacuum. A second vexing problem is produced by the timidity and the backwardness of the child. The newness of the work, the strangeness of classroom procedure, the consciousness of personal limitations make these children unable to forget themselves, to come out of their shells, to lose themselves in the subject that the teacher suggests. It is obvious that much coaxing and emotional sympathy are necessary. The difficulty of these circumstances is increased by a third problem, viz., the deficiency of expression. The vocabularies of these children seem too meager to enable them to express themselves even if they have ideas that crave communication.

In the light of the basic difficulties that we have enumerated, what must the method of instruction be? The answer was suggested in the observation above: the method must be governed by these problems; it must seek to counteract them at every step in the lesson. With this end in view it can readily be seen that the method must be, in the main, an oral one—almost exclusively so in the first two years of the course—with only a crude attempt at written composition in the third year. It is through skillful oral instruction that the patient teacher strives to awaken in the mind of the child preferences and interests that crave expression; it is through the interest and the ingenuity of the treatment that she hopes to attract the child until he becomes so absorbed in the topic that he forgets himself and is thus no longer conscious of personal limitations, and talks freely and spontaneously; it is through proper gradation and organization of the oral lesson that a few words and expressions are made central in each topic and by dint of repetition become part of the child's vocabulary; it is through constant and untiring corrections in oral drills that incorrect forms of speech are undermined and finally eradicated. We must turn then to a consideration of the nature, the organization and the method of oral work in composition in the early grades.

ORAL WORK IN THE PRIMARY GRADES

A. Conversation and Reproduction Lessons.—1. *The Choice of a Subject.*—The most common form of oral composition is the conversation, and the reproduction lesson. The terms are self-explanatory and make formal definition unnecessary. The first problem that challenges the teacher's thought in these oral lessons is the choice of the proper subject. The teacher must exercise great care that she presents no subject that has a thought difficult for the child. It must be a topic with which the child is conversant and which immediately suggests a host of ideas in his mind, pressing for expression. Secondly, it must be a theme replete with action. Every sentence must have a "doing word" in the predicate. These immature minds find no fascination in qualities, observations and inferences. Thirdly, the topic must be, if possible, one about which the child has a preference. "Shall We Have a Relay Race or a Ring Game at Recess?" is bound to elicit an answer from a normal child. "The Kind of Dog I Want for My Pet," prompts eloquent speech in every boy.

It is well to select for this oral work a series of stories which are told by the teacher and are then used as material for reproduction lessons. These stories, properly selected, become a source of far-reaching values for the development of the child. They afford the child an informal and very agreeable means of developing sustained thought; they add to the child's stock of words and expressions; they introduce the child to idiomatic English; they give the children their heritage of fable, folklore and stories that have inspired the race to higher ideals of life; and finally they furnish excellent material for self-expression because these stories, by their interesting content, stir in each child a strong motive for communication.

2. *Mode of Treatment.*—Having selected a suitable topic for oral composition, the teacher is now occupied with the method of presenting it to the class, and with the conduct of the lesson. We must be sure that the facts of the topic are not the goal of the lesson, hence we need have little concern about how *exhaustively* the theme is treated. Take only the surface facts, talk about the topic rather than on the topic, follow a free and easy sequence if the children are happier in this development. *Freedom* is the keynote of the course of the lesson. Hence it must not be considered amiss if the pupils change details, or make personal additions or rational modifications. This is not a test period and the lesson must not be conducted in a "quiz" spirit. The main object is to arouse such interest and enthusiasm in the subject that the children will lose themselves in it.

Nevertheless, we must guard against mere prattle. The lesson must possess definite teaching characteristics. Chief among them we must mention the following:

a. Real Motive and Social Spirit. Unusual care must be taken to prevent the discussion from becoming perfunctory. Children must be made to feel that they are talking not because they must but because there is an urgency to communicate a conviction, to narrate a personal incident, or to give pleasure to others through the telling of interesting experiences. These promptings must serve to make the oral language work in the class as natural as oral communication in everyday life and thus infuse real motive into class discussions.

b. The Teacher's Aim. Before each discussion or reproduction the teacher must decide on the ultimate purpose of the lesson. If vocabulary is to be increased, what words are the children to acquire and what means must be adopted to make these words part of the pupils' expressional stock? If new type forms of phrases or sentences are to be learned, what shall the teacher do to introduce these naturally and frequently and to insure their use? It may be that the aim is to give pleasing content, stir imagination, provoke personal opinion—but in all cases the teacher must have an aim which molds the lesson and determines its organization.

c. Logical Organization. The theme must be unfolded with due regard to rational sequence of ideas.

d. All Children to Participate. It is necessary that every effort be made to have all children take active part in the discussion. Many lessons in oral compo-

INFORMAL COMPOSITION: FIRST FOUR YEARS

sition fail because the teacher neglects the backward and the diffident children who are crowded out of the lesson by the brighter and the more responsive pupils.

3. *Dramatization an Aid in Oral Reproduction and Conversation Exercises.*—The teacher who finds the diffidence of some of her children a vexing problem and a cause for their failure to participate in the class discussions and reproductions may enlist the enthusiasm of these timid pupils by an emphasis on dramatization. No appropriate theme that can be motorized should be overlooked, or, if selected, should be developed by exclusively verbal means. Dramatization has much to contribute to oral composition. It gives the retiring child a new interest in self-expression; it dispels ultra self-consciousness; it gives to expression a naturalness which it may otherwise lack and thus makes self-expression the pleasurable exercise that it is under normal conditions. But these ends of dramatization are lost unless it is spontaneous, and has its origin in the child's craving for motor expression. Successful classroom dramatization is free from affectation, and never degenerates into mere entertainment. In planning a lesson in oral composition, the teacher must seek to incorporate as many motor aids as possible for only then will the children be caught by the enthusiasm of the situation and experience the joy of communication.

4. *Systematization of the Daily Topics.*—The suggestion for freedom and spontaneity in the conduct of an oral composition lesson does not argue for a

lack of organization in these conversation and reproduction lessons. While the children are permitted to develop the topic in any way that gives maximum expression, the subjects that are offered must follow a rational system. Monotony is the pitfall that must constantly be avoided in all this work. The only way to guard against it and insure stimulating variety is to change the nature of the topic daily. Thus, on Monday, it is a personal experience; on Tuesday, it is an ethical topic; on Wednesday, a theme in nature study is selected; on Thursday, the reading lesson offers interesting material for reproduction; on Friday, an exposition of a process learned in the manual training period affords material for conversation. How varied a list the teacher has at her command may be seen from the following table:

Partial List of Appropriate Topics

1. Narration of Personal Experiences: "What I Saw Coming to School," "An Accident on the Street," "Going to a Fire," "The Game at Recess," "Our Outing to ———," etc.
2. Nature Study: Conversation Lessons on "Birds," "Insects," "Flowers," etc.; topics that form the assignment in the course of study for the grade.
3. Description: "Pets," "Playthings," "Pictures," "Places Visited," etc.
4. Story of the Occupations Seen in the Child's Environment: The work of the baker, shoemaker, carpenter, policeman, fireman, etc.

INFORMAL COMPOSITION: FIRST FOUR YEARS

5. Habits of Cleanliness: "How to Have Clean Teeth," "How to Look Bright and Attractive," etc.

6. Habits of Politeness: "How to Behave at Table," "How to Behave in a Conversation," etc.

7. Commands by Children to Class: Pupils take turn in giving orders to class at dismissals, at recess, while passing or collecting various materials, etc.

8. Reproduction of a Story: The original story may have been told by the teacher, read from a book to the class, or read by the children themselves.

9. Number Lessons and Number Games.

10. Exposition: "How to Set the Table," "How We Made a Picture Frame," "How to Make a Kite," etc.

11. Argumentative Conversation: "Where to Go on an Outing," "What Game to Play at Recess," etc.

12. Finding a Story in a Picture.

13. Guessing Riddles. The riddle is stated. Children try to justify their guesses. The author of the riddle proves them wrong. He gives the correct answer. The doubting pupil is answered.

14. Talking about poems on the same topic, for example, the wind. Read Stevenson's "The Wind" and "Windy Nights"; Field's "The Night Wind"; Stedman's "What the Wind Brings"; Howitt's "The Wind in a Frolic." Or, a discussion of the following lullabies: Tennyson's "Sweet and Low"; Field's "Japanese Lullaby," "Dutch Lullaby," "Norse Lullaby"; Holland's "Rock-a-Bye"; Scott's "Lullaby of an Infant Chief."

15. a. Complete a story the beginning of which is given.

b. Complete a story the bare outline of which is given:

Camping party retires for the night—approaching stranger—Rover on the watch—barks—scolded for his noise—barking persists—party aroused—stranger discovered—who is the stranger?

16. How to Be Helpful, (a) at home; (b) in school; (c) in your community.

17. Imaginary Conversation and Conversations on the Telephone: employer and applicant; calling the doctor on the telephone in an emergency, etc.

18. Dramatizations: The parts of a book in a quarrel; the holidays come to life; the seasons in a dispute, etc.

19. What would you say in answer to a letter?

20. Proverbs. A dozen well-known proverbs discussed; their meaning; their applications; which teach the same lesson; which illustrated in the life of Washington, of Columbus, of Edison, etc.

21. Biographies: real and imaginary.

22. Anecdotes narrated and interpreted.

23. The Best Jokes I Collected.

24. Imitation of Fables.

This is only a partial list to which the teacher can add by drawing on her fund of experience. It is submitted merely to show the primary teacher that despite the simplicity of the work and the limited mental resources of the children she nevertheless has material rich enough to afford interesting variety and an opportunity to break away from the dulling sameness which is characteristic of much of the oral composition work in the lower classes.

5. *How Do These Oral Lessons Solve the Basic Difficulties?*—We must now interpret these oral lessons as remedial measures for the difficulties that were outlined at the beginning of the chapter and show how they are designed to answer the needs of the teacher of primary composition. Let us review, briefly, the three problems, the children's lack of material for expression, their backwardness, and their expressional limitations. It is evident that the variety and the nature of the topics that are selected are designed to counteract the first two of these limitations for they give the child plenty of subject-matter that is intensely interesting and capable of arousing such enthusiasm as will transcend the bonds of self-consciousness. Once the child has caught the joy of self-expression, the final problems, limitations of vocabulary and inaccuracies of speech, can be solved. As each child errs, the teacher judiciously makes the correction. Constant repetition of the same corrections of typical errors will soon show positive results. In each topic the teacher selects a few words and expressions, possibly five or six, that are most peculiar to it. In the conversation and dramatization lesson of "How to Pass a Person," such expressions as "excuse me," "beg your pardon," "polite," "impolite," and "rude" are indelibly impressed upon the mind of the child through repetition. In the lesson "The Kind of Dog I Want for a Pet," such words

as "good appearance," "handsome," "brave," "courageous," "loyal," etc., are made central until the pupil carries them away as his own. The teacher must be ever ready to offer those words which each lesson is to contribute toward a richer vocabulary. As the child hesitates for want of a word, the teacher suggests it and thereby keeps the thought running in the pupil's mind and saves him from the paralyzing effect which a consciousness of his verbal limitations is sure to produce. But these results will not follow from a haphazard series of conversation lessons. The topics must be carefully selected and organized into a progressively graded series. Each lesson must be planned to enrich the vocabulary and to correct the most flagrant inaccuracies in the speech of young pupils.

6. *The Danger of Formalism in Early Work in English: Impression, Expression, Formal Instruction the Desired Sequence.*—The great danger in early composition lessons is the introduction of a crushing formalism which robs the lesson of all expressional pleasures and renders the topic under discussion a mere excuse for a drill in mastery of words or in idiomatic or grammatical forms. It must be remembered that all technical elements of speech must grow naturally out of preceding discussions of interesting themes. The steps in early language work can therefore be summed up as three: (a) *impression;* (b) *expression;* (c) *formal language instruction.*

The first concern of the teacher must be to stir the child's self-activity, so that it acquires a liberal stock of experiences, together with a rich imagery of all of them. Hence the lessons in nature study, in reading, in local history and geography and in manual training must be regarded as forming the first step in composition, for in all of these the child is acquiring a large variety of ideas. But class instruction in all these subjects that is properly motivated stirs in each child a desire to reproduce what it sees clearly or to communicate to others convictions that have been implanted. The more interesting the impression, the more intense is the child's yearning for expression. The expressional phases in all lessons must therefore be looked upon as exercises in composition, for they train children in the art of self-expression. Errors of vocabulary, of grammar, etc., made by children in the course of natural speech should now form the basis of formal instruction in English. To deviate from this order, *impression, expression, formal instruction,* is to court a formalism which deadens all language work in the grades.

Opportunities for Oral Language Lesson.—In concluding the chapter on conversation and reproduction lessons, we must again emphasize the principle that was made basic in the initial discussion, viz., the manifold opportunities that the teacher finds in the curriculum for giving children the necessary practice in language work. Every subject, even manual training and calisthenics, can be utilized as material for language lessons. The less we rely on the formal language period and the more we look upon all subjects in the curriculum as agents in developing the art of speech, the surer are we to give children the language proficiency that should ultimately be developed. In addition we must urge the values for composition, of memorization and recitation of selected prose and poetry. These memory selections give children, among other returns, models of correct speech, enlarged vocabularies and beautiful sentiments beautifully expressed. Unless we look upon the whole curriculum as a scheme to develop proficiency in language, formal composition lessons become both sterile and stupid.

SUGGESTED READING

The suggested reading for this chapter will be found at the end of Chapter III.

CHAPTER III

FORMAL COMPOSITION IN THE FIRST FOUR YEARS

The Need of Formal Language Drills.—The discussion of the teaching of composition in the first four years of the elementary course has thus far concerned itself exclusively with the means of stirring and sustaining natural and enthusiastic speech in the classroom. The method outlined in the preceding chapter sought therefore to free itself from all formalism, from all rules of language, and from conscious focalization on the technique of speech. The child saw no serious object in the conversation or reproduction lesson; the teacher, not the child, was aware of an attempt to introduce a series of model expressions, to occasion natural communication, or to increase vocabulary. We come now to a discussion of the more formal side of language work in the first half of the school course. If the environment of our pupils were thoroughly Americanized in language, as well as in customs and ideals, there would be no need of adding to the informal work in composition previously outlined for the early years. But when we realize the foreign influences and languages that make up the environment of many of our pupils, it becomes apparent that merely hearing correct and corrected speech in the classroom, will not serve to counteract the persistent impressions of incorrect speech which are borne in on the vast majority of children of foreign parentage. Even in the early years formal language lessons must be given, drills must be had on set language forms, and typical errors of speech must be systematically undermined and supplanted by correct forms. This formal work in the primary classes can take three forms, viz.: (1) *memorization and recitation,* (2) *teaching necessary language facts,* and (3) *correction of common errors of speech.* Let us turn to these in the order in which they are enumerated.

Memorization and Recitation.—It is obvious that memorization and recitation of properly selected prose and poetry tends, among other ends, to enrich a child's stock of words and phrases, to give him a series of interesting ideas and inspiring ideals in a form truly artistic, to train in organizing ideas and to discourage self-consciousness. The value of this form of language work in early classes is obvious, but the method that is followed determines the degree to which these ends are attained. Few lessons are as stilted and depressing as a perfunctory recitation of a memorized selection in which each child recites merely to satisfy the teacher that he has memorized the words and lines in proper sequence. As the method of conducting these lessons is treated fully in the latter part of the book, the reader is referred to a subsequent chapter.

FORMAL COMPOSITION: FIRST FOUR YEARS

Learning the Necessary Language Facts.—*Their Use for Certain Classes of Children.*—We took occasion to note in a preceding discussion that the child whose own language abounds with barbarisms, and whose environment tends to perpetuate these, must be given a series of language drills which will tend to teach the basic forms and constructions of our tongue. Mere imitation of the teacher's English is not efficacious, for it cannot counteract all the contrary forces in the child's environment. Rigorous and persistent drills are necessary to teach these children not to say: "I *brang* my books," "He *writ* his lessons," "He *hurted* himself," "It *growed* there," "*He learns me out*," "*It stands written*," "Every morning I *put myself on*" (dress myself), "*a* eye for *a* eye," "*five mans and six mans is eleven*," "*five gooses*," "This is *more heavier* than that," "The boys *is* good," "*Me and him* went," "*Me* hat and *me* coat is on the nail," etc. These errors are not imaginary. They form part of a list that the author gathered in the primary grades in one school. True, no one child made all of these errors, but every child heard all of them. It is evident that the informal work outlined in the preceding chapter lacks the vigor and the concentrated effort necessary to banish such barbarisms from the speech of these children.

Cautions in Early Language Lessons.—Great care must be taken in planning these formal drills for the early grades. There are a number of cautions that must be observed lest we dissipate the worth of these language lessons.

THE TEACHING OF ENGLISH

1. The teacher must realize that these drills on language forms are not lessons in elementary grammar. No attempt must be made to introduce terminology or rules. It is not necessary that the child know why *"me* hat and *me* coat" must give way to *"my* hat and *my* coat." In the grammar lesson, the justification for the use of the possessive form *"my,"* and the reasons for the condemnation of the objective form, *"me,"* must be given; in these early lessons the child takes language forms on faith and the teacher is concerned primarily with the problem of developing in the pupils the habit of using *"my"* rather than *"me"* in these expressions.

2. It must be remembered that an isolated language form does not become part of spontaneous speech. The child who recites "my hat," "my coat," "my book," "my ring," etc., nevertheless falls back to "You should have seen *'me'* team play," when engaged in natural conversation. Unless the form is taught in natural context, it will not serve to rehabilitate the speech of the child.

3. It is obvious that an occasional lesson on any correct form of speech will not insure its use. Unremitting drills, well-graded and varied drills are necessary to put our pupils on their guard against the influences of the incorrect language that may assail their ears.

4. The supervisor of this work must remember that this part of the curriculum must be very flexible, for the language facts to be taught vary with each school district in the cosmopolitan cities and

FORMAL COMPOSITION: FIRST FOUR YEARS

towns of the country. It is evident, therefore, that in some schools the list of language facts to be taught will be long, while in others it will reduce itself to only a very few facts, or even none at all.

Method of Teaching Necessary Language Facts.— It remains for us therefore to indicate clearly how these necessary language facts are to be taught. To give this work natural context, it is best to group these language drills around a motivating center. A few illustrative themes are here suggested: What men do for a living. What does our Board of Health do for us? What kind of men and women do we honor? What do proverbs tell us? What does America do for its foreign population? What can her foreigners do for America? How did school pupils help win the war? How can we develop habits of thrift? What expressions best describe a thunderstorm, a snowstorm, a busy street corner? What advice would we give to avoid street accidents, fires, ill-health?

Let us develop the necessary language facts around the first topic in the list above. The teacher announced the topic. After a few questions or judicious suggestions, she obtained from the pupils the following:

"The farmer plants corn and wheat."

"Soldiers fight battles."

"The jeweler makes rings and pins,"

"We honor those who think of others," etc.

At the next lesson the problem was to list what the city does for us. In like manner the following was obtained from a fourth-year class:

"New York City gives us many parks."

"It sends its children to school."

"Its fire department puts out many fires."

"Its health department saves many lives."

Each lesson, limited to about ten minutes, develops a series of related sentences. Care must be taken not to allow these sentences to become heterogeneous; each day's work must have its distinctive center around which these sentences are grouped. Interest in the work is sustained by the variety of ideas contributed.

After children can give sentences with a fair degree of fluency, each group of expressions may be reviewed in an exercise in which they try to find the "who" or "what" word and the "doing" word of each sentence. *"The farmers plant corn and wheat"* is therefore submitted to this analysis and the children conclude that *farmers* is the "who" word and *plant* the "doing" word. In like manner, *"New York City gives people many parks"* is analyzed, and the children conclude that *New York City* is the "what" word and *gives* the "doing" word. This exercise is continued for a number of lessons until children gain facility in recognizing subject and predicate.

The next step in the lesson is to take known sentences and require the children to keep the "doing" word and change the "who" or "what" word. *"The fire department puts out many fires"* thus becomes, *"The firemen put out many fires," "Policemen put out many fires," "Brave men put out many fires,"* etc. In the same way children are required to keep the "who" or "what" word and change the "doing" word.

FORMAL COMPOSITION: FIRST FOUR YEARS

The original sentence quoted above then becomes, *"The fire department saves many lives," "The fire department answers the fire alarms," "The fire department sends out the engines,"* etc. Such synthetic exercises give children practice in making sentences and develop in them a feeling for the function of the subject and predicate.

The next progressive set of drills requires a change of number of the "who" or "what" word. Thus, for the first of these drills the teacher gives only regular nouns, the plurals of which are formed merely by adding "s" or "es." The sentence *"The farmers plant corn and wheat"* is written on the board and the children are required to change to the singular, *"The farmer plants corn and wheat";* or the teacher may give the singular, *"The jeweler makes rings and pins,"* and ask for the plural, *"The jewelers make rings and pins."* In the succeeding drills the children learn of nouns, the plurals of which are formed by changing "y" to "i" and adding "es"; of others where "f" is changed to "v," and "es" is added, and of still others that must be changed in form entirely, like "ox, oxen," "tooth, teeth," "child, children," etc. In this series of drills the child not only learns the plurals of useful nouns but also develops a sensitivity for the agreement of subject and predicate. After much repetition the child learns that it is wrong to say "the farmers plants," just as it is incorrect to say "many tooths." In neither case does the teacher give the reason.

Up to this point the sentences have been declarative

THE TEACHING OF ENGLISH

in form. Interrogative sentences are now taken up. The teacher asks, *"Do the farmers plant their corn?"* and, *"Does the farmer plant his corn?"* and the children reply respectively, *"Yes, they do plant their corn,"* and *"Yes, he does plant his corn."* The same groups of sentences are now reviewed in their interrogative form and the child receives further drill on plural forms, learns the use of the auxiliary "do," which is peculiar to the English language and acquires a feeling for the agreement in number of pronoun and antecedent.

The negative statements are now the subjects for a series of graded drills. The teacher asks, *"Do farmers waste any time?"* and the children reply, *"No, they do not waste any time,"* or, *"No, he does not waste any time,"* if the singular is required. These negative drills, given patiently and consistently, will undermine the double negative, so frequent in the speech of those children whose English is acquired on the street.

Similar sentences now introduce the forms of important irregular verbs by indicating in a simple way a change in tense. Thus, *"The farmer now brings his plow,"* and *"To-day, it costs the farmer much money to raise his crop,"* become, *"The farmer then brought his plow"* or *"It has always cost the farmer . . ."* In like manner, the correct use of regular and irregular adjectives and adverbs and their comparisons can be taught. Let us sum up the important language forms that can be taught in these highly informal and non-technical lessons.

FORMAL COMPOSITION: FIRST FOUR YEARS

1. Ability to sustain a central thought or theme.—"The Park": The park is large. Its trees are tall and beautiful. The fountain sends its spray high into the air. . . . It is wrong to throw litter on the lawns . . . etc.

2. Knowledge of parts of a sentence through analysis showing "who" or "what" word, "doing" or "being" word and "quality" word.

3. Knowledge of sentence forms: declarative, interrogative, negative, positive, etc.

4. Ability to make full sentences from such expressions as, *the green grass, the tall trees,* etc.

5. Vocabulary increased. (a) State whether the following things are hard or soft, cool or warm, large or small, rough or smooth, etc. Give a list of nouns, and elicit the sentences from the children. (b) State opposite qualities or state other words to express the same quality: The day is *warm*, The day is *cool*, The day is *chilly*.

6. Plural and singular forms of nouns and pronouns.

7. Interrogative form and use of auxiliary *do*.

8. Negative statements and the avoidance of double negative.

9. Important agreement, noun and verb; pronoun and antecedent.

10. Irregular forms of important verbs.

11. Use of adjectives and adverbs.

12. Correct form of comparative and superlative degrees of irregular adjectives and adverbs.

13. Change from active to passive voice and the necessary changes involved.

14. A feeling for the sentence is developed.

15. Habituation of correct forms of the type of: "There *are* many . . ." "This *is* one who . . ." "I *have* a cold," but, "I *got* my reward." "He fell *off* the pier," *"He doesn't,"* and, *"they don't,"* etc.

Here we have, then, in non-technical form the minimum essentials of English grammar. Drills which habituate these language forms not only insure speech of reasonable correctness but also give the child a solid basis for advanced work in formal grammar and composition. This method, with obvious adaptations, is very effective with adult foreigners who have had a year or less of instruction in evening schools.

The Systematic Correction of Common Errors of Speech. —*When Necessary.*—There are two methods of teaching children the necessary language facts and instilling in them habits of correct form in elementary language structures. The first is by the method just outlined—by a systematic, graded, positive series of drills on language forms. The second method is the negative which teaches only those language forms that children habitually misuse. The first is the method of prevention; the second the method of cure. Courses of study in cosmopolitan cities prescribe the systematic correction of typical errors of speech for all grades beginning with the second or the third year.

Limitations in the Prevailing Method of Dealing with Common Errors of Speech.—What is the usual method which teachers follow in their attempt to rid the speech of their pupils of the typical mistakes? Very often a teacher culls all the common language errors which experience has taught her abound in children's speech. These are taken up, one by one, corrected arbitrarily, drilled on in appropriate exercises and dismissed for a second common error which is similarly treated in the next language drill. One day the lesson is on "seen and saw," a second on "done and did," a third on "haven't no," a fourth on "brang and brung," until every error on the list has been dignified by a separate period. Very often, the lesson ends with an arbitrary generalization of the type, "Seen can be used only with *have* or *has*."

What is the usual result of such pedagogical practice? In each grade the entire list of common errors is corrected but in each succeeding grade the very same errors are again studied with the same futile result. There are two reasons which account for this waste. The first reason is lack of drill. We need a sledge-hammer blow; the common method of dealing with these errors of speech makes them all pass before the class in a happy merry-go-round while we apply the feather duster to each. These incorrect forms are habits; the problem confronting us is how to break an old habit and inculcate a new one. Hard unrelenting drill, untiring repetition, are the price of habit formation. The prevailing method described above surely fails to pay the price. Secondly, the lessons are too formal. The drills are not natural enough, nor are the correct forms learned through natural context in the course of natural expression.

A Method of Dealing with Common Errors of Speech.—What mode of teaching can we suggest in dealing with common inaccuracies of speech? The following procedure offers a more rational and natural form of exercise and also provides sufficient drill. All the common errors found in children's oral speech and written work should be listed and arranged in a graded series by the supervisor. Such a tabulation would give about thirty to thirty-six common forms that children constantly misuse. Each grade, beginning with the second year, should have a definite number of these errors assigned, three or four in the lower grades, five or six, in addition to a review of those already studied, in the higher grades. With responsibility limited to five or six forms, each teacher could give such drill and application as would permanently undermine these common errors. Let us assume that the teacher of a third-year class must undermine, (1) "it is me," (2) double negative, (3) "I seen it," (4) "I done it," and (5) "I brang my lunch." The first error is selected for study and drill. The teacher puts on the board or better still on a long cardboard the following model sentence: "It is I who am knocking," said Little Red Riding Hood. Then comes the following drill:

Teacher: "What was Little Red Riding Hood asked?"
Pupil: "Who is knocking?"
Teacher: "What did she reply?"
Pupil: "It is me."
Teacher: "Look at the blackboard." The child who made the mistake is given a chance to correct his answer.
Teacher: "William, who spoke when——"
Pupil: "It was me."
Teacher: "Answer as Red Riding Hood would."
Pupil: "It was I who spoke," etc.

The type sentence is kept in full view of the class for a week or two, depending upon the gravity of the error and the frequency of misuse of the correct form. It becomes the basis of short daily drills of two or three minutes in the morning and again in the afternoon. Other model sentences of the same grammatical construction are presented and the drills are continued. The initial sentence seems to become part of the children for it is a permanent standard for reference in the future. At any time when the child gives the objective "me" for the nominative "I," the teacher simply refers to the standard sentence by asking, "What did Little Red Riding Hood say? Now correct your own sentence."

In the same way, this series of drill lessons is followed by, " 'I am not afraid; I have no fear,' said the brave Columbus." This becomes the standard or type sentence for a series of questions in which the child is asked, "Have you money?" "Have you paper and pencil?" "Has he courage?" etc. In each case the teacher requires the two forms of expressing the negative. The child may reply, "I have no fear" or "I haven't any fear," but he is led to avoid, "I haven't no fear." These daily drills are again continued for about a fortnight, when the correct form of the negative becomes part of the child's expressional stock. When, in the future, a pupil tells his teacher, "I haven't no pencil," he is promptly told to recall the type sentence about Columbus and model his answer accordingly. In such a method of organization and procedure the necessary continued and persistent drill can be given to each error, and natural context is used to make permanent the correct form. Each teacher can now be held responsible because the assignments are definite for each grade. Through such a method the flagrant errors of common speech can be eradicated by the time the child completes his fifth year in the elementary course, and teachers in the last three years would then be spared the discouraging task of repeating the unsuccessful work of so many lower grades in addition to teaching the advanced language lessons which presuppose a foundation of elementary knowledge.

Language Games and Pictures.—It is obvious that auxiliary aids are necessary to vitalize these persistent drills in language forms. Any games played by children, such as relay races, baseball, tag, catch the ball, etc., can be adapted for drill purposes. One child who is *"It"* is not permitted to see whom the class monitor touches. *"It"* must then guess who was tagged. *"Was it you, Sophie?"* he asks. To this Sophie replies, *"No, it was not I."* The first child who says *"it was me"* or *"it was not me"* becomes *"It."* Should *"It"* guess the child tagged, he becomes monitor.

Another device is to use pictures that focalize attention on the correct form. Thus, these simple representations show the difference between *off* and *from:*

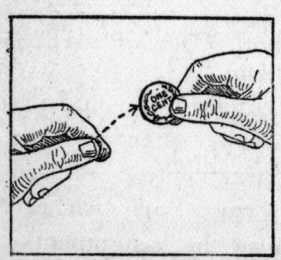 

HE TOOK A CENT FROM ME   THE CENT FELL OFF THE TABLE

FORMAL COMPOSITION: FIRST FOUR YEARS

A word of caution is necessary. Merely labelling a prescribed procedure a game does not make it one. Unless the game played is real and the child's pleasure spontaneous, it is no better than the unmotivated drill. Nor must the game become so elaborate that its procedure overshadows the language form. Drill lessons will always be with us. Too often, in our efforts to lessen the monotony of the work, we completely destroy them.

Development of Efficiency in Early Language Work Is Slow and Difficult.—Throughout the slow, tedious and persistent drills that characterize the language lessons of the early grades, the teacher must not become discouraged. Experience alone can impress the teacher with the slowness and the difficulty of developing efficiency in oral expression among children. The teacher inexperienced in this phase of elementary instruction loses heart at the slow rate of progress in the linguistic development of her pupils. But this slow maturing efficiency in language is to be expected when we consider the many causes that are operative in producing it. We must now turn to them.

1. *Efficiency in Oral Expression Is Usually Special, not General.*—People often speak fluently and coherently on one subject but are exceedingly poor in conversational powers on other topics. The proverbial example of the professor who is an interesting speaker in his specialty but a bore in other fields of human interest, illustrates this phenomenon. There are students who are exceedingly intelligent in dis-

cussing athletic topics but who are inane when they participate in general class discussions. Children who are alert and winning in speech during play may show a decided lack of linguistic ability in formal classroom recitation.

2. *Efficiency of Speech Is Often a Native Endowment.*—Linguistic ability is with many children a birth gift. This explains why so many people are delightful speakers on any topic and can spin a clever verbal thread around any idea. We listen to them with rapt attention, giving ourselves to their every word, only to find in the end that they have contributed nothing of value.

3. *Oral Speech Is Usually Developed as Need Is Felt.*—The individual who lives a life of social contact that prompts expression soon finds that the ability to express himself grows in proportion to need and use. Country children are hence more retiring and less communicative than their talkative and impulsive city cousins.

4. *The School May Repress Linguistic Development.*—The school with its organization and discipline, recognizing not the individual but the group, is usually repressive. Free and spontaneous speech is not allowed; the child as a member of a class has not the opportunity to express himself as often as he ought to, and finally the systematic recitation kills voluntary speech, for the child must express the book or the teacher rather than himself.

Lessons for the School.—This analysis of the causes of slow and labored development of efficiency in oral expression has its lessons for the school. (a) It shows us clearly that every study must be a language lesson. Correct speech cannot be habituated unless we make this concession to the place of English in the curriculum. (b) Wherever possible, children should be encouraged to talk freely in the course of the recitation. Topics assigned to a pupil should be broad and should call for expression in a number of sentences. The recitation that is made up of a series of close-fitting petty questions, whose answers require the mere ejaculation of a word or a phrase, is a means of repressing speech and retarding linguistic progress. The topical method, rather than the petty question method of the recitation, should be followed wherever convenient and practical. (c) Overconscientious and painfully accurate teachers must remember that it is not advisable to curb the child's flow of speech by minute corrections. Let the child have his say, let him speak his mind, then offer the corrections, the changes, and the modifications that are necessary. There is no reason why the child should always be interrupted with such petty suggestions as, "Answer in a full sentence." This sacred regard for the "full sentence" produces artificiality and stiltedness of speech characteristic of classroom recitations. Adults do not always speak in complete sentences; what justification have we for imposing this standard on pupils? (d) Finally, teachers should always encourage fluent and coherent speech among children. If we are to seek the larger values in our work, petty facts must be sacrificed for proper form. When a child formulates his answer in well-rounded, sequential sentences, it must be received with words of praise and held up to the others in his class as an enviable model worthy of their imitation.

WRITTEN WORK IN THE PRIMARY GRADES

Its Minor Position.—In the early years written composition can be accorded, at best, a subordinate place when compared to the varied forms of oral exercise. Too early an insistence on written composition works irreparable harm. The child loses in expressional power, for when the difficulties of penmanship, form, spelling, capitalization and punctuation confront him, all expression is at once killed. We must wait until the elementary requirements in spelling, capitalization, penmanship, etc., have become habituated before written work is begun. Written composition in the first three years is hence almost negligible, for the child is then acquiring technical and formal habits in language. It is in the fourth year that the written work assumes any seriousness of form and content, for now written compositions of two paragraphs should be attempted. The methods to be suggested are very much like those that we shall study for the upper grades with, however, such modifications as common-sense and practical experience would dictate. Thus, for example, in the primary classes the child follows the model more faithfully, imitation is more slavish, the preparatory oral drill deals with a greater number of details of spelling, capitalization, punctuation, etc., and the models are imitated for their very form as well as for their spirit.

The Transition from Oral to Written Composition.— It is well, however, to note how the first written composition is to be introduced, how the transition is to be made so that whatever efficiency the child has acquired in oral expression can be transferred to the written exercises. It must be remembered that ability in oral expression is no guarantee of equal efficiency in written expression. Graphic expression differs psychologically as well as physiologically from oral expression. This is why children efficient in oral composition find that all ideas seem to disappear instantaneously when they are confronted with pen and paper. How shall we aid them in their difficulty?

Let the teacher assign the topic, "Yesterday's Fire Drill," and put it on the blackboard. The children are now told that they are to write a composition on it, hence they copy the title on their papers. The teacher then puts on the board the first question, the answer of which will be the first sentence of their composition. The questions are so worded that they contain the words and phrases necessary in the formulation of the answer. After the answer is elicited orally the children write it on their papers. The following form may be used both for the blackboard work of the teacher and the children's exercise on paper:

THE TEACHING OF ENGLISH

Teacher's Blackboard Questions	*Children's Answers on Paper*
1. Did we have a fire drill yesterday? 2. Did the four bells ring out loud and clear? 3. Did you know whether there was a fire or not? 4. Were the children quiet and quick? 5. Was the teacher pleased with the drill?	1. We had a fire drill yesterday. 2. The four bells rang out loud and clear. 3. We did not know whether there was a fire or not. 4. The children were quiet and quick. 5. The teacher was pleased with the drill.

The answers written by the children are only transcripts of the words used by the teacher. Nevertheless, when taken together, they show good sequence and make up a well-organized paragraph.

Another transitional device is to ask pupils to write a composition which requires only a few minor changes in a model that is before them. Thus, a simple letter, inviting a friend to one's birthday party, is put on the board. The pupils are then asked to write a letter, patterned after the one before them, inviting a cousin to a birthday party of a much younger brother or sister who cannot write. It is obvious that almost all of the model on the board will be appropriated by these pupils.

These methods are pursued until some confidence is developed and transitional difficulties are in a measure overcome. After that, the model is presented and studied, transcribed or imitated as the case may require, but the general method will be only a modification of the procedure to be suggested for the grammar grades.

SUGGESTED READING

Bolenius, Emma M. Everyday English Composition. American Book Co.

Carpenter, Baker and Scott. The Teaching of English, pp. 121-144.

Chubb, P. The Teaching of English, chaps. III and IV. The Macmillan Co.

Cooley, Alice W. Language Teaching in the Grades, especially chap. III. Houghton-Mifflin Co.

Driggs, Howard R. Live Language Lessons. University Publication Co.

Hosic, James F. The Elementary School Course in English, pp. 11-26; pp. 57-96. University of Chicago Press.

Klapper and London. Modern English. Book I. Revised Emerson and Bender text. The Macmillan Co.

O'Shea, M. V. Linguistic Development and Education, chaps. I, II, VI, X, XI, XII. The Macmillan Co.

——. Elementary School Curriculum, First Year, *Teachers' College Record*, Jan., 1906.

Pearson and Kirchwey. Essentials of English, I, II. American Book Co.

SIMONS, ORR and GIVEN. Better English, Book I. John C. Winston Co.

WOHLFARTH-MAHONEY. Self Help English Lessons, Book I. World Book Co., Yonkers, N. Y.

YOUNG and MEMMOTT. Methods in Elementary English, also Good English in Speaking and Writing, Fourth Year. D. Appleton & Co.

CHAPTER IV

COMPOSITION IN THE GRAMMAR GRADES

THE SELECTION OF A PROPER SUBJECT

The Method-whole in Composition.—Careful and thorough treatment of a composition lesson necessitates three periods that are distinct in aim and procedure. Briefly we may characterize these as follows: (1) the *period of oral preparation* in which the science of composition is taught—this is the oral teaching period in which the teacher leads and the child is learning the laws of language; (2) the *period of written composition* in which the child is given every opportunity to express himself and acquire the art of composition, and (3) *the period of correction,* the aim and scope of which are apparent.

These three periods are usually given on three separate days but any two of these may follow on the same day as the exigencies of special circumstances and classes may demand. The teacher seeking constructive programs of work need hardly be reminded that no method has universal application *in toto*. Some parts must be omitted, others modified, and new devices introduced to adjust any method to the specific problems of a particular class. But every method that merits pedagogical approval is based on sound principle and worthy aim. In applying a method, the teacher must be sure that despite the changes and the additions that are made, the justifying principle has been retained. Any method that is not subjected to personal scrutiny, to modification in an attempt to adjust it to specific needs, becomes a pedagogical strait-jacket and inevitably leads to failure.

The Preparatory Period.—The method of teaching composition in the grammar grades is determined by the same considerations as those which govern the method in the primary grades, viz., the basic difficulties that confront the children. We must stop, therefore, to note the problems that make composition teaching a difficult task for the teacher. In the main we may group these under three heads:

1. *Lack of Material Worth Expressing.*—At first thought this difficulty seems slight and only of passing importance, but a moment's consideration brings conviction to the contrary. College students when asked to select their own topics for debates, essays, and the like, experience a feeling of hopelessness as they take mental stock. They have many ideas, they have studied many subjects, but none of them seems big and urgent, and worthy of expression. If this is true of students who have attained some degree of maturity and whose minds have been subjected to the broadening influence of study, how true is it of the child with immature mind and narrow personal aspect of the world.

2. *Lack of Organization of Ideas.*—Children do not feel the need for sequence and systematization of facts. They ramble through their subject in aimless, discursive style; they do not know that "to compose" one must systematize his ideas before giving expression to them.

3. *Limitations of Speech.*—Having met the first two difficulties, we are confronted by the third—expressional deficiencies. These may be summed up under (a) involved and confused forms of expression, (b) incorrect forms of speech, and (c) limitations in variety and extensiveness of vocabulary. In developing the method of teaching composition in the grammar grades we shall follow the sequence in which these difficulties are stated. We turn then to the main problem of the present chapter.

THE SELECTION OF THE SUBJECT

The Sources of Subject-matter.—Every child has two rich sources of subject-matter for expression; two great reservoirs which can be tapped for material for compositions. These we may term the direct source and the indirect source.

The Direct Source.—The direct source sums up all composition material that can be obtained from the child's fund of experience, from his creative imagination, and from the host of incidents and stories that were heard or read. The mere fact that the child is normal and has lived his short life in an active society, guarantees a response from this personal source. The responses which can thus be elicited from the children are limited only by the ingenuity and the sympathy of the teacher.

Concrete illustrations are more suggestive and convincing to the teacher whose composition work does not progress because of the limited number of appropriate subjects. Let us turn to a few. What a host of possibilities do we actualize when we ask the child to begin its composition with, "The match that was dropped on the floor of the barn was not lost because——" Children in a sixth-year class suggested the following developments in their compositions. These are given in a summarized form.

Child A: A tramp in search of shelter steals into the barn. He accidentally steps on the match and sets fire to the structure. The peril of the tramp; the rescue. The tramp turns out to be the long lost and wayward son of the owner. Reconciliation and reform.

Child B: A rainy and dismal day. The children of the owner at play in the barn. The match stepped on. The spluttering not heard in the general noise of the game. The fire. The rescue by the arch enemy of the boy at play in the barn. The reward of the rescuer; friendship renewed.

Child C: A rat in the barn. The fire. Total destruction of the barn with its stock of the owner's wealth. Poverty of the farmer. Moral of the tale.

The conceptions of these three children are given to illustrate the many possibilities suggested by such an appeal to productive imagination. Similar topics can readily be invented by the sympathetic and resourceful teacher, who can enter into the spirit that must pervade the composition lesson. In a fifth-year class, the topic, "What I Found Under a Stone," was assigned for plot invention, preparatory to the writing of the composition. Through questions and suggestions the teacher stirred the children's memories of such incidents and experiences as would readily lend themselves to the building of a new situation suited to the given topic. The richness and diversity of the results may be seen from the following plots evolved, in the main, by the children:

Plot 1

The stone lifted. The opening of a cave. The cave entered. The home of a robber band. Death threats. Joins robber band. Gains their confidence. Leads an expedition. Leads robber to capture.

Plot 2

Cave, robbers, death threats, as in first plot. Pleading by a masked member of the band. Life spared. Escape with this unknown friend. Recognition—lost and wayward friend. Reformation.

Plot 3

Stone lifted. Bag of money found. Seek owners. None found. Money divided with friend. Story of the life of evil and ruin of the one and the life of social service and happiness of the other.

Plot 4

An inventor, unsuccessful and discouraged, walks in the woods. Sits on the stone to rest. Stone moves and he lifts it. Finds a motto, "Perseverance brings success." Curiosity as to meaning. Search for meaning. A message of hope for him. Perseverance and final success.

Excellent results are obtained by appealing to this direct source by such a model as "Der kleine Johannes," given in Maxwell and Johnson's "School Composition." It is reproduced for the convenience of the reader.

LITTLE JOHANNES

It was warm by the pond, and still as death. The sun, flushed and tired from its day's work, seemed to be resting for a moment on the top of the distant ridge of dunes before diving below. Almost perfectly the smooth water reflected its glowing face. The overhanging leaves of the beech took advantage of the stillness to gaze intently at themselves in the mirror. The solitary heron, who was standing on one foot between the broad leaves of the waterlilies, forgot that he had gone out to catch frogs, and stared in front of him, lost in thought.

Then Johannes came to the little grass-plot to see the cloud grotto. Plump! plump! the frogs sprang from the shore. The mirror broke into ripples, the sun picture separated into broad stripes, and the beech leaves rustled crossly, for they had not looked at themselves sufficiently.

Fast bound to the naked roots of the beech lay a little old boat. Johannes had been strictly forbidden to get into it. Oh, how strong the temptation was this evening! Already the clouds were forming themselves into an awful gateway, behind which the sun would go to rest. Glittering little clouds ranged themselves in lines at the sides, like a bodyguard in golden armor. The surface of the water glowed also, and red sparks flew like arrows through the reeds.

Slowly Johannes unfastened the cord of the boat from the beech roots. To float there in the midst of that splendor! Presto, the dog had already sprung into the boat, and, before his master had made up his mind, the reeds bent and pushed them both forward in the direction of the setting sun.

(Translated from the Dutch of "Der kleine Johannes," by Frederik van Eeden.)

The children study the model until they see the grandeur of the picture; then they are required to complete the story as their fancies see it. The range of dramatic possibilities varies with the age, the grade, and the native abilities of the pupils. A few of many good results are given.

Martin S., aged twelve, in a sixth-year class, suggested that a sudden storm which came, "soon broke the mirror with angry waves that rocked the boat to and fro." *Der kleine Johannes* now became frightened and clung to the floor of the boat for safety. "As darkness fell the rocking boat put Johannes to sleep." In the fury of the storm that followed the boat capsized and the unfortunate lad "never awoke to realize that he too 'had set off in the direction of the setting sun.'" This little drama, charming and tender in its conception, bespeaks an emotional refinement not usual in the impulsive and ruthless lad of twelve.

Such a model opens up a vista of possibilities which make it appropriate for almost any grammar grade, as is proved by the following two products written by children in the last year of the school course. The compositions as given are accurate reproductions of the children's results except for the correction of a few minor errors, which they themselves corrected when the compositions were returned to them.

THE TEACHING OF ENGLISH

Little Johannes

Par. I. Introduction.
    a. Time.
    b. Place.
Par. II. Little Johannes.
    a. His longing.
    b. His dream.
Par. III. Home again.

It was a warm, sultry day in summer. The lake lay without a ripple on its face. Above, the silver birch stood majestically reflecting its leaves and form. Somewhat off from this stood a lone heron solemnly standing on one foot like a sentinel gazing at its own reflection in the lake, forgetting that it had come down to the lake to catch frogs.

All of a sudden this tranquillity was broken by a litle boy making his entrance upon the scene. The birch rustled its leaves in disapproval as some of the frogs having been scared jumped into the water and wrinkled the surface. This little boy's name was Johannes. He owned a little boat which was moored to the shore. He was strictly forbidden to go out in this boat. The little boy had a strong temptation to take just one ride. But he overcame his temptation and sat admiring the old boat, for he had had much fun in it. Night was coming and the little boy finally saw a great many little frog-men dancing around his feet. Then some of the elder ones took him by the hand and took him through a wonderful land. This land was all illuminated with colored crystal-like lights. This was the festival of the frogs; there were some who had the greenest dresses on, with big brown spots on them, and others with brown dresses with white underneath the throat. In one part of this great land there were tables set and great dishes of good things to eat. In another there were frogs dancing and singing in frog language, but the little boy understood them, for the fairy frog had put him under a spell. Finally the frogs started to eat and when they had finished they started to depart. Johannes could not go, for he did not know the way. When the last one had departed he heard a great noise and clamor and looking around he saw that everything was dark, and that his father and a number of men were standing around. He had been asleep and his father had been out hunting for him with a number of other men until he found him. His father took him in his arms and carried him home, where he told of his adventure.

Johannes' Adventure

It was near the close of a sultry day in summer. The sun, tired from its day's hard work, seemed to say "Good night" to the world before it was wrapped up in the darkness of the coming night. The frogs seemed to have stopped their din, as if in awe of the setting sun. Little Johannes thought it was the most beautiful sight he had ever seen as he came tripping lightly down the path. At the sound of his feet the frogs seemed to awaken from their trance and one after another their plump! plump! showed they had retreated into the forest of water-lilies.

Tied to a tree was a small boat, which was the property of our hero's father. Little Johannes thought that his mother would like to have some lilies. But really he only wanted an excuse to go out in the boat. He set the boat adrift. After half the distance had been covered little Johannes sat back on the seat and fell asleep.

He awoke with a start, for he had heard his name called. He listened for some moments to make sure that he was not mistaken.

"Johannes!" said a soft voice behind him. He turned and saw before him a beautiful girl.

"What do you want and who are you?" asked Johannes, rubbing his eyes to make sure he was awake.

"I am the Queen of the Lily-pads," said she, "and I have

come to warn you that if you disobey your father again and come out in your boat after dark, the Frog King will surely catch you and he is a very bad man."

"All right, your majesty," answered little Johannes, "I'll go right home and never go out again, if that nasty old King will let me alone this time."

"Oh, there you are," said a voice, and little Johannes awoke and stared around him, thinking that it was the Frog King who had come to get him, but it was only his father. While he slept the boat had drifted ashore and the little lad's father had found him, after a long, exhausting search.

The Indirect Source.—The second, the indirect source, sums up all the knowledge the child has, or can obtain from class teaching, textbooks, encyclopedias, and magazines. Whenever we appeal to the indirect source we have composition through correlation. In history, the children write on "The Battle of Bunker Hill," "The Voyages of Columbus," or "Daniel Webster." In geography the topic selected may be, "The People of China," "Notes of a Traveler," "Pictures of Places I Visited," etc.—in a word, the host of topics to which mentally lazy teachers have recourse.

The Danger in the Indirect Source: Overcorrelation.—There is great danger in resorting to the impersonal source for subject-matter. The composition lesson is usually regarded by many teachers as a period in which we can elaborate and "fill out" what was neglected in geography, history, or nature study. We must never forget that the primary object of a composition lesson is expression and not the mastery of information, however important. The most pleasing element in any pupil's composition is its spirit of originality, of spontaneity, and freedom. Composition cannot show these characteristics if it is a mere repetition of the formal lessons in which the child learns to express the textbook or the teacher, but not himself. Injudicious correlation saps life and virility from all composition exercises.

The Test of Good Correlation in Composition.—In all correlation in composition the child should be encouraged to introduce his own individuality into the narrative. He should write his story from his own point of view, as if he really had lived through it. The autobiographical element often makes correlation helpful and suggestive. Therefore, the topic, "Columbus," becomes "The Conspiracy to Throw Me Overboard—Extract from the Autobiography of Christopher Columbus"; a cold recital of facts in a composition on "Lewis and Clark" takes on a glow of life when the topic becomes "A Page from My Diary Kept During the Lewis and Clark Expedition"; when the topic is merely "Bunker Hill" we get from the children a mere enumeration of events such as can be found in any history; but when the topic is changed to "Watching the Battle as an Aide to General Warren," the composition thrills with real excitement. The dispirited narrative when the composition is on "Arnold's Treason" becomes fascinating correspondence when it is turned into "The Letters Exchanged between Arnold and André." In this lesson one child impersonates Arnold and makes the offer of betrayal, and another is André who writes his acceptance and the details of the meeting.

The following composition is a good example of the kind of correlation that we must seek in composition:

The Bowerie, New York,
August 19, 1807.

Dear Lucy:

I don't believe any one in merrie England ever had such a wonderful experience as I did Wednesday.

Do you know that Brother Robert has made a very wonderful invention?

Don't you think I ought to feel proud to say that I was one of the first people to ever ride on a steamboat? Just imagine! a large boat going up the Hudson without sails!

Along the Hudson River there are beautiful palisades and the river lies smooth and calm.

At New York the people were thronged at the wharves.

I felt so queer with all the people gazing upon us and if the boat hadn't gone Brother Robert would have thought his invention worthless.

Soon he began fooling with some machinery; the engine made a great noise and smoke came from out the funnel.

The people laughed, hooted and said she would never go.

Then the boat moved! You can't even imagine how funny I felt and also how happy. The crowd was astonished.

On we went up the beautiful Hudson against the current O! it was a wonderful ride, I could scarcely sleep for joy. Only thirty-two hours to go from New York to Albany! That was perfectly wonderful. Now the world wont have to wait for the wind to blow her ships over the ocean.

Your American friend,
Edith Bast (Fulton).

COMPOSITION IN THE GRAMMAR GRADES

Two Versions of the Purchase of Manhattan Island

The White Man's Story

Those Indians do love trinkets. They sell their lives for them. Knowing this we flashed our mirrors and tempted them with colored beads. We never dreamed that they would part with such an island for a bag full of beads.

The Indian's Story

We certainly fooled those white men. They think they are smart. We pretended that we would never give up the island. They offered us more and more. We refused. At last they had to offer all their wonderful mirrors and beads. There is so much land here that we shall easily find as good a place. But where could we get such jewels!

In contrast to the above, let us see the following example of correlation, suggested as a model by the principal of one of our city schools:

London, England,
June 2, 1905.

Dear William:

I reached London at ten o'clock Monday morning and the first thing I went to see was Westminster Abbey, a very large church which is one of the largest in the world.

It was built by King Edward the Confessor in 1065 and the first great service was held in the Abbey Christmas Day of that year. A few weeks later King Edward took sick from old age and died and was buried there.

The Abbey is built in the form of a Latin cross and in the south transcript is the Poets' Corner, where there is a bust of Longfellow, a tablet to Shakespeare and a memorandum window to Lowell. King Henry added another chapel, in which there is the tomb of Queen Elizabeth, and the choir is as large as a good-sized church.

Your friend,

———— ————.

This composition is a stupid reproduction from the "Encyclopedia of Persons and Places"; the composition is dead and was written because it was an assigned task. The errors of speech, of grouping, and of facts which occur would not have been made if the child understood and felt what he was writing. All this is justified in the name of correlation for the principal's conference notes add: "The children are benefited not merely in the line of letter writing, but their language is improved and they gain valuable, curious, and interesting bits of information concerning different countries of the world, old and new."

What Is a Good Subject for Composition?—We can best sum up our inquiry concerning the choice of a subject for composition by noting the salient characteristic of a good "composition subject." The difference between a "good" subject and a "bad" one is the difference between "having something to say" and "having to say something." When the child is told to write on Westminster Abbey, he has to say something. All inspiration, all ideas that may be lurking in the mind are at once dispelled. When the child is writing because he has something to say, success is guaranteed because the subject of the entire composition is really "I." In the teaching of elementary composition a good subject allows the personal pronoun of the first person to be the real if not the nominal subject.

In the light of this standard, how stupid and inane are the following models, offered by principals to teachers to be imposed on the children. They have all been gathered in the last three years from conference notes and direct "Orders to Teachers."

The East River Bridges

There are four great bridges connecting the boroughs of Manhattan and Brooklyn. Each of them is more than a mile in length. You can walk across them, or you can go over them in a car or a carriage.

From these bridges you can see steamers with their tall pipes and masts passing up and down the East River. Ferryboats, too, are seen going back and forth between the two boroughs.

The ferryboats used to be the only means of crossing from Brooklyn to New York. Now the bridges make it easier for the people to go from one borough to the other.

Coal

Hundreds and hundreds of years ago there were great forests. In these forests there were no insects; nothing was there but large trees. These trees sank into the earth and have become coal.

Men go down into the earth in small elevators to get the coal. These men are called miners. They have little lamps on their hats. It is very dark and dangerous down in the mines.

Many years ago children worked in the mines.

There are a great many halls in the mines. Coal is very opaque and it is shiny and very brittle.

The Earthworm

The earthworm's body is made up of many segments. He has no bones. Fowls and birds eat him.

He needs no eyes because he lives in the dark earth. He destroys the roots of plants by eating them.

When he dies his body mixes with the soil and makes it richer.

Kindness

I should always treat others kindly. I should be especially kind to all the members of my own family.

I should be kind to all with whom I have anything to do, even if they are not such children as I would choose for companions.

If I have pets, I should be very kind to them.

How far superior are the following, personal expressions of the children!

The Sciences

Though I have read few books on science, I have noticed that, with but one exception, they merely gave the facts. For this reason I had almost formed an opinion that science was interesting, but that books on that subject were dry.

But when I came in contact with a certain book that opinion vanished into thin air. The cause of this sudden revolution of ideas was a book with the dull title—"The Sciences." Edward S. Holden is the author of it. Perhaps I liked the book because the topics were explained in nothing more nor less than a conversation. The illustrations, too, were the best I have ever seen. The experiment was always explained underneath the diagram.

I do not know why I grasp the facts better in reading

conversation than facts. Maybe because the one, being more interesting, engages my attention more. Before reading the book I knew nothing of electricity. Now I know a little at least. The book did not take up much about electricity or I would have learned more. My only unfavorable criticism is that the children knew too much and spoke too well for their age. For instance, a girl of nine is not likely to know much about diving bells, planets, etc. But on the whole the book is excellent.

"Cherry Ripe"

"Cherry Ripe" is a little girl sitting on a huge boulder, with her little toes turned in and her little hands clasped. Beside her on the boulder, on a large leaf, are a number of ripe cherries. "Cherry Ripe" must be a very old picture, for her dress, shoes, gloves and hat are of the fashion of years gone by.

Around her neck is a scarf which looks like a bertha. Around her waist is the wide girdle. The long, full skirt comes to her ankles, out of which her little feet just peep. Her gloves come halfway up her arm.

Above her the May blossom and wistaria are twining and form an arch. Below her the lilies and tall grass come up and form a frame, but I think that the artist of this picture intended that she should be the sweetest and prettiest flower of them all.

It is evident, therefore, that a subject, per se, is neither good nor bad. The point of view and the interpretation of it always determine its value in elementary classes. The topic, "The Snowfall," gives a stupid and lifeless composition if the children are required to treat it in the following topics: In what season does it come? What temperature is necessary? Its relation to rain? What forms may the flakes take? What are the uses of snow in preserving plant life? etc. What is here offered the child is an adult's composition on snow, written from a scientific point of view with a serious aim. This is what snow may be to the teacher but it is not what snow is to the child. To him, it has no scientific cause, it justifies itself merely by the fact that it adds to his joy. How truly a boy's composition on snow is the following!

A Winter Day

"I'll bet you that we will have some snow this week," my friend had declared the day before the snowfall, and all of us agreed with him, for the wind was cold and biting and the clouds low and dark.

The next morning when I awoke I instantly saw that my friend had been right. The windows were frosted and the streets spotless white, as traffic had not yet begun. The adjoining roofs looked as if they had been covered with a huge sheet, while in the park every twig and branch was clothed in its winter garments. The street was as quiet as a graveyard, except for an occasional rattle of a truck as it rolled over the frozen pavement.

After eating breakfast and taking as few books as possible, I started off for school and met a number of my friends. "Hello, Willie," I cried to one of them, "how do you like the"—when, biff! came a snowball, which found lodgment in my ear. "Say, Is, how do you like the"—came derisively from Willie, while several boys laughed heartily at my misfortune. Then began a battle, which soon ended, as time was flying and we did not care to be late.

After school we met in our clubroom, and together we went to some building lots, where the snow was undisturbed, and began building a fort, for which we were to have a battle. When the fort was completed we chose sides, and I was put on the force which was to capture the fort. As I am not an accurate thrower, I was given the position of supplying snowballs. We soon overpowered the enemy and with a loud cheer took possession. We kept on playing until dark and then went home, hoping that there would be a blizzard during the night, which would insure some fun on the morrow.

The practical teacher may admit the possibilities of these results with classes in the upper part of the school course, but may insist that in the lower grades the expressions must be more or less formal and the content must possess a simplicity that seems insipid to the adult mind. It is evidently such lack of confidence in the imaginative products of children that prompted a principal of an elementary school to suggest the following models for fourth-year classes:

My Doll

My doll is a toy. It looks like a baby girl. Its head is made of china; its arms and legs are of plaster. The body of the doll is sawdust and rags. It has glass eyes that turn down when the doll is put to sleep.

The Trolley Car

The trolley car is a combined wagon and big machine. It moves by electric power. The motorman makes it go by turning a handle. The trolley car can draw heavy loads. It travels on wheels; these wheels turn on tracks. The machinery is under the car.

THE TEACHING OF ENGLISH

Principals and teachers possessed of sympathetic insight see at once that to the child the doll is more than a composite of china, clay, glass and sawdust. It is a living object upon which are spent all the emotions of latent motherhood. In the second model the trolley car is not an object of wonder and awe, a monster of strength and speed. These models do not lift the child above the level of the commonplace or the cold realities of life. Contrast them with the following compositions written by second- and third-year children whose teacher's sympathy enabled her to stir the magic force of their imagination, so that the results are rich in imagery and poetic charm.

Where Does the Wind Begin?

The wind begins in the sky. The wind talks. What does the wind say? The wind says, "OOOOO."
Angelina L.

The wind begins in the clouds. The wind goes to sleep in the forest.
John H.

I know where you live wind you live in the tree you are laughing wind.
Albert V.

Where does the wind begin? A big man blows it out of his moth.
Philip V.

The Robin's Song

I hear the robin singing in the trees. He sings "The butterflys are angel flowers."
John R.

Wake up! Wake up! Wake up! It is robin Readbrest. Sunny warm weather is coming.
Angelo S.

COMPOSITION IN THE GRAMMAR GRADES

The robin sings the spring is coming. The spring is waking the green grass. Little green buds are coming out of the trees.
Joseph G.

The robin sings to the Daffadils, "open your yellow eyes." The Robin's sits on my window and tells me a secret of spring-time.
Mary R.

I see the robin on the bushes. The robin is singing me a lovely song. The robin is telling me a secret. The flowers are bursting out of their buds because it is spring.
Clara B.

The robin sings Twee! Twee! Twee! The robin says "Appleblosoms come out of your buds." He tells me to be happy for spring is here.
Cornelius O.

The Dark

The dark keeps me warm. I see a lady dancing on the spark of the moon. The sun eats all the little people up.
Mary R.

The dark is all around. I see emporers and kings marching by. The sun swallows them up. Albert P.

In the night it is dark. At night I see strange people and I hear strange music. In the morning the dark goes away. In the morning the strange people fade away. Clara B.

ORAL COMPOSITION

Written Composition Must Be Subordinated.—The general tendency in the teaching of elementary composition to-day is to stress oral rather than written composition. This emphasis is due to many governing conditions. (1) The composition of the average person is limited almost exclusively to oral rather than written communication. The needs of life must be the determining factor in the classroom. (2) Written composition cannot be undertaken with hope of success unless the pupil has acquired a complex set of penmanship and language habits. (3) To the child, letter writing is the only form of motivated written composition. All other forms of composition are irksome to the average pupil. (4) Oral composition is richer in opportunities for practice. Time consumed in writing is thus utilized in securing a greater number of personal reactions. (5) In oral composition the children's minds are stirred by the suggestions of their classmates and the criticisms, corrective and constructive.

How to Emphasize Oral Composition.—To give oral composition its due place in language work, we must keep in mind the following suggestions:

1. *All recitations* afford opportunities for natural and *thoroughly motivated oral compositions*. This suggestion has been elaborated in previous discussions in this book.

2. *Not all compositions should be written.* It is an error to conclude that every composition subject taken up in class must ultimately be written about. Time and again, the composition lesson need not proceed beyond the oral stage.

3. In the oral preparation for written composition, *pupils must be encouraged to develop the subject from as many viewpoints as possible.* Let us assume that Santa Claus is to be described. The class is asked to suggest the details which will emphasize Santa's geniality, Santa's dress, Santa's home in the land of per-

petual winter, Santa weighed down by his sack, or Santa's conveyance.

Let us take another illustration. The pupils were asked to develop the story of a picture showing a bear ready to lunge at a man lying face down in the snow. Behind a tree stands another man, with gun raised ready to fire. What is the story that can be evolved from this picture? In the oral discussions the following possibilities were elicited from the children:

(a) A trapper fell ill just before the bear appeared. (b) The prostrated hunter was felled by a blow from the bear. (c) The first hunter stumbled over a stump hidden by the snow just as he was surprised by the bear. (d) The hunter on the ground is merely feigning death. (e) The two hunters are enemies. Will the man with the raised gun forgive in this critical moment? (f) The two hunters are long-lost friends. (g) The man on the ground is the game warden sent out to arrest the other. (h) The two men are keepers in a circus and are in pursuit of an escaped grizzly. (i) The two men are in no danger. They are cinema actors and the bear is well trained. (j) The two men are aviators who lost their way after escaping from a wrecked balloon.

Each story was developed orally. The class was intensely interested as the pupils listened to the stories unfolded by their classmates. Here is opportunity for much intensive oral composition.

4. *Variety of titles, introductions, and endings.* An interesting oral composition lesson can usually be obtained by inviting the class to suggest various titles,

introductions, and endings and then to weigh their respective merits. After evolving the various possibilities for the story that might be read out of the picture of the two trappers and the bear, the class was asked to suggest suitable titles.[1] Eighth-year children gave the following:

1. The Shot That Told the Tale
2. Friendly Enemies
3. The Test of Manhood
4. Northern Dangers
5. A Comrade in Peril
6. Where Comradeship Was Born
7. Saved from Death
8. The Last Cartridge
9. Suspense
10. In the Wilds of Canada
11. One Good Turn Deserves Another
12. Cheating Death
13. A Trapper's Tale
14. In the Jaws of Death
15. A Long Anxious Moment
16. The Unfaltering Hand
17. Just in Time
18. Which Will Reach First?
19. Lost and Found
20. The Escape
21. The Fallen Monarch.

Similarly, the pupils may be asked to suggest dramatic introductory sentences and surprising denouements. A spirited discussion usually follows such a question as "Which title gives most promise of attract-

[1] Following suggestion in *Composition Standards*, Savitz, Bates and Starry.

ing a reader?" A good picture, a vital incident in history, or a dramatic literary situation will afford rich opportunity for this type of exercise.

5. *Topics that lend themselves to oral treatment should be reserved for special oral compositions.* Children grow impatient when these themes are subjected to written exercises. Among these topics we may list: (a) Discussion, argumentation, and exposition of current events. (b) Debating the merits of various questions of pupil politics. (c) Debating the merits of candidates for school positions. (d) Dictating telegrams and advertisements. (e) Exposition of a personal preference, my favorite game, pet, book, vocation, etc. (f) A humorous or tragic incident in one's life. (g) Asking riddles and charades. (h) Slogans for various community projects. To these we must add many of the suggestion on pages 147-168.

The Conduct of Oral Composition Lessons.—The success of the oral composition lesson is determined primarily by the character of the subject. If it is natural and presents a real motive for discussion, there will be lively participation by the pupils. The recitation must be thoroughly socialized. Each pupil should talk to the class and not to the teacher. Every objection, disagreement or agreement should be directed to a definite pupil. Each participant must be actuated by a real desire to convince others and to give expression to his ideas. If the children are old enough, they should select their own chairman.

The teacher need not eliminate herself. She must make judicious comments or ask directing questions to keep the discussion alive and relevant. Corrections should be incidental. The teacher should occupy herself with making notes, chiefly mental, of the children's errors, refraining from becoming censorious during the discussion and reserving all drills on correct form for special short formal periods. Only as mind plays on mind does oral composition become real and vital and, therefore, a significant means of enriching ideas and developing language power.

SUGGESTED READING

The suggested reading for this chapter will be found at the end of Chapter VIII.

CHAPTER V

COMPOSITION IN THE GRAMMAR GRADES
(*Continued*)

HOW SECURE ORGANIZATION AND SEQUENCE: THE OUTLINE

The Tendency to Ramble.—Of the three basic problems that confront the grammar class teacher in composition, lack of subject-matter, lack of sequence and expressional limitations, we have considered only the first. Our immediate task is, therefore, a consideration of the problem of organization of ideas for rational expression. Children's compositions often lack this primary requisite, proper sequence of ideas. The child's tendency to ramble is responsible for his characteristic composition which lacks clearness and force. But we need not ascribe this weakness solely to children; adults, too, are often guilty of flagrant violations of the simple principle of logical sequence. Examine the trend of conversation in any ordinary gathering; every important topic is touched on and passed over in the "drift" of discussion because every new interest challenges attention. Class discussions of mature students are often examples of verbal spirals. Listen to the average adult as he tells of some incident or expounds some principle, in which there is no inherent sequence of events—what a heterogeneous composite of facts!

Illogical sequence of ideas and lack of coherence of thought are general failings. Teachers must not, therefore, be surprised to find these defects in children's work. Just as adults are unconscious of their limitations in this respect, so, too, are our immature pupils. The first problem that presents itself, therefore, is not to teach the principle of organization but to bring home the consciousness of its need and its importance. This can best be done by a method of *reductio ad absurdum*. After the child realizes his limitations, present the positive aspects of the lesson, teach him how to secure organization through the elaboration of the outline.

The Principle of Organization Taught by the Outline. —Let us suggest a lesson designed to bring home to the child the inherent tendency to ramble and to teach him a method of securing rational and systematic ordering of ideas. A descriptive composition on a well-selected topic can readily achieve this double end. With this purpose in view, the subject, "The Circus," was assigned to a fifth-year class. The children were made to understand that they must write such a description of the circus as would give one who has never seen it a clear idea of what he will see, and stir in him a desire to see the wonderful feats of skill and daring. Every child was then told to be ready to make a contribution of fact, each to tell what he would include in his own composition. The teacher took these items in the order in which they were suggested by children who were called upon promiscuously. Such a request for material brought the following data from the class: the daredevil acts, the animals, the great tent, the three rings, the large signs, the group of small tents, the crowds, highly colored pictures, the peddlers selling refreshments, the horse riders, the acrobats, the "barkers" at the "side-shows," the band, the apparatus, the funny sights, the freaks, the arrangement of seats, etc.

A few judicious questions and suggestions soon led the children to realize the utter absurdity of such an arrangement and to feel the need of systematic presentation of details. That done, the teacher elicited from the children a suitable sequence. "What would one see on first approaching the circus ground?" The conclusion reached by the class was: "The first paragraph ought to treat of the outside of the circus." The question, "What would one see on entering the circus inclosure after passing through the admission gate?" suggested to the class the theme for the second paragraph, In the Circus Grounds. The teacher then asked, "What would attract one's attention in the main tent?" and brought the children to a realization that the concluding paragraph must tell of the Great Circus Feats. The paragraphs with their respective headings were then written in separate columns on the blackboard and the first step in the development of the outline was completed.

The children then folded their papers into three divisions, each part to serve for the outline of a single paragraph. They were then led to take up each item in their original promiscuous list of data and decide for themselves in what paragraph it belonged. Thus the first contribution, "daredevil acts," is evidently part of the paragraph on The Great Circus Feats; the second, "the animals," part of the paragraph on Within the Circus Grounds, etc., until every fact worth including in the composition was properly placed. The result presented an appearance similar to the following:

Par. I. *Outside the Circus*	Par. II. *Within the Circus Grounds*	Par. III. *The Circus Feats*
1. stretch of canvas	7. the animals	2. the three rings
4. the great tent	1. group of small tents	1. the audience in seats
2. large signs	4. the peddlers selling refreshments	6. horse riders
5. the crowds	2. "barkers" at "side-shows"	5. acrobats
3. highly colored pictures	3. the band	7. the races
	5. the funny sights	4. the apparatus
	6. the freaks	3. the clown
		8. the daredevil acts

This done, the children were asked to examine the items in each paragraph and determine the logical position of each. With the aid of prefixed numbers, they worked out the sequence of ideas in each paragraph as is shown in the outline above.

Values of the Outline.—The values of such a lesson in sequence and organization are many and significant. It is obviously an effective means of teaching the child the need of rational sequence of thought, and the mode of grouping ideas for clear and forceful expression. The outline, properly used and elaborated, also trains the child in systematic thought, in clear and continued development of a line of thinking. As a formal classroom exercise for challenging the child's powers of judgment and concentration, it is excellent. Another inestimable value of the outline is that it is the most concrete and the most efficacious method at the teacher's command of teaching the paragraph, its meaning, its development and its unity. This is true because the nature of a paragraph can best be taught through a form of contrast. There must be a number of paragraphs developing under the pupils' hands, otherwise they carry away notions that are vague and inaccurate. Then, too, the child learns best through some form of motorization. The method suggested for teaching the outline enables the child to learn the organization of paragraphs by actually evolving a number of them simultaneously and noting the various basic ideas that determine the unity of each.

The Drill to Insure Mastery of the Outline.—Since the object in all language teaching is to habituate the correct form it is evident that vigorous and persistent drill must follow this lesson. This drill must be varied as well as thorough so that interest in the lesson will not be endangered. To this end we may suggest a number of exercises:

1. Similar topics are suggested to the class and the method is applied to each of these by the steps

that were outlined in the model lesson. Such topics as, "Our Church," "The Polo Grounds," "Our School," "A Sporting Goods Window," "The East River Bridge," "The Peddler Selling Mechanical Toys," etc., allow for a simple application of the method learned to the new topic.

2. Incidents, descriptions, expositions and the like, which abound in the children's textbooks, are taken up one by one and analyzed into component ideas in order to lay bare the outline which the author had in mind when he wrote the particular selection under study. The children are taught to point out the topic of each paragraph and then to test its paragraph unity.

3. The next form of drill should take up varied topics of narrative, argumentative, expository and descriptive nature, which should be used in oral exercises. A few minutes after a new topic is announced the children must be ready to tell the number of paragraphs they would use in developing it and the theme of each paragraph. When a tentative set of paragraphs has been accepted the children must quickly evolve an appropriate content for each and offer it to the class orally, when called up. After the last paragraph is given, a new topic is announced and the same rapid oral drill takes place.

The subject given to a 6A grade in such a drill was, "The Breakdown of the Trolley Car." By skillful leading and emphasis of correct answers the teacher elicited from the class the following development:

Par. 1. The Trolley Car Collides with a Wagon.

Par. 2. Impatience of the Passengers.

Par. 3. Examination of the Extent of the Accident and Attempt at Repairs.

Par. 4. Arrival of the Emergency Wagon and the Repair Crew.

These four paragraph headings were put on the board and attention was then directed to the development of each one. In attacking the first one for elaboration, the children were able to work out a good opening sentence. After a few colorless attempts in which the teacher indicated the cause of the weakness, a sentence offered was, "While I sat in a Third Avenue trolley, impatient at the slowness, the car came to a sudden standstill." The teacher's commendation of the opening sentence soon provoked from another child, " 'What terrible service! What a snail car this is,' I said to myself, when all of a sudden there was a crash and the car stopped with a terrible jerk"; and from a third, "No trolley car travels so fast as when the motorman loses control of it." One development of this first paragraph, as given orally, was, "We were all shaken up a bit but soon recovered from the fright and the noise of crashing window-panes. There was great excitement for a minute as the people rushed to the doors. When they realized that the danger was over they became calm and went to their seats again. It seemed that the wagon that collided with our car got the worse of it."

Paragraph number 2, on the "impatience of the passengers," brought sentences which told of the straining of necks, of complaints, of people who left in disgust, of women who wanted their fares back, and of men who lost themselves in newspapers. The third paragraph dealt with the examination of the accident by the motorman and the conductor, their quarrel with the wagon driver who caused the accident, their conference, their futile attempt at repair, and then their telephoning for help. The concluding paragraph, developed orally in the same way, told of the arrival of the emergency wagon, the business-like procedure with which these expert workmen set to work, the policeman taking notes, the final repair and the relief of having started again.

All this work was oral; only hints and outlines of paragraphs were jotted down either on the board or on the children's cards. Every child's answers were examined and the class as a whole passed upon them, deciding whether particular facts were appropriate in the paragraph under consideration, whether the sequence of paragraphs was correct, etc. In the same way the following topics might be treated: "A Sporting Goods Window," "A Mounted Policeman," "Joe, the Pretzel Man," "A Beggar," "Report of a Game," "An Athletic Meet," etc. Three or four of these topics could be taken up orally in one period.

Cautions in Developing Outlines.—There are common but erroneous practices in developing outlines that we must constantly guard against if we are to secure maximum results in this type of exercise. We must now turn to these cautions in this form of language work.

1. *The Outline Must Be the Child's Outline.*—Every part of the lesson must be the result of the children's self-activity; they must suggest every fact in the outline; they must evolve the number of paragraphs; they must judge each item and decide upon its place in the general organization. Unless every act of judgment is performed by the pupils, the maximum results of such a lesson cannot be realized.

2. *Too Many Details in the Outline Must Be Avoided.*—It is important that the outline should not be laden with too many minute details. There should be a general organization, a broad suggestion of the line of development and of the proper sequence. An outline that gives an enumeration of petty details crushes individuality, kills spontaneity and robs the final composition of its best expressional elements.

3. *Avoid a Stereotyped Class Outline.*—A final word of warning counsels that we avoid such outlines as will give a set of compositions bearing remarkable similarity to one another in every detail—exercises that seem as if they were printed from the same type and cast in the same mold. How can we guard against this slavish imitation? How can we introduce individuality of expression and variety of form?

How to Secure Variety in the Outlines.—1. *Outlines Should Not Be Copied Verbatim.*—Despite the fact that the class as a whole or a particular division may be writing on the same subject and from the same general outline, variety of expression and individuality in the final product need not be stifled.

After the outline is elaborated and the final form is shown on the blackboard, it should be erased and the children should be required to construct their own, each child thus producing an outline reflecting his own point of view and his own individuality. No matter how retentive the children may be, a delightful variety can be secured.

2. *Encourage Variety of Grouping.*—After the children have learned the *modus operandi* in the construction of an outline, the teacher must not rest content with one grouping of facts. Show the children that the number of paragraphs is not fixed, provided the items in each are shifted and rearranged under their logical heading. Variety will invariably result. Thus in a composition on "Our School," let it be supposed the visitor arrives in a carriage and enters at once, then what is the sequence of paragraphs? Evidently, paragraph 1, Interior Structure; paragraph 2, Decorations; paragraph 3, Activities; paragraph 4, Exterior. Or, the visitor on entering is attracted by the work that is being done; hence the paragraphing is, paragraph 1, Activities; paragraph 2, Structure That Makes This Possible; paragraph 3, Teaching Apparatus; paragraph 4, Decorations; paragraph 5, Exterior Structure, etc. Each child may therefore select that grouping which appeals to him most.

In the description of the circus the teacher and the children should evolve other forms of paragraph development than the one suggested in the lesson, viz., paragraph 1, The Parade Before the Opening of the Circus; paragraph 2, The Circus Grounds; paragraph

3, The Circus Performance; or, paragraph 1, The Circus Grounds; paragraph 2, The Performance in the Main Tent; paragraph 3, The Side-shows; or, paragraph 1, The Preparation Before the Circus Comes to Town; paragraph 2, How the Circus Is Put Up; paragraph 3, The Rehearsals; paragraph 4, The Performance. A child who experiences difficulty with one arrangement of paragraphs may find another suggestive and interesting. He must therefore be given free choice and be allowed to follow a paragraph grouping that is entirely original, should his ingenuity suggest one.

3. *Allow Personal Choice of Details.*—Once the paragraph themes have been suggested, teachers must allow children perfect freedom in the choice of details. Thus in the paragraph on The Circus Feats in the composition on "The Circus," children may omit any data offered in the outline and incorporate any other feats of skill and daring that have greater attraction for them. What children are to say about the various suggestions in the outline about the "side-shows," "the barkers," "the acrobats," "the clown," etc., should never be indicated. Whatever the word suggests to their minds they should write, unhampered by injudicious direction and dictation, and thus again offset the undesirable sameness of class productions.

4. *Encourage Variety of "Attacking and Closing" the Subject.*—Another means of securing variety of form and showing personality in expression is to elicit a variety of beginnings and endings. The com-

positions on "Our School" showed the following in a 5B class:

1. "I am very proud of my school for it is so attractive."
2. "Every visitor who comes to this section of the city is attracted by our school."
3. "I praised my school so much that my uncle finally made up his mind to visit it. I met him at the teachers' entrance."
4. "One of the very beautiful buildings in this city is . . ."
5. "My country cousin was never so much surprised in all his life as he was when he visited my school."

Then came a contrast between the city school and the country school.

5. *Avoid the Wordy Outline.*—A final suggestion for securing variety in the organization of composition is to suggest each item in the outline in only a word or two. Outlines made up of sentences or long phrases are bad, for the children soon learn to supply a few predicates, an adjective or an occasional modifying phrase or clause and the composition is complete. The scantier the outline, the better.

How Closely Shall the Outline Be Followed?—A final problem which arises in the course of the employment of the outline is the extent to which the children shall consciously follow it. The answer cannot be didactic nor positive. It all depends upon (a) the nature of the composition, and (b) the age and capabilities of the children. When the topic is one of exposition, or narration, or argumentation, then logical sequence is exceedingly important in securing clearness and force. But in writing a description of a person, a sunset, a brook, or a quaint room, the ultimate aim is to give a lasting and vivid impression of the picture; here the choice of detail rather than the sequence of facts is the vital problem, hence the outline need only be followed in its general trend.

As far as the child's age and capabilities are concerned, it may be safe to assert that through the sixth year of the elementary course, the outline must be a conscious prop in composition, and must inevitably take a considerable part of the oral period which prepares for the final expressional exercise. But thereafter, it should gradually begin to assume a minor place in the preparatory period, not that the outline is now less important but because a habit of mind should have been formed in the fifth and sixth years of the school course. Where the outline is properly taught and impressed through drill of sufficient frequency during these two years, the child should be able in the later years of the school course to organize facts without aid or direction. Pupils of the seventh and eighth years when confronted by a composition subject, should habitually think: (a) What is the subject as a whole, i. e., what mass of facts comes under it? (b) What are the best groupings of these facts, i. e., how many paragraphs do I want and what are they? (c) How shall I organize each paragraph?

and (d) what is an appropriate opening sentence and closing sentence? Before writing his composition, the child should give evidence of having accomplished this organization. The outline should be made a part of the composition and may even be placed at the head of the sheet.

Teaching Organization Through Pictures.—A second method of teaching organization of ideas is to use serial pictures, each of which tells one phase of a story. Let us assume that "The Picnic" is the composition subject. The first picture, "Getting Ready," shows grandmother preparing the lunch while mother is putting finishing touches to the children's clothes. Father is testing his fishing reel. In the second picture, "The Trip," we see a crowded train with others bent on pleasure. Despite obvious discomfort all are happy in the anticipation of what the day holds forth. The third picture, "The Picnic," shows the lunch spread under a tree, the boys among its branches, the mother looking up nervously at them, the girls romping in the field, while father is casting tragic glances at the dried brook. The fourth picture, "The Bedraggled Homecoming," contains the denouement—the price of pleasure. The children look unkempt, the younger ones sleepy, all are tired and father not yet over his fishing disappointment. With four such pictures, properly labelled and simply but effectively drawn, organization of ideas around central themes can be taught concretely. The problem, of course, is to obtain necessary pictures. A teacher with only moderate gift in drawing can readily make these sketches on large pieces of cardboard not only for her own class but for her colleagues as well. We must hope that the many excellent language books now available will include such serial pictures in forthcoming editions.

Limit the Scope of a Composition Subject.—Another means of training in organization is through the definiteness of assignment. Ask pupils to write on "The Battle of Gettysburg" or on "Lincoln" or on "The Founding of the Colony of Georgia," and they begin a long story that runs in fairly intelligent order because the subject itself is narrative and has an inherent sequence. Evidently, there is no training in organization because the pupil does not consciously plan the sequence. But when the subject is limited to a specific incident, the pupil must deliberately decide on the organization of details. Such subjects as "Pickett's Charge," "Lincoln's Boyhood Home," "Our First Day in Georgia," have no inherent sequence and tend to discourage long rambling compositions. Unless each pupil deliberately plans his work, he can hardly proceed after the first sentence or two.

Similarly, the story of Cinderella can readily be subdivided to yield at least six good composition subjects that demand careful planning—"Why They Called Me Cinderella"; "My Godmother Heard My Call"; "The Magic Change of a Cinder Girl"; "How I Went to the Ball"; "Finding the Owner of the Slipper"; "My Sisters' Amazement"; "Returning Good for Evil." Each of these definite subjects stirs the imagination, arouses the child's inventive power and gives training in sequential thinking.

Supplementary Means of Developing Power of Organization.—In addition to the formal lessons on the use of the outline, various supplementary methods can be incorporated in all periods for developing in children a sense of logical organization. After a story is read to the children, or by them, a few minutes may profitably be spent in eliciting from the pupils the outline that must have guided the author. Various games and processes, that make up the work of the physical training and the manual training periods respectively, may be submitted to careful analysis, and the steps in the procedure listed in proper sequence. In all lessons the teacher should take occasion, in the summary, to call the attention of the pupils to the organization of the facts that guided her in planning the topic for the period. Thus, after a geography, a history or a nature-study lesson, the teacher naturally calls upon the class to summarize the most essential facts. As the lesson is retraced, step by step, by the children, the main topics and subtopics should be listed on the board. When this summary is completed, the children see the sequence which governed the organization of the lesson. Then, too, all study lessons can be made informal but nevertheless direct means of teaching children the art of organization. The child who studies his lesson in geography tries, first, to ascertain the meaning of the text and then to group the most important facts in a logical outline before committing to memory any of the data. These study lessons make unmistakable contributions to the child's growing sense of organization.

COMPOSITION IN THE GRAMMAR GRADES

SUGGESTED READING

The suggested reading for this chapter will be found at the end of Chapter VIII.

CHAPTER VI

COMPOSITION IN THE GRAMMAR GRADES
(Continued)

EXPRESSIONAL LIMITATIONS: THE MODEL

The method of teaching composition in the grammar grades, it was seen, must be governed by the basic difficulties which confront the teacher, viz., lack of content, lack of organization, and expressional limitations. The first two of the three have already been considered in detail in the preceding chapters. We must now turn to the third factor which makes children's work poor and the teacher's problem difficult —expressional limitations, which consist of (a) ungrammatical forms, (b) confused and awkward expressions, and (c) paucity of vocabulary of necessary words. Time and the influences of general education tend, in a measure, to overcome these three limitations and strengthen the child along these very weak lines, for as the child's education progresses he learns the primary laws of grammar, gradually acquires better expressions, and in the course of his daily reading, conversation, or study, enriches his limited stock of words. But all these modes are governed by chance. What specific means have we of bringing about progress in these directions? In the main, these are four:

COMPOSITION IN THE GRAMMAR GRADES

(1) *group teaching,* (2) *a wise use of the outline,* (3) *establishing an intimate relationship between grammar and composition,* (4) *the use of the model.*

1. Group Teaching.—It is the common experience of all teachers that children usually vary greatly in expressional ability. Natural gifts seem to assert themselves in composition in most unmistakable terms. Some children are precocious in their expressional work, some are exceedingly good, while others seem hopelessly behind. The following compositions were selected from a sixth-year class. The first was written by a child who had been only eight months in America; the second by a pupil who was born in this country.

The Garden in Winter

As soon as the winter comes the garden loses its beauty. Instead of the beautiful foliage the trees are covered with snow. The brook is quiet, the flowers are gone and everything is asleep under the snow. The only nest on the tree is empty and looks as if it is waiting for its possessor the sweet singer. Only the evergreen tree is standing without changing. All these things have their own beauty. Oh! How beautiful the trees are against the sky at sunset. Would all those beautiful things be alive again? I hope they will.

The Garden in Winter

The garden in winter is very dreary. Because the birds are gone and the brooks are froze. It is bare. Oh! the garden is very beautiful. The snow hides the flowers under the ground. There are many buds on the trees and the nests are waiting for the birds. And the sun shining threw braches of the trees.

What a ludicrous attempt, therefore, is the composition lesson which assigns the same topic to all children, presents the new principle simultaneously to them and expects the same standard of result from such varying abilities! What a wrong to neglect those able and gifted in expression or to stultify their power by dragging them down to the level of the mediocre! How stupid to expect the backward and hopelessly deficient to keep up with the standard of general class progress! When shall we realize that indiscriminate class teaching which neglects personal aptitudes or weaknesses and individual needs, stifles unmeasured ability on the one hand and perpetuates hopeless ignorance on the other! The need for group teaching, for teaching according to personal capacity, is more urgent in composition than in any other elementary school subject. The possibilities for grouping are here more numerous and the conveniences for group teaching are greater, yet teachers are less prone to group in this subject than in others. The difficulties that a pupil encounters in composition are peculiarly personal, hence, only as we try to approximate individual work in composition, will the child outgrow his personal expressional limitations.

2. **The Outline.**—A good outline, it was shown, is a great help toward clear and direct thinking. But expression follows thought; hence, clearness of expression is the inevitable sequel to clearness of thinking. The outline, by systematizing the child's ideas, guarantees the necessary antecedent of clear and forceful expression.

3. **The Intimacy of Grammar and Composition.**—A third factor that seeks to minimize and correct ex-

pressional limitations is the close relationship of grammar to composition. The ideal course in grammar is so planned that it emphasizes those parts that can be of service in writing, or can become standards of judgment and correction; the ideal grammar lesson has its origin in the faults committed by the children in their composition and finds its application in correction of these same faults. For purposes of illustration let us suppose that an examination of a set of compositions shows a tendency toward sentences related in thought but independent in construction, giving a very amateurish and childish effect. Examples of this prevalent weakness are, "Columbus was a bold navigator. He never feared to sail unknown seas"; "The Civil War was a long and bloody conflict. It brought untold human misery." A number of sentences similar in looseness of structure are put on the board. By a few well-chosen questions the teacher elicits that each pair of sentences has the same subject and that they can readily be united into one. The ever ready "and" will undoubtedly be offered but again the children can be led to see that the same looseness of structure is still present. If no pupil can combine the first two sentences to produce a suspended sentence, the teacher offers, "Columbus, who was a bold navigator, never feared to sail unknown seas." As the loose sentence, "Columbus was a brave navigator and never feared to sail unknown seas," is compared with the suspended one, the children readily feel the difference in force and the superior ability of the latter to command attention to the very last word. It is now a simple matter to elicit from the class that the word "who" made possible this improvement in their loose sentence structure. In the same way the succeeding pair of sentences are taken up and the children led to see the value of such words as "which, who, whose, whom," etc. The question, "What shall we study in our grammar lesson to-day?" brings the answer, "The words, *who, which, whose, whom.*" The lesson is thus justified, a vital motive that prompts dynamic interest is supplied, and a definite aim is established for the period. At the end of the lesson each child carefully reads his last composition and improves every loose construction by a form of the relative pronouns he has learned. Such lessons make grammar real and enable the child to improve his speech by intelligent self-criticism and correction.

THE MODEL

The most potent single factor in elevating standards of expression is the model. Its place in the teaching of composition must receive our attention for the remainder of the chapter.

4. Basic Principle of Teaching Language Through a Model.—The psychological principle which justifies the emphasis that is to-day placed on the model as an aid in the teaching of composition, is the oft-quoted dictum, "Language is learned through imitation." The model is studied appreciatively until its appeal sinks deep and becomes part of the pupils, so that unconsciously a child reproduces its wording and its phrasing in his own speech. This method of teaching composition based on imitation is not a process of instruction peculiar to the school; it is the method followed by writers of the first rank. Stevenson tells us, "I always kept two books, one to read, one to write in. . . . Whenever I read a book or a passage that pleases me, I must always sit down and ape that quality. . . . I have thus played the sedulous ape to Hazlitt, to Lamb, to Wordsworth. . . . That is the way to learn to write." Many of the great masters have developed technique by this method. We see then that we need not concern ourselves very vitally with those teachers and principals who refuse to use the model because "it means imitation and a curbing of individuality of expression." Properly used the model discourages that peculiar individuality of expression that children can well afford to lose.

The Selection of the Model.—The proper choice of a model will often determine the spirit, the enthusiasm, the efficiency of the lesson itself. What consideration should guide the teacher in making the selection for a particular class?

1. *The Model Must Be Above the Children in Tone but not in Comprehension.*—The trite advice, "Use models of plain everyday English," has little to justify its application. The model must present no thought difficulty; it must be on the child's level of comprehension and interest. But its tone and spirit must be literary and lofty, so that the child consciously looks up to the model. Many a school supervisor of elementary grades or junior high schools persistently cautions teachers not to make up their own models.

He insists that their source should be of some standard literary repute.

But it is important, however, that the teacher realize that there is a sharp distinction between the literary standard of the child whose appreciation is crude in the extreme, and the literary requirement of the adult whose linguistic taste has been refined through years of cultural pursuits. Judged by literary canons, a particular selection may possess unusual merit, but its very excellence may make it inappropriate for the pupil of school age. We must see the model through the child's eyes and interpret it in terms of the child's interests, otherwise we may thrust the child into deep waters from which he cannot emerge, and he drowns in utter discouragement. O'Shea, in his "Linguistic Development," warns us therefore:

The pupil must feel the limitations in his present equipment before he can appropriate readily and effectively the means of extending it. So it is poor policy to give pupils in the seventh and eighth years and even in the high school, models in literary expression taken from the involved writings of Milton, Shakespeare, Bacon, Tennyson, Addison and the like. The formal grammatical and rhetorical textbooks are full of complicated but excellent examples of expression, judged from the standpoint of the appreciative adult, culled from the world's great literature, the aim being to illustrate every quality of strength and grace and efficiency in style by the best instances to be found anywhere. But there is an error here which runs through much of our educational theory; what is logically "best" in adult appreciation is interpreted to be most suitable for the child at every stage of his development.

COMPOSITION IN THE GRAMMAR GRADES

Bearing this warning in mind, the following letter of the late Richard Mansfield to his son Gibbs meets the first requisite of an appropriate model. It is charming in its simplicity. Its diction, its force, and its ease raise it to a literary plane.

> Private Car 80,
> Colorado Springs, May 27.

MY DEAR, DEAR BOY:

I received your beautiful letter, and I was proud to think that you could dictate it yourself. Of course, you want to go fishing, so does your Dada, and also to go rowing, but he is sorry you do not want to play Indian. Playing Indian is great fun, for you carry a gun or a bow and arrow, and you lope all day long after somebody without stopping to eat or drink, and, when at last you find this somebody that you have been looking for you get down on your stomach and wriggle like a snake without making any noise until you reach him.

Then you give a dreadful whoop and cut off his hair, if he has any, and hang it up in your wigwam.

There are lots of other things you can do, but it is time for me to talk of something else now. I am sitting in my car and the lamps are lighted and are covered with pink shades, and outside it is raining (it wouldn't be pleasant if it were raining inside, would it?) and the drip, drip, drip of the rain on the roof makes me feel very cosy and sleepy. If you were here, I would give you some beautiful marbles to play with, and you could sit on the rug and roll them.

To-day it rained so hard that all the little streams drank so much water that they grew and grew and grew until they became giants, and then they were proud and naughty, and took the bridges and the rails in their quivering hands and tore them away, so that your Dada's train could not go any farther. When you are a grown-up engineer you will build bridges and rails that the giant streams can't tear away, won't you?

On Sunday I went for a drive with Mr. Dillon, and we went to a spring where real soda water bubbles out of the ground, and then drove home through a place called the Garden of the Gods, where there are rocks formed by Nature to look like eagles and frogs and little old men and all kinds of people and things, and we saw a little baby donkey, a real one, and your Dada bought it for his little boy, and if he is as good as he always is (not the donkey, but the boy), then Dada's boy can ride and drive it next year, please God.

And now Dada kisses his boy just one hundred and one times and fifty and a half are for mudder. Jefferson is bringing Dada's supper, and Dada is going to eat it and thank the Lord he has such a good boy and such a dear mudder. DADA.

Compare this literary letter, charming and appealing in its simplicity but essentially on the child's level of comprehension and interest, with the following flat and insipid models offered to teachers by principals who believe that "models must be on the plane of everyday English."

JACK AND THE BEANSTALK

Jack lived with his mother. She was a poor widow. A giant had killed her husband and stolen her gold.

One day the widow told Jack to sell her cow. The foolish boy sold it for a few beans. His angry mother threw the beans out of the window. The next morning Jack found a beanstalk growing outside his window. It seemed to reach the sky.

COMPOSITION IN THE GRAMMAR GRADES

The Golden Touch

There was once a king named Midas. His little daughter's name was Marygold.

The king loved gold very much. So he was given the golden touch. Then everything he touched became gold.

At first this made the king feel very happy. One day he touched his little daughter. She became a golden statue. Then the king was glad to get rid of the golden touch.

These pseudo-models lack zest and inspiration; they are entirely devoid of literary merit and cannot therefore stir in the child a spark of enthusiastic appreciation. How inferior does the second selection appear in contrast with the composition written by a fourth-year child in spite of the repressive influence of the principal's literary sense.

King Midas

Many hundreds of years ago there lived in a far-off land a king whose name was Midas. He had a beautiful little daughter named Marygold. The king loved her very much.

Midas was very greedy. One day, a fairy came to him and told him he could have any wish he pleased. The king said, "Oh, kind fairy, please give me the gift that everything I touch should turn into gold." The beautiful fairy touched him with her wand, and said, "King Midas, you may have your wish." Then Midas was very happy.

His happiness did not last very long. He wanted to eat a piece of bread—it turned to gold. He touched an apple—it turned to gold.

One day he was in his treasure house counting his gold. His little daughter Marygold came in to kiss him good morning. He kissed her and she turned to gold. Then the king fell to the floor in a swoon. When he recovered he wished that he could lose the gift. Soon the fairy came back and Midas begged her to take back the gift. She took it back and changed everything back to its proper form.

YETTA H—— 4A

The two models quoted fail badly because they violate the very first of the cardinal principles of selection,—they are not above the children in tone and spirit.

2. *The Content of the Model Must Appeal to the Child's Interest.*—The model must at all times reflect the child's life and environment. However beautiful in form, however lofty in appeal and literary in style, the content and not the form of the model will, in the last analysis, attract the child. We must be sure that there is something active, urgent and personal in the selection that is presented for analysis and study. The two models that follow illustrate the point under consideration,—the first, however, by its neglect of this requisite quality.

How to Play Tennis

Tennis is a game played very much by both men and women. A ball, a racket for each player, a net, and a marked court are needed.

The ball is hit with the racket by the first player. He must place the ball within certain lines or the hit counts against him. If the ball is placed properly, the second player must hit it with his racket. The object is to keep hitting the ball and placing it within the lines. The player, who has the highest count, wins.

How "flat, stale, and unprofitable" is this impersonal, lifeless explanation when compared with the following personal, active, and natural exposition!

How I Built Davie's Wagon

Little David is but six years of age, and like many other youngsters is determined to have his way. It was a hot day in June and David wanted to have some fun. His heart was set on a wagon. He stepped up to his hard working father and said, "Papa, make me a wagon." I, a friend of the neighboring carpenter, was standing nearby. So Mr. Abelman, turning to me, said, "If you don't mind, George, here is a box, some tools and a plank. I am confident you like carpenter work. Go into the back yard and make Dave a wagon." Having nothing to do, I agreed to this. I secured wheels and set to work.

The first thing I did was to nail a plank to the bottom of the box exactly in the center, extending it a yard beyond the front of the box. I next nailed on the back axle and attached its wheels. I afterward took the front axle and nailed it to a small piece of flat board. I bored a hole through the center of the plank, three inches from its end, and another through the small piece of flat board on which the axle was nailed. Then I put a large screw through these holes so as to make the steering apparatus. Last of all I attached the front, smaller wheels and a cord to both ends of the axle. Now everything was complete; the wagon was finished and a pretty good job it was.

You can imagine David's joy after the completion of the wagon. He owned a wagon he could call his own and made the other little fellows envious.

3. *The Model Must Illustrate Only One Specific Principle.*—The model that exemplifies many principles of composition usually teaches nothing, for in

the end it entails diffusion of attention and results in no permanent acquisition. Select a model because it shows how to describe a person, how to describe a place, how to tell an incident, how to write a dialogue, how to give a clear exposition, etc. At the end of the period the child must consciously feel that at least one lesson has been made central, at least one principle of composition has been learned and mastered.

4. *Models Should Be Reasonably Short.*—Another consideration governing a good choice of the model is its length. Models should be short, seldom exceeding two hundred and fifty words. The long model dissipates energy and attention and weakens the point to be taught. The short model allows for closer concentration on the vital point, deeper and more lasting impression, and easier grasp of the underlying principle that is involved.

5. *All Models Need Not Come from "Reputed Literary Sources."*—A final suggestion counsels that we use the best compositions of the last class as models for the succeeding pupils. This is in direct contradiction to the prevalent belief that all models must have "reputed literary sources." The model of "reputed literary source" may discourage; its very perfection may preclude any attempt on the part of the child to imitate and approximate it. In all practical higher endeavors in life we usually strive to attain the possible, not the perfect. Confronted with the perfect literary model the child may feel his helplessness and thus put forth no effort in his discouragement. One of the great limitations of the old en-

graved copy-books was that the copy represented perfection; hence failure seemed to the child a foregone conclusion. But with the product of one's own classmates as a model, a child is roused to healthy emulation, for the goal is possible and probable.

General Treatment of the Model.—Now that we have justified the use of the model and have considered the guiding principles in making the most appropriate selections, we must turn our attention to the method of presenting it to the class. To make it easier to follow the lesson through its progressive steps, we must take a specific illustration and refer all procedure to it. "Gellert," a narrative model offered by Sykes in his "Elementary English Composition" (p. 16), will serve this purpose admirably.

Gellert

Prince Llewellyn had a favorite greyhound named Gellert, gentle at home and valiant in the chase. One day the prince was about to go hunting and blew his horn for his dogs. All his dogs came save Gellert. He blew again and called but Gellert did not come. He could wait no longer and set off without his favorite. He had little success and returned to his castle vexed at his ill luck.

As he came up to the castle-gate Gellert came bounding out to meet him. But the prince noticed that his lips and fangs were dripping with blood. The prince was startled. He thought of his infant child who often played with the dog. Rushing to the child's room, he found everything in disorder, the cradle overturned and daubed with blood. More and more terrified at the signs of conflict, he sought for his child but in vain. At last he felt sure that the hound had destroyed his son, and with the cry, "Monster, thou hast devoured my child," he plunged his sword into the greyhound's side.

As Gellert gave his dying yell, a cry was heard from beneath the overturned cradle and there Llewellyn found his child unharmed and just awakened from sleep, and beside him, torn in pieces and covered with blood, lay the body of a great gaunt wolf.

Llewellyn was grieved to the heart; but nothing could bring his faithful dog to life again. He buried him by the castle wall, and over his grave he raised a great cairn of stones so that every passer-by might see it and remember his story. And the place to this day is called Beth Gellert or the Grave of Gellert.

The Model in the Hands of the Children.—Each child must be supplied with a copy of the model. Merely to hear the model read by the teacher will not suffice for the auditory appeal is of the very weakest. To see it on the blackboard may help, but too many children cannot see all of the writing and proper concentration is impossible with the disconcerting circumstances attending such a presentation. With the model in the hands of each child, the proper appeal can be made and the necessary concentration and attention can be given.

The Reading by the Teacher.—The lesson itself should begin with a reading of the model by the teacher, the children following on their individual copies. To call upon the children is not the most advisable procedure; they stumble and hesitate, new words confuse, new constructions fail to arouse proper meaning and the necessary expression is lost; all these circumstances militate against the success of the lesson. The teacher's reading gives meaning and spirit to the selection; the expression of the reading will give comprehension even where words and phrases may be unfamiliar to the children. The lesson is thus begun with proper interest and attention and the proper attitude toward the work is aroused.

The Outline of the Model Developed.—The next step is to trace the structure and the organization of ideas in the model. With this end in view the teacher must elicit the outline of the model. The children read it silently and then give (1) the name of each paragraph by pointing out the topic sentence. (2) They then analyze the contents of each paragraph and test for paragraph unity. Is the topic sentence justified? Does every sentence in the paragraph treat of the theme announced in the topic sentence? (3) Attention is next directed to the sequence of the whole series of paragraphs. What guided the author in making his paragraphs follow as they do? (4) The children are finally asked to consider, What are the opening and the closing sentences? Are they effective? Why?

The Comprehension of the Model.—Now that the children have seen the organization of the model and the development of the theme, the detailed study is begun. The teacher must see that all necessary words and expressions are made familiar, that unusually effective expressions are emphasized, and that the children are led to imitate them orally and to attempt variations upon them. Let us refer to "Gellert," the illustration selected. Do the children know the meaning of "greyhound," "save Gellert," "fangs," "conflict," "devoured," "gaunt," and "cairn"? If they do not, all further study must wait for the acquisition of this information. "How shall it be given?" the teacher asks—"through the dictionary, through the context, through sentences, through word study and etymology, or through direct telling?" Any method will suffice, but in the main, the direct telling, the much condemned didactic method, must be used, for the governing object of the lesson is not to study words but to carry away the spirit and the form of the model as a whole. Since mere words must be subordinated to the thought and its expression, the shortest method is the best.

Drill on Superior Forms of Expressions.—The teacher now turns attention to the best phrases in the model and tries to bring out their force and their worth as media of expression. Thus, "valiant in the chase," is subjected to a little exercise like the following: "How would you express the same thought?" To this query of the teacher, children in a fifth-year class replied, "Brave while out hunting," "Courageous while out hunting," "Fearless while chasing the deer," "Brave while pursuing the deer," etc. The statements offered by the class as equivalents were compared with the original expression in the model and the children were led to note its superiority. To cap the point and make the drill effective, insist on original application. Let the children give a list of situations where the phrase can be applied, e. g., to the fireman, policeman, soldier, sailor, etc. Then have them construct sentences about these situations, using the expression that is to become part of their vocabularies, *e.g.*: "The fire captain was *valiant* at the scene of the rescue of the old woman," "The policeman was *valiant in* the pursuit of the burglar," "The general was *valiant in* the attack," etc., until an effective impression has been made and the expression is on the highroad to the goal of habit. A similar drill can be given on "dripping blood," "vexed at his ill luck," "The prince was startled," "but in vain," etc.

But the teacher may object, "When will the oral period come to an end if each good expression be made focal in such a drill?" Much time would undoubtedly be consumed. Since the time is necessarily limited, we must sacrifice the number of expressions studied to the thoroughness of the drill. The teacher must select only two or three of the dozen admirable phrases and make sure that these become part of the children. If each model could be made to contribute two or three of these expressions toward the child's permanent linguistic possessions, each term would witness unmistakable progress.

Emphasis on the Principle of the Composition Illustrated by the Model.—The next point, and the most important part of the lesson, is the emphasis on the specific point that led to the selection of the model, the drill on the principle of composition which the model illustrates.

If the model was selected to illustrate an argumentative composition, then it becomes the aim of the teacher to show the children that the organization requires successively, (1) that the topic or the question be stated, (2) that the outline of the arguments be foreshadowed, (3) that the first argument be posited, (4) that the proof for the first argument be given, (5) that the following arguments and their proofs be stated in the same way, (6) that the conclusion be drawn to bring home the contention that is upheld throughout. In the following composition, these points are attempted after a study of the model. The child's product lacks much that is desirable, but it is nevertheless a good statement of what the child feels and thinks.

Resolved: That Examinations Are Unnecessary

1. Examinations are given every term to test the pupil of his or her knowledge of different subjects. It is done from the lowest grade in the primary to the highest department in college. The question arises, "Are these necessary?"

2. I firmly believe that examinations are entirely unnecessary because, first, they make the pupil nervous, and

3. second, marks can be obtained in other ways. When the pupil is in the examination hall, things taught her leave her head entirely, therefore they are not a fair test of

4. the pupil's knowledge. It is much better to count the pupil's recitations during the term than for them to be sent on short notice to the examination hall, as one is more familiar and feels more at home in one's own classroom. It's hurtful to the pupil's health as it works the pupil up to a nervous pitch and many pupils become very ill after them.

COMPOSITION IN THE GRAMMAR GRADES

5. My opponents may say that the pupil has to be marked so that the teachers may know whether he or she is fit to go on to another grade, but that can be done by marking the pupil on his or her daily work, and averaging up the marks on the different subjects at the end of the term. Then again the other side might say that the pupil might become more nervous standing up and facing the class while reciting than just answering an examination paper, but again I say one feels and is more at home in the classroom and with the teacher than in the examination hall. They also might say that if one

6. is not healthy enough to stand an examination they should not be at school, but it is just the examinations that make them unhealthy and nervous after the examinations.   ANNETTE H—— 8B.

When the model is used to teach the art of exposition, emphasis is laid on (1) how the topic to be expounded is announced, (2) the importance of careful sequence, (3) the need of sentences that are distinguished by their simplicity and clearness. As a final point we may mention that the child should be taught the test of good exposition. To do this let the children follow out the directions and see if the result is the desired end. Thus, in the composition on "How to Lay off a Baseball Diamond," the child should actually "lay off," to a scale, the measurements and the lines on a sheet of paper, and test the clearness of the exposition and the logic of the sequence. Whenever an exposition is written, each pupil should be required, if feasible, to express diagrammatically or graphically the directions in his own composition as a test of the efficiency of his written work.

In the case of narration, the analysis of the model must be such as will reveal the four component elements of a good narrative:

1. The Plot, "The What?"
2. The Characters, "The Who?"
3. Situation, "The Where—The When?"
4. The Purpose, "The Why?"

The introduction must give the "who," the "where" and "when," and the "why"; the succeeding paragraphs offer the "what," the plot. The child thus learns that the organization of a narrative lies in the sequence of events as they happened in time, that the series of occurrences begins with the preliminary events and the setting of the scene, and gradually works up to the climax which in its turn is followed by the denouement, the surprise in outcome or ending. An analysis of the model on "Gellert" reveals, very readily, this structure. Of course, it is obvious that not all these elements and principles of composition would be taught in any one period. A whole lesson may well be spent learning how to write a climax. The children analyze the model and note that the climax is preceded by rather slow movement, long sentences, discursive style, that the climax has maximum movement and is made up of a number of short sentences and independent clauses. Thus, in the model studied, we find, "The prince was startled . . . rushed to the child's room . . . everything in disorder . . . cradle overturned . . . daubed with blood" . . . Every verb is an action word. This is followed by a series of imitations by the children, in which

COMPOSITION IN THE GRAMMAR GRADES

they take first the same subject and then similar subjects for their themes. The teacher takes one or two topics and gives his climax as he would write it; the children then try their own. Thus, the teacher offers, as the climax in a composition on "A Fire":

> The smoke was now curling out of each window. It became blacker and denser. The crash of breaking glass filled the air. Above the din, a sharp cry rang out. A helpless woman stood on the third floor fire-escape. A sheet of flame now leaped out of the story above. The upper structure was almost entirely enveloped. "Help! Help!" was taken up by all bystanders. But help was almost beyond human power.

The children are asked to suggest a similar situation and the teacher offers to give the climax in appropriate form. Suppose that the children suggest "The Fire Engine and the Child." The teacher proceeds:

> The sharp shrill whistle of the engine is piercing the air. The heavy wagon is rounding the corner. The strained face of the driver changes. He pulls frantically at his reins. What can be the matter? See! . . . a child in the roadway! The mother's screams ring out wildly. The bystanders are in dismay. Horror-stricken they stand motionless. I shudder to see what the next moment will bring!

As the children's imaginations conjure up new situations of hairbreadth escapes and breathless excitement, the teacher gives, on the moment, the fitting climax. This arouses great enthusiasm and the teacher need only challenge the children to imitate this construction in new topics that he may assign. A competition is started, to see which pupil can, by using short sentences and independent clauses with action verbs, give the greatest feeling of suspense and excitement in the situations of "A Man Overboard," "The Stranded Ship," "Columbus Sighting Land," "Pocahontas Saving Captain John Smith," "Crashing into an Iceberg," and the like. Only as one point is made focal in the lesson, harped on, imitated, and repeated from varied views and angles, is the child's language ability developed.

In the same manner we treat in the formal lesson, a model description. Now the teacher carefully brings home the fact that in effective description we should give: (1) *the general impression*, "As I looked up, a most delightful spectacle confronted me," etc.; (2) *the point of view*, "There, before me, stretching to the right and left, lay a beautiful sheet of water"; (3) *the general comparison*, "It resembled those charming oval lakes that stud the landscape of Northern Maine"; (4) *choice of details*, use of color and picture words—those words and details which emphasize the calm of the lake, and the feeling of quiet satisfaction, and which give the most vivid picture; (5) *the lasting impression*, "It was one of those haunts of Nature where peace and contentment reign."

Here again, we must remember that for any one lesson only one point is selected and the drill is given to make that a permanent acquisition. Let us suppose that details and color words are to be emphasized in the study of a particular model of description. "Der Kleine Johannes" is studied and the children are

COMPOSITION IN THE GRAMMAR GRADES

led to see that all details, all words, suggest tranquillity, peace of nature and of man. A new topic is given, the dominant characteristics are elicited and suitable adjectives listed on the board in preparation for the drill.

Topic	Characteristics	Adjectives
1. A Rapid River	1. movement mass of water noise	1. noisy turbulent rushing whirling, etc.
2. A Snowfall	2. slow quiet calm pure	2. Same words as characteristics
3. A Beggar	3. pity fear disgust	3. ragged hungry thin pale sickly dirty shaking pleading, etc.
4. Brooklyn Bridge by Day and by Night	4. Contrast of impression	4. Contrast of adjectives
5. A Street Scene	5. noise rush hurry scurry insignificance of the individual	5. Same words as characteristics

Each topic is now taken up and with the aid of the suggestions on the blackboard, the descriptions are attempted orally by the children. In this way a number of themes can be outlined and elaborated in the oral period and the child learns that in writing the description of a place, a person, or a thing, only such characteristic details and color words are selected as will give the auditor or reader one predominant and permanent impression.

But it may be argued, "Why study these forms in the elementary school?" It is true that when children leave school they will not indulge in descriptive paragraphs nor does their correspondence require an intimate knowledge of the technical structure of narration or exposition. While this must undoubtedly be admitted, we cannot, however, draw the conclusion, "Therefore do not teach these." We are engaged in teaching correct expression; and these forms are the media. Even though letter writing does constitute the sum total of the written composition in the later life of most people, a letter which rises above the level of personal twaddle and gossip shows touches of description, of narration, of exposition and of argumentation. And, finally, we must remember that these composition exercises have their value and application in the literature lessons. When in the course of future reading, the child sees a passage that interests him, he can analyze it and criticize it in terms of his standard. His eyes are open, for instance, to the masterful picture of *Ichabod Crane,* to Irving's happy choice of characteristic details and rich picture words. These exercises, properly presented and stressed, teach the child the technique of expression and give drill until correct forms become habit in both oral and written speech.

The Final Reading of the Model.—The topic under discussion is the consideration of a method of teaching the model. The mode of procedure follows a number of steps: (1) the reading of the model by the teacher, (2) the outline of the model for the study of its sequence, (3) a study of unfamiliar but necessary wording and phraseology, (4) a study of the basic principles for which the model is chosen. The final step in the study of the model requires that we have a final reading of it, either by the teacher or by one of the best readers among the pupils. The reasons for this last reading are many and obvious. In the course of the analytical and detailed study, the model was well dissected. It is now necessary to give a unified impression. The final reading leads not only to this end but to an increased familiarization. In addition one always experiences a keen pleasure from an increased appreciation of old knowledge. It is in this final reading that the child sees how much the lesson has meant to him, how much more he now reads into it, and consequently how much more he reads out of it.

How Closely Shall the Model Be Followed?—Having presented the model systematically and thoroughly, the teacher must next concern herself with the problem of how closely to follow it in the course of conscious imitation. A moment's thought will show the futility of a positive answer. Any degree of imitation may be encouraged depending upon the language ability and the experience of the pupils. Unusual care must be taken to make *imitation progressive through the course and to adjust the degree of imitation to the capacities of individual pupils.*

Let us examine the graded steps that show progressive imitation, varying from slavish reproduction to free personal expression:

1. Transcribing the model
2. Writing on the same topic with free access to the model studied
3. Writing on the same topic without access to the model studied
4. Writing on a topic related to the model studied
5. Writing after more than one model is studied
6. Writing an original composition before model is shown

Even in the seventh year, it may be necessary to ask children markedly behind grade to transcribe the model while another group attempts a personal composition on the same subject as the model that was studied. This latter group has permission to refer freely to the model. More advanced pupils are required to write without reference to the model once it has been studied. The most advanced group may be asked to write not the story of "Gellert," but of human bravery and sacrifice.

Should the Model Precede or Follow the Composition? —A source of endless contention is the time when the model is to be studied—before or after the composition is written by the children. The debates are spirited. The verdict, however, cannot be given to either side, for both are correct, each, of course, in its own circumstances. What are the merits in the dispute?

Those teachers who argue, "before," that the model must precede the child's written composition, insist that language is learned through imitation. If the model is not given the child before the written composition, he has nothing to imitate. When a new topic is presented or a new form of composition is assigned, the child feels lost. All expression is paralyzed in the face of the technical difficulties. Let the child learn the mode of procedure, the organization, and the attack, from the model, and the feeling of confidence which ensues, guarantees free and easy expression, for the child, unhampered by formal problems, expresses his mind freely.

Those who champion the opposite side of the controversy are much perturbed by such a contention, for they argue that to present the model first kills all originality and deadens every spark of personal interest. The child is too immature to see the literary value and beauty of the model. Let the child, therefore, write his own composition, replete with crudities and flagrant errors. Then let him study the model, compare it with his own product and see its inferiority in the contrast. Thus there will be aroused in each child a feeling of discontent with his limitations and he will be spurred on to greater effort. But may it not entirely dishearten the child when he perceives his own inferiority?

These contestants do not realize that there are two uses of a model, viz., a standard for imitation and a standard for correction. In discharging the first function, the model must naturally be used before the composition, but for purposes of correction, it follows the child's own production. Realizing the limitations of any arbitrary law, it may nevertheless be stated as a safe tendency that through the sixth year all models should precede children's compositions, for the pupils are still too poor in language possession to launch out for themselves. In the seventh and eighth years the model should be used as a standard for imitation in new and difficult forms, i. e., in descriptions, in argumentations, and the like. But, when the topic is of an old form, a narration, or a business letter, or a biography, the children should write their own compositions first and then use the model as a standard for correction. The model is studied very carefully and then the original compositions are corrected in the light of the lessons learned and the limitations noted.

How to Prevent Slavish Imitation of the Model.—The final topic in the discussion of the model is the means of guarding against overimitation, which makes composition little more than a transcription exercise and kills whatever originality and enthusiasm the child may have in his self-expression. The suggestions that are offered for guarding against slavish imitation are simple indeed, though often neglected in the routine of teaching.

1. *Variety of Organization.*—The simplest method of introducing a personal note in the compositions written after the model is studied, is to evolve with

the children all the possible forms of organizing the facts of the subject. At the end of such an exercise each child decides for himself, the number of paragraphs he will have, the theme of each, and the grouping of facts under them. It is evident also that each mode of organization will have its appropriate opening and closing sentence. In discussing the element of originality in the outline, instances were quoted from children's work illustrating the point under discussion.

2. *Drill on Synonymous Expressions.*—In the study of the model entitled "Gellert" it was shown how rich and varied an exercise can be worked out by eliciting synonymous expressions for "valiant in the chase." Such a drill entails a verbal stock-taking which leaves the child with a more varied and richer vocabulary. In the "Pied Piper of Hamelin," we find among others, the expressions, "The town was infested with rats," "The people were beside themselves," "His clothes were variegated," and "gray rats, brown rats, young rats, old rats." These were made basic in a drill on variety of synonymous expressions with a fifth-year class. The children gave, "The town was rat-ridden," "It was a town of rats," "The rats of the universe seemed to collect there," "The rats made the town their home," "It seemed as if no rat was happy unless it got there," etc., for the first. "The people hardly knew what to do," "The people were driven to desperation," "The problem seemed hopeless to the townsfolk," "The townspeople despaired of ever getting rid of the rats," are

types of equivalents that were elicited for the second. Such a drill is therefore an effective means of guarding against too close an imitation of the model.

The Variation Method.—A special method known as the "variation method" is gaining much popularity in many schools. Teachers who follow this method select a story which is read to the class. The story is then outlined and subdivided into logical parts. The first logical subdivision is treated somewhat as follows. The first sentence is written on the blackboard. Subject, predicate, complement and important modifiers are marked off by vertical lines. Each part of the sentence is then subjected to variations and each contribution that is accepted is put on the board in its proper column. The writer observed such a lesson in which the sentence for the day was, "The old scholar arose early each day to study the holy law." For the subject, "the old scholar," the children offered: "the old prophet," "the prophet of old," "the pious old man," "the God-fearing rabbi," "the religious teacher," "the old religious student." For the predicate verb, the teacher elicited, "awoke," "bestirred himself," "left his bed." For the adverbial modifier, "early each day," the children offered, "at the dawn of day," "at the first sign of day," "at the coming of daylight," "before the sun showed his face," "before the darkness of night had left," "when the world was still wrapped in the darkness of the night." Toward the end of the period, the blackboard work took on an appearance like the following, each contribution being in different colored chalk:

The old scholar	*arose*	*early each day*	*to study the holy law.*
The old prophet	bestirred himself	at the dawn of day	to learn God's word.
The prophet of old	left his bed	at the first sign of day	to study the holy books.
The pious old man	awoke	at the coming of daylight	to read the commandments of the Lord.
The God-fearing rabbi		before the sun showed his face	
The religious teacher		before the darkness of the night left	
The old religious student		while the world was still wrapped in the darkness of night	

Three twenty to thirty minute lessons were devoted to this work every week in this class. At the end of each lesson, each child selected the sentence that appealed most to him. Thus, one child selected, "The pious old man bestirred himself at the coming of daylight to learn the Holy Book," as his synthetic product, while another thought, "The old prophet arose at the first sign of day to study the holy law," the best combination. The sentence selected was copied into a notebook. Each lesson, therefore, enriched the story by a sentence which each child selected for himself. When the whole story was thus gone over, each child had the same story told in a different way.

The worth of such a procedure is unquestionable. It enriches the vocabulary, giving it greater flexibility and breadth; it teaches variety of sentence structure; it maintains active interest through friendly and helpful rivalry; and exercises to a large degree, the self-activity of the child. As a device in composition, it is of rare worth. But as a method to supplant all other ways of teaching composition, it must be condemned. Composition teaching means training in logical organization, in sustained thinking, in accurate and intelligent observation, in spontaneous expression. These ends are obviously and necessarily lost sight of in the variation method.

3. *Vary the Topic.*—In selecting the topic for composition the teacher should usually take, not one identical with that of the model, but rather one that al-

COMPOSITION IN THE GRAMMAR GRADES

lows general imitation only. Care must be exercised not to select a topic so similar that all a pupil need do is to change the name from "A Fireman" to "A Policeman"; from "A Sailor" to "A Soldier." If the model studied gave a description of a mounted policeman, the topic for composition should call for the description of a beggar, a peddler, a foreigner; in a word, a topic in which the principles learned in the model will be applied, but the point of view, the phraseology, and the specific organization will allow for welcome variety.

Actual experience convinces the teacher of the deadening effect of choosing too similar a topic. In a 4A class, the model studied was "Little Marie of Lehon." The model that was presented for the literary inspiration of the children ran as follows:

There she was, trotting toward us in her round cap, blue woolen gown, white apron, and wooden shoes.
On her head was a loaf of buckwheat as big as a small wheel. In one hand she held a basket full of green stuff, while the other led an old goat which seemed in no hurry to go home.
She was a rosy bright-eyed child. She looked rather shy and always seemed in haste.

After an analytical study of this lifeless and insipid model the children were told to write a similar description of a personal friend. A typical result of such an assignment is quoted so that the reader may make the comparison and draw the obvious moral.

My Friend Jennie

There was my friend Jennie. She was jumping a rope. In one hand she carried a loaf of bread and in the other she carried a pitcher of milk. She used to be a rosy child but she is pale now.

4. *Every Composition Should Be a Personal Composition.*—In all topics the teacher must have the children so change the items and facts of the model that there will result an intensely personal expression. An illustration of this suggestion is found in a common form of business correspondence, a letter of application for a position. But no matter who the child may be who writes it, in what class it is written, or what position is applied for, it is always the same, stupid, stiff and stilted meaningless formality,—"Having seen your advertisement in this morning's . . . I herewith beg leave to offer myself as an applicant for the position." There is no justification for such formality, for few letters are more personal and urgent than an application.

If one were to try to convince an employer to let him have a particular position what would be his line of argument? First, he would analyze the position and make a list of the necessary qualifications that one must possess to fulfill the requirements. Second, he would proceed to prove that because of special training and experience, he possessed these qualifications in so strong a measure that the employer could not, in justice to his business interest, refuse the applicant. This, at any rate, seems to be the course dictated by the urgency of the situation. Why should we teach a set form and inflict it upon our children, with all its meaningless words, when it is precisely the kind of application that would never make a favorable impression?

Let us assume that a boy is writing a letter applying for a position as errand boy; what should he include in his letter? What are the demands of the position? One must (a) know the city, (b) be quick and alive, (c) be honest and reliable. In the light of these requirements a boy should say (a) that he was born in the city, hence the inference is that he knows the city streets and highways; (b) that he sold newspapers for two years and is therefore alive and alert; (c) that he served as cash boy in a department store on Saturdays and during the holiday season and can bring references, thus showing that he is honest and trustworthy. These essentials are precisely the very items that children who follow the set model always fail to mention.

Another illustration will suffice. The position applied for by a class of sixth-year boys was that of "wagon boy" for John Wanamaker. They all informed the gentleman that they noted his advertisement in the morning newspaper, that they begged leave to offer themselves as applicants, that they had completed the sixth year of the public school, that they lived with their parents, that they could bring references from principals or teachers. But the employer is not interested in all these estimable things. They are all beside the mark. To qualify for the position one must know the streets and avenues of the city; be able to understand more than the English language, because so many foreigners purchase at the store; know something of automobiles; be alert and active, and honest. Let the children list these requisites. What can they offer? "Born in New York City" is certainly an asset. "I can speak or understand Italian as well as English," is worth adding. "I helped on a milk route," is another qualification that has a direct bearing on the position. In the class referred to almost every lad spoke one other language besides English, but the fact was not mentioned; ten lads knew the operation of an automobile, but not one said so. Every bit of personal appeal was lost in the dead formalism of the model.

5. *Teach Through Many Models.*—In teaching any principle of composition in grades above the sixth year more than one model may be used; two or three may be presented and the principle of composition evolved from them. The point is taught, but the variety of the appeal guarantees a rational rather than a slavish imitation.

6. *The Model after the Child's Effort.*—A final suggestion advises that just as soon as it is feasible, the model should be used as a standard for correction rather than for imitation, hence the model is to follow rather than precede the child's original composition.

SUGGESTED READING

The suggested reading for this chapter will be found at the end of Chapter VIII.

CHAPTER VII

THE CORRECTION OF WRITTEN COMPOSITIONS

In introducing the subject of the teaching of composition in the grammar grades, it was observed that the method-whole in composition required three separate and distinct periods, each having its own aim, function and organization. These were designated (1) the period of oral drill and teaching, (2) the period of written composition, and (3) the period of correction. The three preceding chapters concerned themselves with the conduct of the first of these periods; the present chapter must give itself to the second and the third. We must pass, therefore, to a consideration of the second period.

The Period of Written Composition.—In the first period the science of composition is taught. But this aspect of the subject finds its justification in application and in rational use. The second period, therefore, concerns itself with the art side of teaching. The teacher's task of instructing and the pupils' task of learning give way to a free and personal expression by the children. This is pre-eminently their period.

The Teacher's Function.—But it must not be erroneously assumed that since the period of direct teaching is over, the teacher need only see that the children are amply supplied with paper and ink and started on their written work. The teacher's function, though not instructional, is nevertheless supervisory. Teachers must not conveniently eliminate themselves from this period merely because the burden of the work is necessarily thrown upon the children.

What is the teacher's work of supervision in this period? First we must mention the tireless effort that must be made to correct bad physical posture of the children during written work. Impaired eyesight, round shoulders, depressed abdominal cavities are a few of the many distressing effects due to bad posture in written work. The most essential fact to remember is that bad posture which is not persistently corrected soon becomes a habit from the clutch of which the child cannot free himself.

It is also important that the character of the work should be watched constantly. A word of praise to a child who has begun well keeps the fount of effort freely flowing; a word of warning or censure awakens the child to a realization that he must approximate a higher standard. While the children are writing, the teacher must walk about the room, up and down aisles, and inspect work, not in a spirit of espionage but rather in the attitude of friendly criticism and constructive supervision.

In this period children should feel that they are at liberty to ask questions, consult the dictionary or verify facts in any textbook to which they can have access. It is a grave error to deny to a class the very privileges that we ourselves take in our own written work. The child who asks the teacher whether one says, "None of them are" or "None of them is"; or whether "principal" is correct in the expression, "The principle which explains the workings of the magnet," shows promise and healthy development. He has reached a point in his linguistic growth where it actually makes a difference to him whether his form is correct or not. Most pupils are in a state of sublime indifference to the laws of language and to the unreasonable demands of our unphonetic spelling. The teacher need not answer the pupil directly. The child who wants to know the spelling of "emancipation" is asked to suggest the first two syllables. After he offers "e, man," he is told to look for the remainder of the word in the dictionary. Such questions as, "When was the Battle of —— fought," or "What was the name of the general who . . . " etc., can be answered by "Look for the name in the index of your history textbook." But where a direct and didactic answer must be given, it should be offered in the earnest spirit which prompts the child. Questions that are asked merely for the sake of asking questions must be treated in a manner designed to hastily discourage the offender.

Cautions in Written Composition. — Experience shows a few common errors in the conduct of the written composition period that need guarding, for they are frequent pitfalls for the unwary. We must, at all times, make a sharp distinction between "composition" and "penmanship." All written work must always show care, accuracy, neatness and earnest endeavor to produce results on the highest level that the child can attain. But the desire for good penmanship, for "a fine-looking lot of compositions," must not befog our conception of "composition" as an expressional exercise in which penmanship and technique of language must be duly subordinated. When school authorities require that the written composition be a polished result, perfect in penmanship, spelling and punctuation, it is wise to let the children write their compositions in the rough with all conscious interest on the expressional side of their tasks. This is the freest possible expression. In a later period each child rereads his composition, corrects it in ways that his calmer and more critical judgment may dictate and then commits the final effort to paper. But we must not fail to realize that this is a period of penmanship rather than composition which is given as an expedient when school regulations place undue emphasis on form rather than on content.

Children's compositions should be kept within reasonable limits. In the fifth and sixth years, they should not extend beyond one and one-quarter pages of the regular six-by-nine paper usually used in the schools; in the last two years the maximum should be about one and one-half pages. Long and discursive exercises have serious limitations. They tend to increase the number of errors, to make difficult the regular correction of composition and to produce extreme carelessness. Few children are capable of maintain-

THE CORRECTION OF WRITTEN COMPOSITIONS

ing a uniformly high standard of efficiency in a long effort.

But little need be said of the teacher's supervisory rather than instructional function in this period, if composition is taught by a group system which uses the same method, and sets the same pace, for only those children who are of like ability, and which tries to raise the language level of each child by meeting personal needs and individual weaknesses. The group method would continue the instructional task of the teacher by keeping one set of pupils busy writing while the other would be receiving its oral drill and explanations.

THE PERIOD OF CORRECTION

Correction of written work in its fullest and ugliest sense is one of the banes of the teacher's life. There is so much of it that it is completely overwhelming. The results are most discouraging for the round of irritating errors appears and reappears despite the untold drudgery of constant correction. The vital problem in correction of written work is hence twofold: (1) how to reduce the onerousness of the burden, and (2) how to make the work more telling and productive of greater results. These two pressing needs must be met by a sound method.

Objects of Correction.—But before we attempt to indicate a method we must formulate definitely the reasons for correcting class work. Teachers are required to go through the tedium of correction, first, because there is the need of acquainting the child with his error and the cause of it so that he will be able to correct the incorrect form on his own initiative. Secondly, it is hoped that by dint of repetition teachers will inculcate in each child a habit of self-criticism so that he will examine critically all that he writes and change it in accordance with his better judgment and in the light of what his language lessons teach him.

The Time for Correction.—Much ado is often made about the question, "When shall we correct?" Any answer will suffice, for the question is more or less useless. Let the teacher warn the children against possible errors if they can be anticipated with any degree of certainty. On the other hand, the corrections may be made during the writing of the compositions, if we feel certain that this interference will not curb the expressional tendencies of the children. From the very nature of the case we can readily realize that the bulk of the corrections must be made after the compositions have been written. But at all times we must bear one important caution in mind, viz., that the corrections must never become too minute, lest children become ultra self-conscious. With their limitations constantly confronting them, they fear to write as freely, as fully and as enthusiastically as they feel about their subject and the result lacks the life and the zest that characterize good compositions.

Incorrect Method.—Before suggesting a method of correcting written work we must note, in passing, certain very common though incorrect procedures which must be avoided, for they defeat the twofold object that governs all correction. One of these is the method pursued by teachers who have too strong a sense of responsibility and are therefore prompted to do too much for their pupils. The compositions are taken home, read by the teachers and with the aid of pen and red ink, the children's efforts are slashed most ruthlessly and the correct forms indicated. In the next period the child receives his composition—a veritable labyrinth of red lines. For example, *king Edward* has a line under the small *k* with a capital above it and a small "c" underneath. The child looks up at a complex chart of queer symbols and learns that the "c" advises him to make a capital. The word *akward* is underlined and marked "sp." The chart tells him that he has made a mistake in spelling. If he has no dictionary, he asks the teacher for the correct form. The next sentence has a two-legged "p" with its face turned the wrong way or a large "s" which indicates where to begin a new sentence. The mystic chart tells him that he has offended by violating paragraph unity or sentence structure. A new sheet of paper is now given him and the child begins to transcribe his composition. He carries out the red ink warnings, makes the new paragraph or the sentence, writes *king* with a capital, *awkward* with two "w's" in the right places; never questions the "why" or the "wherefore" for he has full confidence in the teacher. What are the inevitable results? The next composition finds the same errors of paragraph unity and sentence structure. *Queen Elizabeth* is written *queen Elizabeth,* etc. Because the child did not learn the cause of his errors, he is as helpless as heretofore.

He obeys slavishly the arbitrary dictates of the red ink, and does not acquire habits of self-correction. In the light of the two aims that were set up as standards, this method fails woefully despite the conscientious effort and the weary drudgery of the teacher.

The Method of Correcting Written Work.—A pedagogical method of correcting written work requires that the teacher read the compositions but refrain from putting any marks of correction on them. While the children are writing, the teacher can read their compositions over their shoulders and make note of such general errors or class mistakes as merit class study and attention. In this way a number of the compositions are read. The remaining ones are read after class hours, and the common errors noted in the teacher's book. It is imperative that the teacher refrain from marking them. The time now spent is insignificant in comparison with the old method. These typical errors are now embodied in a composition and the result is put on the board to be taken up in the period for correction. The children are made to understand that the faulty work on the board is a composite of their common errors.

Elicit the mistakes from the pupils, then through questions and suggestions lead them to see the reason that explains why the form is wrong. The first inaccurate sentence on the board is "John, with his dog, are in the room." The teacher appeals to their knowledge of grammar, and asks such questions as "What is the subject? the predicate? the rule of agreement? What are the modifiers?" If for some reason,

THE CORRECTION OF WRITTEN COMPOSITIONS

answers to these cannot be obtained from the children, a direct explanation is given and the reason for the inaccuracy is stated by the teacher. The children are then called upon for the correction of the sentence. Under no circumstances should the teacher offer the correct form, for the aim of the lesson and the test of comprehension are both defeated. In this way each general error on the board is taken up, discussed, and corrected by the pupils. When this work is completed, the children read their own compositions with great care and look for such typical errors, which they underline and correct.

In this work a few minor cautions are necessary: (1) The corrections on compositions written in ink should be made with a different colored ink or lead pencil, for if the same colored ink is used, the children's minds become occupied with the problem of how to correct surreptitiously; an "e" is filled up and dotted to become an "i," a small "s" has its head enlarged to become a capital letter, and the like—practices which take attention away from the main issue, the comprehension of the cause of error and the interest in self-correction. (2) Let the children underline each error with ruler and pencil, and refrain from indicating by a confusion of symbols what literary sin they have committed. These symbols cannot anticipate every possible error that children in their ignorance can perpetrate. The period is often wasted with questions of the type, "I put in double quotation marks where I should have had single ones; how shall I mark it?" etc. A line under each error ought to suffice. (3) It is important that children look for only one or two typical errors at a time. To ask them to read their compositions and correct in the one reading all their errors is too big a task for them. In the resulting diffusion of attention, they overlook flagrant mistakes and neglect important corrections. (4) We must stimulate them to set to this task with spirit and avidity. They naturally fear to bring out all their errors prominently. Hence we must put a premium on correction. Let them feel that all errors corrected are excused; all uncorrected, count doubly against them. In this way we reduce the teacher's burden, lead the children to see their errors and note the cause, and to develop habits of self-criticism.

Seeming Limitations of the Method.—But it may be argued that there are serious limitations to this method. To begin with, not all errors will be corrected. This imputation is true, but it is better to have some of the errors corrected and feel that an effective effort has been made to undermine them than to correct them all only to be chagrined by their unwelcome reappearance in the next composition period. A second criticism that can in all justice be urged is that in such a method all typical errors will be eliminated and perhaps eradicated, but how will those errors that are peculiar and personal to each child be brought out and corrected? To reach the child's personal limitations and incorrect forms, this method must be supplemented in a number of ways. Let us consider them.

Eliminating Individual Errors: 1. *Each Composition to be Read by a Critic.*—The first means that we

THE CORRECTION OF WRITTEN COMPOSITIONS

have of undermining those peculiar errors that are made by each child is to arrange to have each composition read by a critic. We have all seen evidences of the children's desire to read one another's compositions. Exchanges are constantly going on behind the teacher's back if such a practice is foolishly forbidden. Such a desire can be utilized for educational ends. Just as soon as the teacher knows her pupils she can group them by two's and have each child act as an assigned critic of his classmate. Thus, a child who writes good compositions is made the critic of one whose work is below grade. The former can receive little constructive criticism from any of his classmates; the latter can gather a great deal of helpful advice from the assigned critic. The teacher must direct the critics' efforts along certain lines by hanging a large cardboard in some conspicuous place, containing these directions:

Critics Look for:
1. Paragraph Unity and Structure.
2. Sentences—
    (a) Capitalization.
    (b) Subject and Predicate.
    (c) "and" habit.
3. Punctuation, Spelling, Capitalization.

Each critic reads the composition three times, each time for one specific error. To add to the seriousness and the dignity of the task, each critic must sign his name and pin his criticisms to the original composition. In marking compositions, the teacher should rate the critic as well as the writer of the composition. The compositions are then returned and each child reads the critic's suggestions, carrying out such directions as appeal to him, and verifying the doubtful ones by reference to textbook or to the teacher. Where class discipline is properly organized, children are allowed to sit together, to discuss their compositions, and decide on the final corrections. However, those whose ideas of discipline call for deathlike stillness, with a repressive silence and military responses, may shrink from such a suggestion. In this form of correction, children take pride in offering good corrections and in bringing compositions to their critics that have as few mistakes as possible; they are at all times kept active learning the art of self-criticism.

2. *Compositions Criticized by the Class.*—A second supplementary device to detect personal errors and shortcomings is the common exercise of having the class criticize the compositions of individuals. To elicit criticism that is direct and pointed, the children should be trained to listen intelligently by having a chart similar to the one mentioned before in front of the class, and requiring "Group I" to listen for paragraph unity and sentence structure, "Group II" for grammatical correctness, and "Group III" for beginnings, endings, kind of facts, etc. In this way much of the stupid criticism that is often made by children can be eliminated. The class should be encouraged to point out commendable efforts so that the child who

reads his composition does not feel that he is running the gantlet of adverse criticism. It is also advisable to allow a child to answer his critics and to defend his stand if he is not willing to accept the criticisms that are too freely offered by the thoughtless.

3. *Personal Correction and Criticism by the Teacher.*—A third supplementary aid to help each child overcome his own personal peculiarities is to have the teacher give his personal attention to each composition. The task is not only colossal, but when carried out in the usual manner is, as we have seen, devoid of results. Hence the teacher should take only one-third or one-fourth of the whole set of compositions each week, the following week the second third or the second quarter, etc., until every member of the class has received the benefit of the teacher's criticism. But it must be remembered that each composition must be read with the child, the error pointed out, and its cause explained, but the pupil himself must indicate the correct form. No mark is made on the composition that the child does not personally dictate. One-third or one-fourth of a large class would rarely give a teacher more than twelve or fourteen compositions a week. The children can meet the teacher in personal conference before school hours, during study periods, or for a few moments after sessions. In this way the teacher is not overwhelmed by a task that saps energy and vitality, the children learn the cause of their errors, habits of self-correction are engendered, and positive and effective steps are taken to improve standards of expression.

Form vs. Content Correction.—We have concerned ourselves thus far with formulating a procedure designed to correct errors of form. But it is evident that a composition may be poorly balanced, trivial facts may be permitted to exclude things vital, the same details may be repeated and repeated, the introduction may be hackneyed, or the conception of the whole rather stupid or absurd. It is evident that we must give pupils an opportunity to improve the content as well as the formal elements of their compositions.

This can best be done by reading to the class a number of carefully selected pupil-products. Those read first should show distinct merit in content. Well-directed questions lead children to see the excellence of the content of these compositions. This is followed by a reading of those that offer much opportunity for improvement. After these latter compositions are criticised and improving changes indicated or made, each pupil is encouraged to reread his own composition critically and decide on necessary changes. Pupils may either write out a list of changes they would make if time permitted, or may actually rewrite the composition so that it embodies their plans for a superior product. A plan for critical self analysis of one's composition is suggested in the introductory part of Chapter IX.

How Shall the Class Work Be Kept?—When the work is completed, how shall it be kept? Surely not in the altogether too prevalent form in which papers of the whole class are collected, fastened tight, adorned with ribbons and elaborate title pages, and hidden in the dark recesses of a closet to await the critical eye of principal or superintendent. These compositions must be kept in individual envelopes or in notebooks so that each child has a cumulative result. At a moment's notice the teacher must be able to see a child's progress or retrogression. The children like this method better, for the pride of ownership and evidences of tasks accomplished are always sources of keen pleasure.

The Rewriting of Corrected Compositions.—The final consideration in the matter of correcting compositions is the problem of rewriting compositions. Not many years ago, the unanimous verdict was, "All compositions must be rewritten." To-day the camp is divided. Many insist that compositions should never be rewritten. Their many arguments, when summed up, reduce themselves to the following: (1) Time is lavishly spent in an exercise that is a matter of penmanship rather than of composition. (2) The period is dull since it is at best a stupid repetition, a mechanical transcription. (3) Such lessons have a deadening effect upon future compositions since no joy is experienced in this kind of expression.

The opponents insist on rewriting, for they argue that in real life the first draft is generally not the final one. We rewrite as a result of self-criticism of the first effort. Second, the habit to polish, to modify, and to correct an initial effort is well worth acquiring. Third, the final rewritten form leaves a good impression upon the child's mind.

Each side has legitimate claims and a pedagogical

basis but nevertheless suffers from the excesses of an extreme point of view. A moderate policy counsels that compositions should never be rewritten for the sake of improved penmanship nor at regular periods, like once a fortnight or once a week. All rewriting should spring from a desire on the part of the children to have an opportunity to improve an unsuccessful first attempt. For purposes of illustration we may assume that a composition was written and the model was studied afterward for comparison and correction. The children now realize how far from the mark they hit, how much better they could do if a second trial were allowed them. If this is the feeling that prevails, the children should be permitted to rewrite their unsuccessful compositions. This second exercise is alive and spirited, for it is actuated by strong motive power and earnest conviction.

SUGGESTED READING

The suggested reading for this chapter will be found at the end of Chapter VIII.

CHAPTER VIII

VITALIZING ORAL AND WRITTEN COMPOSITION

Introduction.—The concluding chapter on the teaching of composition asks how life and enthusiasm can be introduced into the varied expressional lessons of the elementary school, because children generally feel that these are routine drills, devoid of all interest and giving no pleasure. They experience little exhilaration but much fatiguing effort because teachers neglect the basic tenet that was laid down at the beginning of this discussion, viz., "The play spirit must characterize the art of composition, for all art was conceived in a play spirit." We must now turn to a series of miscellaneous suggestions that seek to vitalize composition and infuse into it this play spirit of art.

1. Greater Emphasis on Letters.—Compositions in essay form usually lack the naturalness of letters; they are as stiff and stilted as our own high-school and college essays used to be. The reason, in the main, seems to be that the child sees no use for the composition form just as we saw no use and felt no need for the essays imposed upon us. But a letter stands out as a form of communication that is essentially useful, practical, and personal; these attributes give it spirit and interest. An examination of the term's work in elementary classes reveals a surprising preponderance of the essay form. It is evident that the usual ratio of three essays to one letter each school month must be changed to at least two letters and two essays.

2. The Correspondence Should Treat of Actual Affairs of Real Life.—If letter forms are to be emphasized, we must eliminate at once such letters as are letters in form only and essays in spirit. One may write to a cousin, as is so often done in the classroom, about "How people live in China," or "How the Battle of Bunker Hill was fought," and use the proper form, arrangement, superscription, salutation, etc., but he is, nevertheless, sending an essay, not a letter. A recent publication much used by teachers suggests the following "Subjects for Letters": "Imagine you live in Honolulu; write to a brother telling of the people, their life, occupations, etc." "Write to your uncle on what you think of a book." "You just returned from a visit to your cousin in New Orleans; write him about the return trip." "Write a letter describing your imaginary visit to the South." "Write a letter telling how you spent your last vacation." "Write a letter telling your aims in life." These are a few of numerous suggestions, all violating our cardinal dictum which holds that a letter is a personal expression on a personal theme rather than a general expression or an artificial literary effusion.

Select titles like the following: "Letter complaining that inferior goods were sent by a department store, and the answer"; "Letter of application, and the answers: (a) acceptance, (b) rejection"; "Letter of apology for a business error"; "Letter of introduction"; "Letter asking for an advertisement for the school paper"; "Letter challenging another class to a contest"; "Letter to a hotel asking for summer rates"; "Letter to a summer camp asking for terms"; "Letter to the Association for the Prevention of Cruelty to Animals asking that the authorities send for a homeless cat"; "Letter to the Board of Health complaining of some source of contagion," etc. In all cases the child should be required to write the answers also. Because these relations and affairs necessitate correspondence in actual life, they must be the topics for the letters in the schoolroom.

3. **The Correspondence Itself Should Be Real.**—Not only should the theme of the letters reflect real life and human relations, but the form of the correspondence should be made as actual as possible. In the workaday world one writes because he is actuated by two conditions: (1) He has something to say, and (2) he has someone to whom to say it. In school, children usually write because they must say something; what they say is stored in the teacher's desk in neat packages. It is evident that classroom correspondence must be actualized by having it addressed to a real person who will read and answer it. The letter asking for an advertisement in the school paper should be addressed to one's permanent critic, who reads it and answers it. The exchange of letters actually takes place. This means life and spirit, for the letter is real, it bears a living message, and brings the coveted answer. Every

opportunity should be seized upon to make classroom correspondence real and urgent. Children should write letters to their teachers when they have a complaint to register or when they seek advice. If a member of the class is sick, or is at home because he has lost a member of his family, notes of sympathy should be written and the best ones sent. If teachers keep watching for such opportunities, they will find innumerable ones arising in the course of ordinary routine during the term.

4. The Class Journal with Its Board of Editors Elected or Selected.—A class journal can be organized in the sixth, seventh, eighth and ninth years. A board of editors of three or five is appointed by the teacher or elected by the children. This board is directed by the teacher and brings out an issue at regular intervals of about a fortnight. The journal is of simple construction and can be mimeographed so that each member of the class receives his personal copy. The editors read each week's compositions and select the best three or four for reproduction in the class journal. They post notices on the class bulletin boards calling for original stories, anecdotes, timely clippings, appropriate personals, and the like. They write up interesting classroom incidents, summarize school athletics, give the news of the class teams, hold contests for the best short story—in a word, contribute to the life and spirit of the class.

Such a journal can be made an agent of untold value. There are a number of pupils in each class who like to read, who do read, whose imagination is rich

VITALIZING ORAL AND WRITTEN COMPOSITION

with interesting inventions but who have no motive and no reason for giving expression to these through writing. The journal draws them out and produces surprises for the teacher. It is also a means of revealing the true natures of some children to their teachers. Because a child is not proficient in the work of the grade, he is judged stupid. But his contributions to the class journal may reveal a sense of humor, an originality, a fund of common-sense, and practical judgment which will stand him in good stead in later years. These revelations offer most agreeable surprises. Such a journal will also make for greater class solidarity; it creates good class spirit, acts as a wholesome spur toward better compositions, for children strive to be selected for the editorial board and to have their compositions reprinted in the issues of the paper.

5. Use Debatable Topics.—Debatable topics should be used with greater frequency, for they meet with much favor among the children. They are popular because—if well chosen—they give the child an opportunity to express his personal preference. Hence we must be sure to select a topic that reflects the child's life and desires, his point of view, his yearnings. The following list of topics urged in a standard book much used in elementary grades cannot receive unqualified indorsement: "Physical Training Should Be Compulsory in Public Schools," "Woman Suffrage," "The Civil-Service System Should Be Abolished," "The Term of the Supreme Court Judge Should Be Limited," "Canada Should Be Annexed to the United

States." A more appropriate series of topics would be: "Resolved, That We Have a School Paper"; "Resolved, That We Have a School City"; "Resolved, That the Girls Should Vote in the School City"; "Resolved, That Examinations Be Abolished"; "Resolved, That Pictures of Fights Be Forbidden"; "That Firemen are More Useful than Policemen, or Nurses than Teachers," etc.

The children should be allowed to take sides; an advocate of the negative should be declared a partner of a sponsor for the affirmative, and should be required to exchange his composition with him. The succeeding composition lesson should continue the same subject so that each child has an opportunity to answer his opponent. The results, when the topic is appropriately chosen, are most satisfactory because the two governing motives which prompt natural expression are present, viz., the children have something to say and they are addressing their views to some definite person who will read them. Enthusiasm and pleasure are guaranteed to the children in such work.

6. **Aim at Variety of Form and Content.**—An examination of a term's compositions usually reveals one marked limitation—there is woeful lack of variety of form and content in them. If one were to check up the titles of these compositions, he would find that biographies lead by a large margin. When in doubt as to a subject, a teacher usually selects a character about whom the children have read in history or literature and tries to make him yield the inspiration for the week's composition. These biographies are simple

to write, for these persons were all born, lived their eventful lives, and then died, thus affording an obvious sequence and a stereotyped organization. There is no reason why we should lack variety of subject-matter if we consider the many possibilities that are at hand.

The outline here given suggests types of compositions appropriate for the range of grades in the elementary and junior high school:

I. *Narration*—
  1. Reproduction of
     - a. Story Read or Told
     - b. Incident Witnessed
  2. Imaginative Incident
     - a. Personal Anecdote, Humorous
     - b. Serious Story, Result of Child's Imagination

The following compositions are types of imaginative incidents taken from the work of school children. They are quoted not because of unusual merit but rather because they are typical of the humor and the tragedy that most children feel and can express.

THE EXPECTED GUEST

On Monday afternoon my uncle from Boston was expected to pay us a visit. I had never seen him, because he had not visited us for fifteen years. We occupied a flat in the house situated in the upper part of Manhattan, and mother and I were alone.

At about two o'clock the bell rang and I answered the

door. A man entered and inquired if Mrs. Green was at home. I replied, very politely, "Yes, sir; walk right into the parlor and sit down. Mother will be in in a minute."

Then going to the kitchen where my mother was, I said to her, "Mother, uncle is in the parlor." So she slipped off her apron and went in. As she came near the door the man arose and said, "Madam, I would like you to try a new brand of coffee which I am advertising, and if you like I will leave a sample with you and call to-morrow for your order." My mother did not feel like ordering coffee that day because she was sadly disappointed. But we had a good laugh, and about nine o'clock that evening my uncle arrived.

A Daring Rescue

On the evening of November 22nd I was seated in my father's store writing a composition, when I was disturbed by a great hullabaloo outside. Whenever I am occupied in this way the least disturbance irritates me. So, throwing aside my work, I ran to the door to find out the cause of the disturbance.

I was horror stricken at the sight which met my gaze. The whole street was lighted up with a red glow. Glancing up at a house nearby, I saw flames belching forth from a first-story window. A great crowd of furious people had been attracted to the spot and the street was crowded. Some daring boys had climbed up the fire-escape and one of them had muffled a blanket around his face and had gone into the burning flat. He immediately withdrew and in his hand he clutched a chair. He was just giving it a final tug when he was overcome by the pungent smoke. He hurled the chair back and ran down into the street, closely followed by the other boys.

The sea of expectant faces was suddenly turned upward. For on the top floor, the figure of a girl was seen standing on the window-sill ready to jump. The flames could never have reached that height, but the girl had probably been crazed by fear, and had acted upon the impulse of the moment. "Would nobody stop her?" I kept repeating to myself. To jump would be fatal. One of the men in the crowd had courage enough to climb swiftly up the fire-escapes. He reached her just in the nick of time. Bidding her be brave, he gripped her around the waist and cautiously climbed along the narrow ledge to the opposite window, where the fire-escape was situated. Their forms were plainly silhouetted against the white wall of the building. Every neck in the crowd was craned upward. The girl had now collapsed and the burden was entirely upon the man. He descended slowly, oh, so slowly, until he reached the first floor where the flames were snarling, hissing, and crackling from the window. He paused a moment! Would he falter after having gone so far? Gathering all his remaining strength in one last effort, he made a desperate spurt into the very heart of the flames, and just when his strength was deserting him a fireman snatched the girl from his now feeble arms and lowered her down to a waiting comrade below. For meanwhile the firemen had arrived. The girl and her rescuer were badly scorched and they were both carried to a neighboring drug store.

At this stage the fire was at its height. The flames had burst through the ceiling into the flat above. The owner of the burning flat, who occupied a store directly below it, was crying piteously, for, said he, "My wife and baby are above." With difficulty he was assured that they were safe. Meanwhile the firemen were exerting every effort and soon had the fire under control.

Not a pin was saved from the ruins after the fire. But what is of more importance no lives were lost. The following day the papers had a thrilling account of how "A driver at the risk of his life saves a girl of eighteen."

II. *Description.*—A descriptive composition may vary considerably so that the child never realizes that he is writing the same literary form, for it may be a description of a place, of a person, or of a thing. But in all description we should bear in mind the fact that the child is not interested in writing a description merely for the sake of description, merely to give to someone a rich, detailed picture which he himself sees. Every description that is written in the elementary school should have either a personal touch or a story element in it; it must always be a description for some definite purpose; to give the setting of a story, a picture of the main character in an incident, or the like. A child's language stock is too poor to enable him to indulge in description freely, and to give a vivid impression of characteristic details merely through the use of rich color words and suggestive phrases. In describing a person the child must be made to realize that he can give us a picture of the person by telling what the character does and says as well as by giving an enumeration of the distinguishing features. What is meant by having children write description with a personal touch or a story element, can perhaps best be seen from an analysis of concrete illustrations.

  Illustration A. A boy is about to start out from a country town to try his fortune in the city. Describe him.

  Illustration B. "Der kleine Johannes"—Description of a lake. Its beauty and splendor tempt Johannes to row in the boat, in violation of his mother's commands.

  Illustration C. My Classmate.

My Classmate

On coming into the classroom every morning it is a habit of mine to glance at a certain individual whose antics are quite amusing. There are very few characters in our class whose descriptions would be as interesting as that of my hero's.

He is as tall as the average fifteen-year-old boy. Perhaps not many peculiarities as to traits can be seen unless he is closely watched. He has a kindly disposition and is at peace with all. The mention of black hair, dark brown eyes, prominent nose and rather thin features will suffice for a description of his appearance. One of his chief characteristics is modesty. Of course he knows grammar, but when he gets up to recite he misses because being so modest he is satisfied that somebody else should get the glory. Many times in the different rooms of the departmental section, he can be seen gazing out of the window, watching the clouds as they sail gracefully by. I remember distinctly on one occasion, while he was in one of his favorite reveries, I arose to read a composition about a diamond necklace valued at $10,000. At the mention of such an enormous sum of money his eyes grew as large as saucers, his mouth expanded to twice its natural size, and his face was aglow with excitement. So noticeable was this that the teacher on seeing it remarked, "Master X has really awakened."

I might relate some more very interesting incidents regarding him but I am afraid my narrative may become tedious. Hoping the one of whom I write will not in any way be offended, as I have tried hard to say nothing that would embarrass him, I will close feeling certain that my description has not been in vain.

Pupil in 8A Grade.

Illustration D. The Beggar. Turgenieff: "Dream Tales."

THE BEGGAR

I was walking along the street. . . . I was stopped by a decrepit old beggar.

Bloodshot, tearful eyes, blue lips, coarse rags, festering wounds. . . . Oh, how hideously poverty had eaten into this miserable creature!

He held out to me a red, swollen, filthy hand. He groaned, he mumbled of help.

I began feeling in all my pockets. . . . No purse, no watch, not even a handkerchief. . . . I had taken nothing with me. And the beggar was still waiting. . . . And his outstretched hand feebly shook and trembled.

Confused, abashed, I warmly clasped the filthy, shaking hand. . . . "Don't be angry, brother; I have nothing, brother."

The beggar stared at me with his bloodshot eyes. His blue lips smiled; and he in his turn gripped my chilly fingers.

"What of it, brother?" he mumbled; "thanks for this too. That is a gift too, brother."

I knew that I too had received a gift from my brother.

III. *Exposition.*—The next form that composition may take is the expository one. But here, too, it must be remembered that in the question of form *vs.* content, form always proves—to the child—to be less interesting. The teacher must make sure of a fitting content, hence children should not be required to write expository compositions merely for the sake of learning the technical requisites of literary exposition. There must be a personal element, and an individual expression throughout the essay. From this point of view, models like the following are poor, for in the final analysis they have no reason for being and are expository merely for the sake of expounding.

How to Play Ping-Pong

Ping-pong is a game played by men, women and children. A light, hollow ball, a pair of rackets, a net and a table are needed. Boys often use small boards and a cloth stretched across a table, but grown-up people use regulation tables and rackets.

The game is like tennis. Since it is played on a table, it is often called table-tennis. The first player serves the ball. If he fails to "place" it properly, the count is against him. Should he "place" the ball within the correct space, the second player must hit it with his racket. The object is to keep hitting it and sending it within the proper lines. The player who has the highest count wins. The system of points is the same as that used in tennis.

How a Canal Lock Works

A person who has never traveled on a canal is always interested in the operation of the locks. A lock is a structure in a canal that is designed to raise boats from a low level to a higher one or vice versa. Since the land through which a canal flows is not absolutely level, it becomes necessary to raise or lower a boat with the changing height of the water.

The lock has two strong gates across the canal. These separate the two levels of water. When a boat comes to the lock from the low level, the gate is opened and it is allowed to enter. The gate is then shut and the boat is inclosed between the two gates. The second gate is then opened, and the water from the higher level gradually runs in. The boat is raised slowly. When the gate is opened wide, the water in the lock is the same height as the higher level in the canal. The boat is then pulled out of the lock and proceeds on its way.

Teachers' manuals on the teaching of composition are replete with expositions of this type, excerpts that give a list of impersonal directions, written, as far as the child is concerned, for no other purpose than to illustrate technicalities of formal language. No worth-while effort by the child can find its impulse in the indifference which such models arouse.

How can one add the personal touch and introduce motive in the exposition written by school pupils? An analysis of the following essay written by a 7A boy may give the answer:

His First Swimming Lesson

My last summer was not the happiest one of my life for not many weeks had passed before I broke my leg in a bad fall down the stairs. It was difficult indeed for me to get about with my clumsy crutches and my foot in plaster. The day was hot and I felt that I would enjoy the cool breezes of the East River. I therefore hobbled over on my crutches to the dock which is only three blocks from my house.

I had not been there very long when one of the boys who was carelessly jumping from one canal boat to another and from one raft to another, slipped and fell in. By the terrible struggle to grasp the raft I saw he could not swim. Had I been well I could have saved him. But with my bandaged leg I could do nothing. I rushed to the end of the pier as well as I could. By this time the lad luckily grasped a loose board. As he held on I shouted my directions to him.

I told him to fill his lungs with a deep breath and hold his head above water. As soon as he did this I advised him to kick with his legs and push the board in the direction of the raft. He tried it but was too excited to do it right. I then told him to push the board under his arms to be sure of support. He did it. I then began the arm movement, hands together, all the way out, palms turned out and each arm pushing through the water in a semicircle until the palms touch, then push hands out again. He did as he saw me do and covered a short distance. I then shouted to him to keep his legs working. Just then a swell of a passing boat pushed him with some force and he reached the raft.

It was an exciting day but even if I did not save the careless boy, I gave him his first lesson in swimming.

The feeling one gets on reading this child's effort is that the exposition of the swimming strokes is not forced; it is not written because he was trying to carry out the set formula for this special form of composition. Its setting is natural, its context is real, its explanations are spontaneous, and its very expression intensely personal. The following list of topics may give added illustrations of how to introduce a personal note in exposition in order to produce more spirited and lifelike results:

"The Boy on the Coaching Line Advising the Players."
"The Captain of the Basket-ball Team Explaining the Signals to His Players."
"The Captain of the Baseball Team Giving His Players Instruction in 'Stealing Bases.'"
"How I Won the Championship in the Ping-Pong Tournament."
"How I Made My Record in Tennis."

"How I Made My Radio Set."
"How I Earned Money for My Radio Outfit."
"Why The Apron I Sewed Was Not a Success," etc.

IV. *Argumentation.*—In a previous connection, necessary cautions, suggestions, and a list of appropriate topics for argumentation were given. Nothing need be added here for elementary composition.

V. *Invention.*—This is a form of composition that finds the children most responsive, for it appeals to their sense of originality; it calls for all their ingenuity and for a full and free expression of those ideas that crave most for utterance. It is obvious that the forms of inventive composition can be as varied as the teachers who guide the lessons and the children who write the final product. The forms most frequently used are:

A. Imaginary Conversations.—The success of these compositions is determined primarily by the appropriateness of the topics selected. The following situations have brought uniformly good results:

1. The Little Girl Pleading with Lincoln for Her Brother's Life.

One cold, damp Sunday morning in the spring of 1863 a little girl was seen ascending the steps of the White House. She rushed past the guard at the main entrance and before she could be overtaken was in the large office of President Lincoln. The president, surprised, looked up with a start and then asked:
"What can I do for you, my dear girl?"
"I have come to ask for a great favor."
"To plead for your rebel father, I suppose."

"No, sir, for my brother, John."

"A rebel who should be freed for shooting his northern countrymen, I suppose."

"No, sir, he is a loyal supporter of his country's flag."

"Then why come here to plead for him?"

"Because, sir, he fell asleep while on sentinel duty. For eighteen hours he fought bravely with his regiment and helped win the battle. When the fighting was over, he was put in the first batch of sentinels. He is not strong, he is young, only eighteen. He trotted up and down and, before he knew it, he was asleep at his post. He was caught and is sentenced to be shot."

"His offense is a grave one indeed," said the President, "but so brave a boy and the brother of such a sister can be of greater service above ground than under it. Go home, you have saved your brother."

In her great joy the little girl rushed from the office without stopping to thank President Lincoln.

B....A.... 6B.

2. An Encounter with a Beggar.—The writer of the composition meets the beggar, who solicits aid. A conversation ensues in which the sad life of the beggar, the series of misfortunes, the downward path, etc., are brought out.

3. The Capture of André.—The three patriots stop the inquiring stranger; the conversation in which André raises their suspicions and finally implicates himself, the search, the conference among the patriots, the decision to bring André to the American commander.

4. Columbus Before the Court of Spain.—Columbus explains his ideas and hopes, the sceptical and sarcastic questions of the ministers, the sympathetic

questions of Isabella, the answers of Columbus, the final convincing argument, Isabella's offer of her jewels, etc. This topic allows for a skillful blending of exposition and dialogue, and for effective correlation of history and composition.

5. Cat-and-Mouse Story.—The following effort by an eighth-year pupil shows a commendable result. It is given in full because the topic and the organization will readily suggest to the teacher a host of similar situations appropriate for the needs of any class:

An Incident

Plump! Bing! Tarra-r-r! Bang!

"What in the world was that?" said I, startled by the noises which were heard from the cellar.

"There goes the shelf with the tin cans," answered my brother, turning a white face toward me.

"I guess there must be robbers down in the cellar," said I, trying to look scared, although I could hardly keep from laughing.

My brother looked to see if I was in earnest, but he soon discovered the deception, and we both laughed outright.

"That's Tabby hunting for mice," said I, and with that we each took a candle and crept down to the cellar.

The maltese cat met us with a glad "meouow," and we noticed that he was licking his chops in a satisfied manner.

The Cat's Story

"Well, you see it was this way," said the cat, when asked to relate the incident on the back fence to the assembly, who generally congregated for the usual evening concert. "I had been taking a nap on the trunk, when something stepped on my tail, and, turning around, I found Mr.

Gray Ears and **Mrs. White Tail** sitting there and staring at me. With a cry I sprang toward them, but they succeeded in scurrying away with me close at their heels, but I caught Mrs. White Tail. I could have caught Mr. Gray Ears only I did not want to eat too much, so I let——"

Wiff! Poor Tabby toppled off the fence from the effect of a well-aimed shoe, which had just come from the top-story window of a house nearby. The audience soon dispersed, and all scattered to their respective homes.

The Mouse's Story

"Friends, countrymen and mice, I have just passed through the most thrilling experience that has ever befallen any of our great tribe. I have met our worst foe and vanquished him.

"You knew that I and Mrs. White Tail took a walk yesterday. When happening to cross the wood pile I discovered the cat sleeping on the trunk. I bravely walked over and stepped on his tail, so he would awake. The minute he tried to spring at me, I rushed at him. He turned and was going to run away, when he saw Mrs. White Tail, and quickly grabbing her in his mouth he ran away. I pursued him, but he outdistanced me, and so I had to come home without poor Mrs. White Tail."

6. On Board the Caravel.

ON BOARD THE CARAVEL

The following conversation took place between Columbus and his sailors in mid-ocean:

"Where are you taking us?" shouted the sailors.

"You are going on this journey for fame, and your mothers will be better off when we return," said Columbus. "We will never see our parents any more," replied the sailors sadly. "We will reach land in a few more days," spoke Columbus hopefully. "We will see our death by that time," they shouted as they walked away towards the deck where other sailors were conversing secretly about their plans. Finally one sailor said, "Let's make him reverse the ship and take us home."

"That's a good idea; his life now lies in our hands," said the sailors. "Who will volunteer to take the message?" asked the sailors doubtfully. "I will," answered one sailor, who was attempting to stir up a mutiny aboard ship.

The sailor walking towards Columbus said, "Columbus, reverse the ship, and your life will be saved."

"No; I will keep on the voyage until I discover land for Spain," replied Columbus angrily, yet firmly.

"Is that your final answer," replied the sailor bitterly.

A shrill whistle was heard and the sailors soon appeared. They all crowded around Columbus.

"What does this mean?" asked Columbus, calmly.

"It means that you must reverse the ship, or we will throw you overboard."

"I will have you put in chains when we arrive home," retorted Columbus coolly. "We do not care, but we will give you just a half-hour to think the situation over," replied the sailors as they left Columbus. While looking in a westerly direction Columbus thought he saw land; he took a pair of spy glasses, and, sure enough, it was land. Columbus, now encouraged, shouted, "Land! Land!"

The sailors, hearing the cry, sprang from their seats and rushed upon the deck toward Columbus.

"Where is land?" asked the leader, impatiently.

"Look for yourselves," replied Columbus, handing him the spy glasses. The leader looked and saw islands not far away. They soon reached land, where, falling on their knees, with their faces turned toward heaven, they prayed that God might protect them.

By 8th Year Pupil.

VITALIZING ORAL AND WRITTEN COMPOSITION

B. Imitation of Fables.—A second type of inventive composition that meets with popular response by the children is the construction of a fable in imitation of one that was studied as a model. The fable of "The Wolf and the Lamb" is read and its construction noted. Similar elements are suggested and the children construct their own fables, *e.g.,* "The Pike and the Minnow," "The Hen and the Worm," "The Pigeon and the Hawk." A fourth-year pupil in a foreign section of the city gave the following as his result:

THE HEN AND THE WORM

One bright day a hen started out to find some worms for her children. She right a way met a fat worm. She wanted to eat it, but she wanted, too, an excuse.

"How dare you clap on my door?" said the hen.

"How can I clap on your door, if I ain't got no hand," said the worm.

"You are the loafer that bites my children," said the fresh hen.

"You are wrong," said the worm, "How can I bite your children if I ain't got no teeth."

"If you didn't then your brother or your father did," said the hen. Whereupon she bounced upon the poor worm and carried it away.

A lad whose stay on our shores barely exceeded four months wrote on a topic all his own in trying to imitate the fable which tells of the rats in convention deciding on a plan to tie a bell on the cat's neck. The phase of American street life that struck him most inspired the following:

THE TEACHING OF ENGLISH

THE BOYS AND THE POLICEMAN

One day boys was shooting crap so a policeman caught hime and brought to the station house.

And when they got free thay made a meeting and said, what shel we do to the policeman.

So one wise boy went up and said, we will put a bell on his neck.

So another boy went up and said, who will put the bell on his neck?

C. Ending a Story Whose Beginning Is Suggested to the Children.—This is another form of inventive composition the possibilities of which were discussed in a previous connection in Chapter IV.

D. Personification of Inanimate Objects. — A fourth popular form of inventive composition is the autobiography of an inanimate object. While these topics usually prompt successful results, the teacher must be careful not to personify an object that means little or nothing to the child. The autobiography of an eraser, of a coffee bean, of a package of tea, etc., are topics that allow for much correlation, but the child is nevertheless indifferent to the life history of these articles. The object chosen for personification must be one that thrills the child, stirs his imagination rather than his memory, or is at times a source of joy to him. The following are compositions by school children showing topics that were happily chosen:

THE BASEBALL'S STORY

"I was once a proud baseball, proud of my white glistening cover and the trade-mark so conspicuously placed on my head. My stitches were of the brightest red, and were so becoming to me that I was the most talked of person in our store. In fact the wagon-tongue bat lying on the shelf became so envious of me that he would gnash his teeth and would threaten that if he ever got a chance he would pay back the grudge he owed me. But what did I care for the mutterings of a miserable old bat. So the days passed on without any special happenings.

"One day as I was lying on the counter in my softly lined box a man came in and asked our salesman if he had any good baseballs. I was immediately chosen. 'That one will do,' said the man, taking me out of my soft box and placing me roughly into his pocket. 'Now, I'd like to see a bat,' continued the man. My enemy on the shelf was brought out and he also was purchased.

"I knew nothing until I felt myself being taken out of that hot stuffy pocket. When I beheld the light again, I uttered a sigh of relief. Turning around, I saw my old enemy, the wagon-tongue bat, grinning at me. This mortified me very much. I was then tossed to a man whom I had never seen before and he looked so queer in short trousers and striped stockings that in spite of my sadness I could not resist laughing at him. He took me in the palm of his hand and threw me so swiftly to the catcher, that I barely had time to catch my breath. 'Strike one,' I heard somebody call. One thing that attracted my attention on my way to the catcher was the manner in which the wagon-tongue was eyeing me. I was tossed to the pitcher. He twisted me in his fingers and curved his wrist so that I feared he would break it. I was again thrown, yet so queerly did I twist and turn that I became giddy and knew nothing until I found myself in the catcher's glove as before, and my enemy, the old wagon-tongue bat, rushing at me with great violence, but failing to hit me. 'Strike two,' the same voice cried. I was again thrown to the pitcher, who after twisting me in his fingers as usual delivered me. Crack! Oh, my! The wagon-tongue bat had carried out his threat at last and with a terrific whack sent me speeding into space. 'Ha, ha!' I heard him laugh. 'I have caught you at last, proud one.' I knew nothing until I found myself lying here in this dark crevice. How I came here I am unable to say, but my opinion is that after striking the ground I must have rolled into this dungeon. But now look at me; begrimed and dirty. I, who was once so proud and vain, am hidden from all the world, perhaps forever."

THE WAIL OF AN ACHING TOOTH

CHARACTERS

Aching Tooth; Eye Tooth, his neighbor; Other Teeth, A Dentist

SCENE I. *In a boy's mouth*

Aching Tooth.—Oh! I'm pains and aches all over.
Eye Tooth.—Why! What's the matter, a cavity?
Aching Tooth.—Cavity? A hole as big as a pin head.
Other Teeth.—You have a nerve to kick. What should we back teeth say? I have a hole as big as you are. Master George never reaches us with his tooth brush.
Aching Tooth.—You bet I have a nerve. If I didn't I wouldn't hurt. I am sorry for you.
Chorus.—O, O, we hurt.

SCENE II. *In a dentist's office*

The boy is in the dentist's chair. The dentist leans over and speaks as he examines the patient.
Dentist.—The front one will have to come out. I can save the others.
Aching Tooth.—Hear that, Eye Tooth. I have a pull with the dentist. Hooray, soon, I'll hurt no more.
Eye Tooth.—Do you think our master will learn his lesson?
Aching Tooth.—I certainly hope so. A tooth brush, tooth powder and water and we would all be healthy to-day.

Dentist.—Now open wide. It won't hurt.
Chorus.—Goodbye, Aching Tooth.
Aching Tooth.—Goodbye, Good-bb..........

This last illustrates how effectively the dramatic form may be used in personification.

E. Imaginary Diaries.—These form another type of inventive exercise that brings enthusiastic responses from the children. The diary of a beggar, of a soldier, of a sailor, of Captain Peary at the Pole, of Livingstone and Stanley while on journeys in Africa, etc., are usually productive of gratifying results. These forms of invention can be multiplied to a number limited only by the child's ingenuity and the teacher's ability to conceive new situations.

VI. *Biographical Narratives.*—The lives of the inspirational figures of literature and history supply some of the topics for class composition. But as was observed heretofore, these must not receive more than their proportional allotment of the composition periods. In making the life history of any man the basis of a composition, teachers should try to avoid the old hackneyed sequence of birth, boyhood, manhood, death and lasting results of his work. The children should be encouraged to seek originality in the grouping of the facts, and should emphasize only the one or two great achievements that gave the individual the position he occupies in the history of civilization. There is no reason for such complete categories of details and petty facts as one habitually finds in classroom products. Treated in the traditional sequence

referred to, there can be little or nothing that is inspirational in the biographies studied in the class. But the most distinguishing characteristic of a biographical study must be the inspiration which such a life stimulates. The model on the "Life of Hale," as given in Sykes' "English Composition for Grammar Grades," illustrates the proper organization and the proper relative value of facts in biographical narratives:

Nathan Hale

In 1776 Washington was endeavoring to capture the city of New York from the British. He needed to know the plans of his opponent, General Howe, and to have maps of the shores of the Hudson and the Sound.

Washington asked Knowlton to call his officers together, to tell them of the desperate state of affairs, and to ask for a volunteer. A common spy could not do the work, for it required a man who understood military plans and could make drawings. No one responded to the first appeal. Men who had no fear of death recoiled from the dishonor of a spy's fate. As Knowlton was urging them further, Nathan Hale entered and at once undertook the task. Any service done for one's country, he said, was noble. . . .

Hale received his last instructions from Washington, and, disguised as a school-master, he crossed from Harlem Heights to Long Island. For two weeks he was within the enemy's lines and made plans of all their defenses. His work done, he was staying at a small tavern on the shore waiting for the boat which would take him to safety. In his shoes were the drawings with full notes in Latin. But a Tory, a man said to be of his own kin, recognized him. The man went out, and a few minutes later word was brought Hale that a boat was approaching. He dashed out to meet it, and shouted greetings to his friends, as he thought—but found muskets leveled at his breast.

He was carried to the headquarters of General Howe. Hale made no secret of his name, rank, and errand, and there was no choice for Howe but to sentence him to the spy's fate, to be hanged.

Early next morning Hale stood on a ladder leaned against a tree. A rope was about his neck; the end of the rope was about to be thrown over a limb of the tree. The Provost Marshal asked him for a confession. Hale answered: "I only regret that I have but one life to give for my country." "Swing the rebel off!" was the command, and in a moment all was over.

The Provost Marshal had been unnecessarily cruel to the prisoner, and had destroyed the letters Hale had written to his friends, so that, as he said, "The rebels should never know they had a man who could die with such firmness." But Hale's dying speech was heard by a generous young British officer, Captain Montressor. Sent with a flag of truce to announce the execution, Montressor repeated the words to Captain Hull of the American forces. Such words can never die, and the memory of such men as Hale is immortal.

VII. *Letters.*—Letters, with their complete variety of form and content, come next in this list of types of expression. The early part of this chapter gives in detail suggestions and methods for letter writing. Letters may be (1) business; (2) social. In the latter group, we have (a) the formal, and (b) the informal. It is overstating the case to maintain that formal letters should receive no attention in the elementary school; they should receive but little consideration until the child develops a fair degree of proficiency in writing the informal letter and the business letter. The stiff formal letter with its expression of chilly sentiment is ill adapted to instil the enthusiasm that must characterize the composition lesson.

VIII. *Miscellaneous Suggestions.*—To this long list of suitable topics we must add:

1. Writing Resolutions: To live up to Roosevelt's ideals of an American boy or girl; to honor our country by honoring its language.

2. Writing Pledges: Pledge to be true to country and city, to school, to one's club, to boy or girl scouts. Study scout pledge or Ephebic Oath.

3. Dramatizing a story and adapting a story for the moving pictures.

4. Completing an incomplete story.

5. Writing telegrams and radiograms.

6. Telling the story of a picture.

7. Discussion of the message of poems, for example, "In Flanders Fields" and "America's Answer."

8. Paraphrasing narrative and dramatic verse.

9. Reports to class or to school paper of games, books, class incidents, accidents, community projects, etc.

10. Personal anecdotes.

In addition, many of the suggestions for the lower grades can readily be adapted for the fifth and sixth years and for the junior high school.

7. The Composition Project.—A teaching project, like a project in life, is a unit of purposeful experience. Any real experience which is presented in its natural background and which invites solution of a series of closely related problems is a project. Compositions presented in relation to a project must necessarily be real and vital.

A local community is conducting a campaign for funds to enlarge its hospital and maintain its increased activities. This community project is made a classroom project in composition.

In the first period, the project is set before the children and they are asked to plan the campaign as if they were the active committee in charge. A plan of activity is evolved with the aid of the class.

A. To prepare posters setting forth the medical needs of the community.
B. To prepare pictorial posters of the present hospital and the proposed additions with appropriate legends.
C. To prepare a set of slogans.
D. To prepare copy for newspaper notices.
E. To prepare letters asking prominent people and socially minded persons of means to serve on the committee.
F. To prepare a letter soliciting funds.
G. To prepare subscriptions or pledge blanks.
H. To prepare letters of thanks to contributors.
I. To prepare follow-up letters to those who do not answer the first appeal.
J. To prepare letters to the local newspapers.
K. To prepare letters to clergymen asking them to make strong appeal to their parishioners.
L. To prepare letters to principals asking them to obtain pupil aid and pupil contribution.

It is evident that much can be introduced in this project that will correlate with community civics, hygiene, ethics, arithmetic, and pictorial representation and design. We shall not, for our purposes, elaborate these correlations. The first period ends with the class enthusiastically agreeing to undertake this project.

In the second lesson, the first poster is undertaken. The pupils list all the facts that such a poster must present: the inadequacy of present hospital and free clinical facilities, statistics; the growth of population in the last ten years, statistics; the increased cost of supplies and personal service, statistics; expert opinion of present needs and needs for the next ten years. After all the facts are collected, urgent problems present themselves. How shall we group the facts? How shall we word the poster? How are other posters arranged and worded? What faults are plainly seen in other posters? What is the suitable size? How shall we make our poster attractive? What design should be made for it in the drawing class? Each of these problems presents a natural situation calling for a free expression of opinion. The pupils are carried away by the specific question. In the next lesson, their ideas are crystallized and more progress is made.

All the composition lessons of the semester may be devoted to an earnest attempt to complete the campaign. Three periods of oral composition may be necessary for the formulation of effective slogans. Contests are conducted and the children learn the full power of the correctly chosen word. Every composition lesson is welcomed. Ample evidence is presented to show that the children think of their composition problems between lessons.

In a similar manner such projects as the following

may be made the basis of a series of composition lessons: "How to Prevent Accidents," "How to Celebrate a National Holiday Appropriately," "Planning a Celebration of the Birthday of One of Our Great Writers or Inventors," "A Stay-in-School Campaign," "A Thrift Campaign," "Planning Form Letters to Be Used by a Department Store," "A Campaign to Bring All Non-English-Speaking Foreign Adults to School," "An Advertising Campaign for Our School Paper," "Conducting a Class Paper."

The superiority of project teaching in composition is apparent to any teacher who will select a real project and analyze it into its component problems. At once, composition work becomes purposeful, highly unified and thoroughly motivated. Every recitation becomes socialized, not because the teacher so plans it but because the circumstances prompt a natural exchange of ideas. The children obtain an insight into social relationships not by an objective study of it in history, civics, or ethics, but rather by actually participating in social living.

8. The Teacher.—The final inquiry, "How Can We Vitalize Composition?" was answered in terms of a number of constructive suggestions. The table of possibilities that is offered, though not scientifically accurate nor complete, shows the teacher what a rich field of subject-matter can be brought to the children. But the most potent factor that makes for efficiency in composition teaching is the teacher—his spirit, his zest, his life and enthusiasm, his faith in the ultimate ability of the children. The methods suggested must never be regarded as more than general guides; they show proper tendencies, correct goals, but they are not designed for accurate and absolute imitation. Each teacher must interpret the suggestions in terms of his own peculiar problems and seek to adjust them to the individual needs of his specific class. Without this personal interpretation and specific adjustment all methods are doomed to inevitable failure.

SUGGESTED READING

BOLENIUS, EMMA M. Advanced English Lessons. American Book Co.

CARPENTER, BAKER and SCOTT. The Teaching of English, pp. 121-144. Longmans, Green & Co.

CHUBB, P. The Teaching of English, chap. XI. The Macmillan Co.

DRIGGS, HOWARD L. Live Language Lessons. University Publishing Co.

GOLDWASSER, I. E. Method and Methods in the Teaching of English, chaps. XV and XXII. D. C. Heath & Co.

HOSIC, JAMES F. The Elementary Course in English, pp. 97-128. University of Chicago Press.

KIRKPATRICK, E. A. Fundamentals of Child Study, chap. VIII. The Macmillan Co.

———. How Children Learn to Talk. *Science,* Sept., 1891.

KLAPPER and LONDON. Modern English, Book II. Revision of former text by Emerson and Bender. The Macmillan Co.

VITALIZING ORAL AND WRITTEN COMPOSITION

LEONARD, S. A. English Composition as a Social Problem. Houghton Mifflin Co.

McMURRY, CHARLES A. Special Methods in Language. The Macmillan Co.

———. Oral and Written Composition. *New York Teacher's Monograph,* Vol. III, No. 3, June, 1901.

PEARSON and KIRCHWEY. Essentials of English, III. American Book Co.

SIMONS, ORR and GIVEN. Better English. John C. Winston Co.

SAVITZ, BATES and STARRY. Composition Standards. Hinds, Hayden and Eldredge.

TAYLOR, J. S. Composition in Elementary School. A. S. Barnes & Co.

WOHLFARTH and MAHONEY. Self Help English Lessons, Books II and III. World Book Co., Yonkers, N. Y.

YOUNG and MEMMOTT. Methods in Elementary English. D. Appleton & Co.

CHAPTER IX

HOW TO MEASURE PROGRESS IN COMPOSITION

The Prevailing Method of Judging Ability in Composition.—The problem of evaluating merit in composition is especially difficult. In the other subjects, we deal with experience that is either simple or factual. The child's penmanship is a relatively simple motor reaction when compared to his composition, oral or written. So, too, pupils' answers in geography either agree or disagree with the actual facts. But in composition we have a complex of factors, for the composition is the product of the child's ideas and his mastery of formal language. Originality of composition, logical arrangement of ideas, adequacy of vocabulary, grammatical quality of speech, corrections of spelling, punctuation, capitalization and arrangement—all these determine the merit of a composition.

What is the prevailing method of judging pupils' compositions? The teacher's rating of a composition is an expression of a personal judgment. The worth of all the thought and language elements involved in the child's composition is summed up in the grade which the teacher assigns it. But personal judgment varies with one's experience, training, and natural endowment. The round of petty irritations and minor satisfactions in the day's experience modify this judgment in no small degree. A composition which was rated B (80-89 per cent) by one teacher was rated D (60-69 per cent) by another teacher of the same grade. A pupil's geometry paper was photographed and submitted to a number of experienced teachers of high school mathematics. The grades assigned this paper varied from 30 per cent, dismal failure, to 90 per cent, unusual merit. A teacher rescoring a set of compositions two weeks later and relying again on personal judgment, will in all probability show marked divergences of judgment. Personal judgment is too capricious to be used as a sole basis for grading pupils or their efforts.

Composition is taught in every school year. What standard of result may we reasonably expect from a ninth-year but not from a seventh-year pupil? A representative eighth-year composition was judged by one teacher worthy of any proficient ninth-year pupil and by another distinctly below his expectations from seventh-year children. What shall this composition be rated as a seventh-, an eighth-, and a ninth-year product respectively? Courses of study prescribe for a succession of grades, "development of paragraph sense, mastery of sentences, control of formal aspects of language through habituation." How much of a paragraph sense should sixth-year pupils have? Eighth-year pupils? What degree of control may we reasonably expect from children in different grades? Whose judgment is to prevail in formulating the answers?

Analytic Composition Rating of _____

School _____ Grade _____ Term _____ Teacher _____

Title of Composition	Date	I. Content			II. Language				III. Form							Grand Total
		1. Self Expression	2. Organization	Total I	3. Vocabulary	4. Sentence	5. Grammatical Correctness	Total II	6-A. Form	6-B. Letter Form	7. Spelling	8. Punctuation	9. Capitalization	10. Appearance	Total III	
1.																
2.																
3.																
4.																
5.																
6.																

HOW TO MEASURE PROGRESS IN COMPOSITION

The prevailing method of judging merit in composition is thoroughly inadequate; it is variable, accidental, and as capricious as the personal judgment on which it is based.

The Analyzed Judgment of the Teacher as a Basis for Rating Compositions.—A more helpful but not a scientific system of evaluating compositions is to rate specific elements that make up general composition merits. Merit in composition is summed up in ten points, grouped under three heads, *Content Aspect, Language Aspect,* and *Formal Aspect of Composition.* For each pupil a record card is kept like that opposite.[1]

Explanation of Items in the Analytical Composition Rating Plan.—We must now examine each of the composition elements in the diagnostic table.

I. CONTENT ASPECT OF COMPOSITION.
   1. *Self Expression.* Consider originality of conception of the composition as a whole. Is the title appropriate? Does the child merely reproduce the suggestions offered by teacher, book, or other pupils?
   2. *Organization of Ideas.* Are ideas logically grouped? Is the paragraphing therefore correct? Are irrelevancies suppressed and minor details subordinated?

II. LANGUAGE ASPECT.
   3. *Adequacy of Vocabulary.* Is the vocabulary commensurate with the child's ideas? Are words repeated or incorrectly used:
   4. *Sentence Sense.* Are sentences clearly indicated by period and capital? Does each sentence have

subject and predicate? Are subordinate clauses used as sentences? Is there evidence of sentence unity, or does the child run separate ideas together by using *and* or *so?* Does the child give evidence of ability to use varied sentences and inverted order, for example, *If I were . . . were I. . . .*

5. *Grammatical Accuracy and Use of Idiomatic Language.* Consider such errors as lack of agreement, misuse of tense forms, incorrect forms of plural, pronoun without antecedent, use of unidiomatic forms, etc.

III. FORMAL ASPECTS.

6A. *Correct Forms.* Consider details of arrangement, for example, margins, indentations of paragraph, placing of the title and signature, ability to follow the prescribed form of the school. 6A applies to essay type of composition.

6B. *Letter Form.* It is obvious that any one composition will be rated for either 6A or 6B. Under the latter we must consider the correct placing of the address, date, salutation, body of letter, complimentary close, inside address, signature, etc.

7,8,9. *Spelling, Punctuation, and Capitalization.* In the formal spelling lesson attention is focalized on indicated words. Similarly, in a dictation exercise the pupil is especially concerned with requirements of punctuation and capitalization. But in the composition lesson, when the mind is encouraged to give itself to a free flow of ideas, spelling, punctuation, and capitalization are apt to be slighted. If the pupil is familiar with the analytic rating scheme, he will reread his composition to make corrections in these formal aspects of his work.

HOW TO MEASURE PROGRESS IN COMPOSITION

10. *Appearance.* Consider attractiveness of written work, neatness, and care in penmanship, freedom from careless erasures and changes.

The Use of the Analytic Rating Chart.—Not every written composition of every pupil need be subjected to this severe analysis. Six to ten compositions so rated each semester will suffice. Pupils must be encouraged to familiarize themselves with the details of the rating scheme and the successive ratings given them.

An Evaluation of the Analytic Rating Scheme.— The primary weakness of this scheme lies in the fact that personal opinion rather than objective standards is still the basis of our judgment of pupils' composition. But in the last analysis, personal opinion is the basis of judgments arrived at by the use of any of the objective scales. If our ratings are to have value, we must strive to substitute for untrained and capricious judgment an analytical and critical evaluation. Exception may also be taken to this scale because it regards all the elements of composition as of the same value. Obviously, elements 6, 7, 8, 9, and 10 are decidedly less vital to a free and forceful expression of ideas than those in the first half of the table. It is possible to arrange these elements, by statistical treatment of a variety of judgments, in a scale of descending importance and to assign to each a definite relative numerical weight. But we must ever be mindful that the least important of these items is still very important and is likely, in the ordinary routine of life, to count with a particular reader, as much as the most important. We teachers may decide that, in a relative scale, originality of conception and adequate vocabulary should each be given 3.2 times the weight assigned to spelling. But the prospective employer may reject the applicant whose letter is not arranged in approved form or shows errors in spelling.

This analytic rating scheme is diagnostic. It reveals to pupils their specific weaknesses and suggests to teachers a basis for differentiated language drills. It indicates to pupils the direction in which they must exert special effort. It affords cumulative justification for the ratings teachers give their pupils in composition.

Used in connection with a five-point rating scale, this analytical rating plan will reveal the relative standing of each pupil in his group. Let *3* indicate the middle 40 per cent of the class in any one of these ten elements, say in grammatical accuracy. This group, number *3,* is composed of the distinctly average pupils. Now let *2* indicate the 20 per cent of the class that is below the average and *4* the 20 per cent above the average. Finally, let *1* indicate the 10 per cent of the pupils who are distinctly inferior and *5,* those who are in the best 10 per cent. The highest score is *5,* the lowest, *1.* The maximum for the ten items is 50. Pupil *G* has a score of 39 and pupil *H,* 21. It is a simple matter to rate all the children and determine for each pupil his rank place in his class.

Our plan does not enable us to compare the work

of one class with that of another nor to determine how well any one pupil can do with respect to the normal achievements of children of similar mental age, chronological age, or school grade. To do this with some degree of scientific accuracy is one of the fundamental aims of standardized composition scales. We shall sum up the endeavors to evolve a scientific scale for measuring achievement in composition.

THE MEASUREMENT OF COMPOSITION ABILITY

The Hillegas Scale for Measuring Composition. *Aim.*—One of the early composition scales is the one formulated by Hillegas.[1] Its aim is to present a series of scientifically graded compositions in terms of which merit in composition can be measured.

How the Scale Was Evolved.—As a result of the judgment of over 400 competent readers, ten compositions out of an initial 7,000 were selected and so graded as to range in quality from 0 to 9.3. The second composition has a value, according to composite judgment, of 183 points; the third, of 260 points. The quality is measured on a scale which, theoretically, at least, is made up of equal distances of merit. Thus, the third graded composition having 260 units of merit is about 42 per cent better than the second graded composition whose merit is 183 points. It is obvious that these points are not equivalent to percentages. Sample *0* and two others are artificial. The remaining

[1] M. B. Hillegas, *A Scale for Measuring English Composition for Young People* (Teachers' College, Columbia University, 1913).

THE TEACHING OF ENGLISH

samples vary in length, style and character so that all types of writing, except poetry, are represented.

SAMPLES OF THE SCALE *

THE ADVANTAGE OF TYRANNY

The Third Specimen. Value 260 or 2.6

Advantage evils are things of tyranny and there are many advantage evils. One thing it that when they opress the people they suffer awful I think it is a terrible thing when they say that you can be hanged down or troddon down without mercy and the tyranny does what they want there was tyrans in the revolutionary war and so they throwed off the yok.

[Written by a boy in the second year of the high school, aged 14 years.]

SULLA AS A TYRANT

The Fourth Specimen. Value 369 or 3.69

When Sulla came back from his conquest Marius had put himself consul so sulla with the army he had with him in his conquest siezed the government from Marius and put himself in consul and had a list of his enemys printy and the men whose names were on this list were beheaded.

[Written by a girl in the third year of the high school, aged 17 years.]

DE QUINCY

The Fifth Specimen. Value 474 or 4.74

First: De Quincys mother was a beautiful women and through her De Quency inherited much of his genius.

His running away from school enfluenced him

---

* In these specimens, the content is faithfully reproduced. It has not been possible, in some cases, to reproduce the actual line lengths.

much as he roamed through the woods, valleys and his mind became very meditative.

The greatest enfluence of De Quincy's life was the opium habit. If it was not for this habit it is doubtful whether we would now be reading his writings.

His companions during his college course and even before that time were great enfluences. The surroundings of De Quincy were enfluences. Not only De Quincy's habit of opium but other habits which were peculiar to his life.

His marriage to the woman which he did not especially care for.

The many well educated and noteworthy friends of De Quincy.

[Written by a boy in the fourth year of the high school, aged 16 years.]

Fluellen

The Sixth Specimen. Value 585 or 5.85

The passages given show the following characteristic of Fluellen: his inclination to brag, his professed knowledge of History, his complaining character, his great patriotism, pride of his leader, admired honesty, revengeful, love of fun and punishment of those who deserve it.

[Written by a girl in the first year of the high school, aged 18 years.]

Ichabod Crane

The Seventh Specimen. Value 675 or 6.75

Ichabod Crane was a schoolmaster in a place called Sleepy Hollow. He was tall and slim with broad shoulders, long arms that dangled far below his coat sleeves. His feet looked as if they might easily have been used for shovels. His nose was long and his entire frame was mot loosely hung together.

How to Use the Hillegas Scale.—The teacher must acquire complete knowledge of the scale through careful study of each of its specimens. A pupil's composition is then read and compared with the specimens in the scale in order to discover the one it approximates most closely, and is rated the grade of this specimen.

Evaluation of the Hillegas Scale.—The Hillegas Scale is almost a pioneer effort and must therefore be judged accordingly. Among its limitations, we must note the following: (1) it is long, and the average teacher would not find it easy to master; (2) its samples are stilted, and their topics would not stimulate children to self-expression; (3) it contains three artificial specimens, that is, compositions not written by pupils; (4) only one sample is given for each grade of merit; (5) it contains no sample of correspondence, social or business; (6) it is made up of specimens set at unequal intervals on the scale of merit.

Assume that the line *A-B* is a scale of merit:

$$A \vert \overset{b\ c\ d\ e\ f\ g\ h\ C}{\vert\ \vert\ \vert\ \vert\ \vert\ \vert\ \vert\ \vert}\ \underset{b\ c\ d\ e\ f\ g\ h\ D}{\vert\ \vert\ \vert\ \vert\ \vert\ \vert\ \vert\ \vert}\ \vert\ \overset{b\ c\ d\ e\ f\ g\ h\ E}{\vert\ \vert\ \vert\ \vert\ \vert\ \vert\ \vert\ \vert}\ \underset{b\ c\ d}{\vert\ \vert\ \vert}\vert B$$

Points *Ac; ce; Cc* are known as equal intervals, whereas *Ad; dh; Cf* are unequal intervals.

General Merit vs. the Diagnostic Scale.—A telling defect in the scale is summed up by the author who says, "No attempt has been made in this study to define merit. The term as here used means just that quality

HOW TO MEASURE PROGRESS IN COMPOSITION

which competent persons commonly consider as **merit** and the scale measures just this quality."[2] But we saw that merit in composition is a complex of achievements. To assign a grade, even scientifically, to a pupil's product does the least helpful thing for him. A scale which is diagnostic and gives the teacher a scientific basis for planning specialized activity for a pupil achieves the really highest possibilities of a composition scale.

There are those who distinguish two functions of a scale, (a) the diagnostic, and (b) the classificatory. The Hillegas Scale, they argue, is of the latter type. However analytical and diagnostic a scale may be, it is necessary, in the end, to obtain a gross score for a pupil's effort. They hold that a letter is judged not by synthesizing its varying merits in content, organization and form but rather by the general impression. This is not necessarily a desirable method of evaluation, but it is the way of men. An æsthetic experience provokes a gross or single reaction rather than a synthesized reaction. This is undoubtedly true for the lay mind, and especially so in æsthetic reactions. But the composition scale is designed as a classroom instrument to be used by teachers so that they may acquire the habit of critical and analytical judgment of pupil's work. It must therefore be diagnostic as well as classificatory.

Thorndike Extension of the Hillegas Scale.—Thorndike undertook the task of refining, supplementing and

[2] See p. 174.

SPECIMENS SELECTED FROM THE TRABUE SUPPLEMENT TO THE HILLEGAS SCALE.

3.8

I would like to go out in the after noon and play catching the ball. Go over to Bertha's house and have a few girls to come with me and be on each others side. I have a tennis ball too play with. The game is that one person should stand quite aways from another person and throw the ball too one then another. Someone has to be in the middle and try too get the ball a way from someone then she takes this persons place who she caught the ball from. Then till every person has a chance.

3.84

5.0

Next Saturday I should like to go away and have a good time on a farm. I should like to watch the men plowing the fields and planting corn, wheat, and oats and other things planted on farms.

Next Saturday I will go to the Pioneer meeting if nothing happens so that I cannot go. I should like to go swimming but it is not warm enough and I would catch a bad cold. I should like to go to my aunts and drive the horses, I do not drive without some older person with me, so I cannot go very often.

I should like to see my aunts cat and her kittens, too. I think I can, to.

4.97

6.0

I should like to join my girl friends, who are going to the city on the 9:05 A. M. train. They are going shopping in the morning and will have lunch to-gether, then they are going to the Hippodrome. After the Hippodrome, they are all going home to dinner to one of the girls houses, she lives on Riverside Drive so they expect to take the "Fifth Avenue Bus" up there. The evening will be devoted to playing games, singing and dancing.

6.01

HOW TO MEASURE PROGRESS IN COMPOSITION

7.2

If I had a thousand dollars to spend, I think I would take a trip to San Francisco by train with the rest of the family, and stop at a sea-side hotel. It would be glorious to see the surf again, and to escape from the cold blustering weather of December for the balmy breezes of the ocean, and the whiff of orange blossoms.

We could take long drives under shady trees, visit the orange and olive groves and bathe in the surf. Think of bathing in the ocean in December!

Coming home again I should enjoy stopping at Yellow Stone Park. It would be lots of fun to camp out, and to ride over the prairies on frisky poinies. It would be very interesting to notice the change of climate as we got farther east, and to go to bed on the train one evening feeling warm, and waking up the next morning feeling very chilly.

7.22

I am afraid by the time I would get home a thousand dollars would be pretty well used up; but if not I would like to give a party.

8.0

One Sunday, towards the end of my summer vacation, I was in bathing at the Parkway Baths. In the Brighton Beach Motordrome, a few rods away, an aviation meet was going on. Several times one of the droning machines had gone whirring by over our heads, so that when the buzzing exhaust of a flier was heard it did not cause very much comment. Soon, however, the white planes of "Tom" Sopwith's Wright machine were seen glimmering above the grandstand. Everyone stood spellbound as he circled the track several times and then headed out to sea. He was seen to have a passenger with him. Suddenly, the regular hum of his motor was broken by severe pops, and the engine ran slower, missing fire badly. In response, to Sopwith's movements, the big flier tilted and swooped down to the beach from aloft like an eagle. The terrified crowd made a rush to get out of the way as the airship came on, but Sopwith could not land on the beach, but skimmed along close to the water instead. Suddenly his wing caught the water, and the big machine somersaulted and sank beneath the waves. The aviators soon came bobbing up and were taken away in a launch, but the accident will

8.00

not soon be forgotten by those who saw it.

extending the Hillegas Scale.[3] To seven of the original Hillegas specimens he added two business letters, six book reviews, and three character portrayals. These he arranged in fifteen degrees of merit.

Artificial samples are thus eliminated, real school products are introduced, the number of samples, especially at the middle points in the scale, is increased, and each specimen is long enough to give a better basis for judging quality. But this extended scale still measures composition on the basis of general merit and does not distinguish qualities of form from those of content.

Trabue's Nassau County Supplement to the Hillegas Scale. *Aim.*—Trabue developed a supplement to the Hillegas Scale which not only elaborates and refines the original but also furnishes a measure of specific as well as of general merit.[4]

Description of Nassau County Supplement.—The scale is composed of ten samples graded from 0 to 9.0. Seven of these samples, 0 to 7.2, are narrative and on the same subject, "What I Should Like to Do Next Saturday." The method of developing the original Hillegas Scale was followed in evolving this supplement.

Evaluation of the Nassau Supplement.—Authoritative opinion holds that Trabue's supplement is the most

---

[3] E. L. Thorndike, *Thorndike Extension of the Hillegas Scale* (Teachers College, Columbia University, 1915).

[4] M. R. Trabue, *Nassau County Supplement to the Hillegas Scale* (Teachers College, Columbia University, 1917).

HOW TO MEASURE PROGRESS IN COMPOSITION

effective instrument for measuring merit in composition in the junior high school.[5] It presents, with the exception of the last specimen, real school products in a scale whose distances are fairly equal. But we must note that there is a marked, not a gradual step, from colorless pupil effort to the composition that shows real quality (sample 6. to 7.2). At each step in the scale only one specimen is given, thus diminishing the usefulness of the measuring instrument. Limited to narration, it is not helpful to the teacher who is rating business or social letters or a composition that is expository or argumentative. Then, too, it has not diagnostic value. It measures and classifies, but it does not give specifically a basis on which a remedial program can be planned for a class, or for smaller groups of children.

Ballou's Harvard-Newton Scale. *Aim.*—Ballou set himself the task of formulating a scale for each type of writing, namely, description, exposition, argumentation and narration.[6]

Description of the Harvard-Newton Scales.—Four distinct scales are presented, each made up of six graded compositions written by eighth-grade pupils and placed at equal distances on a scale of merit. After each specimen, there is given a helpful statement of its

---

[5] See report, "English Composition, Its Aim, Methods and Measurements," p. 50, in *Twenty-Second Year Book* of the National Society for the Study of Education (Public School Publishing Company, Bloomington, Ill., 1923).

[6] F. W. Ballou, *Harvard-Newton Composition Scales* (Harvard University Press, Cambridge, Mass., 1914).

merits, its defects and the reasons which justify its place in the scale.

Evaluation of the Harvard-Newton Scales.—The separate scales make the scale more helpful in judging pupils' composition. Each specimen is long enough to reveal its real worth. The explanatory statements for each specimen make each of the scales clearer and simpler to use. The topics selected are attractive and are more like the subjects assigned in a progressive class than those found in most of the other scales.

But these scales still measure only general merit. Experience proves that it is more helpful to have two or three samples for each step in the scale. These scales offer only one. Another reason which accounts for the limited use of these scales is the lack of provision for lower grades. They have no lower register. The upper parts of each of the four scales have proved too high for measuring eighth-, ninth-, and even tenth-year pupil products.

Then, too, this fourfold classification breaks down in actual practice. Most of what we write is a composite of all of these types—narration and description intermingle freely; exposition is not free from argumentation, and pure argumentative writing without free introduction of exposition and description is rare.

Breed and Frostic Scale.—Samples of this scale, which is further described on pages 198-199, are given below:

HOW TO MEASURE PROGRESS IN COMPOSITION

SAMPLES OF THE SCALE

The numbers above the samples represent amounts of merit

.2

The hanjict shop for there
there was so many in it. After
a little they it going. And
they to pleace were the the picine
was. They all get out of the
hounce and but there thing
down
on the table and rain out to
play. After they were platy
the had there lunce. And
They had a very nice time.

2.7

When the engine r stop, one
of the boy took his shoes and
off
stocking √ and got out into the
river and bushe the bout a little
so as to stare the enginer
a going, when that had
stared the bowt went aright.
And they went rideing
around the river where
having a nice time went
one of the girl saw a water—
lillies and they try to pick when she
fell in the river but she got
aright, her cloth were wet
some but they soon try, and

she got her water lillies.
      When they were throu-
ght rideing they got out and
went to the bank and
had their lounce, After
that they play games,
which then they began
to pick flowers in the woold.
But when they went home
they had many beautiful flower
to take their mothers. But
when the departed they
all to their teacher we all
have like you this year and
hope you will teach again
next year. And we all are glady
we have pass this year.

3.7

They were near the park when the ~~enjing~~
engin stoped. They pattled ashore and went on
                                              there
to the parck. ~~There~~ t There,~~ the~~ was a man who
had another f boat. ~~At~~ After a while they
asked the man if he would tow the boat back
when he went and he said that he would. When
evening came the man told the teacher that he
was going f back. The teacher ~~glal~~ gathered the
children together and went to there boat, where
                                              on
the man had already tied the top rope one the
                                          were towed
boat. They all got in and ~~went~~ back ↓ up the
river. Then they departed and went home happily.

HOW TO MEASURE PROGRESS IN COMPOSITION

4.7

Jack the one who was runing
the launch said, "lets take these pales
and push the launch to shore. Yes! Yes!
let do said all; we took the poles
and tu) pushed it to shore. Jack
got out and looked around. He saw
a house over yonder, he went over
to see if they had any gasoline,
when. he got there and ask they
had none. When he came back
we were suprised to (she) see
him without the gasoline. He
said, "lets go out here and walk
the rest of the way. We (w) all
said yes, because it was only about
one and a half (ba) blocks or so.

When we arrived at the wood
we all ran to get a the
tables set and get every thing
ready, that so went we got
through picking a few we coald
eat out lunch. When we got
enough (w) violets, of purple, white
and yellow, dutcchmans breechs,
an liles and etc. we ate our
luanch and had a fine time.

We got ready to go home
and a big cloud of black was
over us, we got ready just the
same and had to push it alone the way hom.

5.7

After a time floating on the river. They got
it started and away they went, It was two
oclock when they got to the picnic grounds.

THE TEACHING OF ENGLISH

All played games till 3oclock, then they
had lunch, and played awhile longer, then
got ready to come back. John took the
baskets to the river to puttin the boat
but it was gone. one of the boys went
up the river a little ways, but
stayed to long, The children thought some
one stole it. They were all there, but where was
Jack? Henery heard the chucking of a boat,
He ran to the river, and saw Jack coming
around the curve, He gave Jack a scolding
for taking the boat. So they loaded the things in
and started for home. They all landed
safe, and were glad that the engine did
not buck, that ended the picnic.

7.0

"Oh," crief Jhoney, "what shall we
do. The teacher who had been
shouting with the children, turned
pale for just ahead of them was
a swift currant which, she knew,
would (lu) hurrel the launch
up side down and drownd them all.

Some of the little girls began to
cry but the teacher relized that
something must be done at once.
She was a brave and gritty little lady
and so she resolved to do
a dangerous thing. She knew that
if the boat could be turned on some
other course that they might
see a boat and be saved but
no body ever ventured in this
dangerous place.

HOW TO MEASURE PROGRESS IN COMPOSITION

~~There was a rope in~~ A little
ways from the launch was a
~~be~~ long board. ~~(If they could)~~
floating around.
If they could but reach this it
might mean safty for they could
push the boat out of this course.

There was a rope in the launch
and the teacher tied it around her
waist and had four of her strongest
boys to hold on the other end.
The teacher jumped over board for
she could swim quite good.

Three times the board slipped
out of her hands and she was almost
discouraged. when at last she got it.

A shout of joy arose from the boat
~~and~~ but the teacher had no
time to join them for in two
more minutes the boat would be
in the currant.

She got on board and ~~in~~
before they could realize what
was happening she was pusshing
the boat out of its course and some
of the big boys were helping her.

At last the boat moved into other

8.0

They had run out of gasoline. Where
they were it was ten feet deep and no
one could swim.

What could they do with all these child
ren, crying and shreiking with the fear of
not being able to have the picnic.

The man that ran the engine told the

THE TEACHING OF ENGLISH

others that they must wait for someone to come along and take them to the dock. Then, the children were getting nervous about staying over night.

Suddenly a bright thought came to the teacher. She said, "Children, can't we have a picnic on the boat? There is plenty of sitting down games, I am shure. "This Idea pleased the children and soon they were very busy laughing. Soon as the big steamer 'Armada' went past and offered to take them in but the children were having so good a time that they asked the 'Armada' to come back at five o'clock.

They had their picnic lunch on the boat at four o'clock, and by five they were willing to go back.

They afterwards said it was more fun than all the other picnics put to-

9.0

"What! the engine stopped, well I declare," ex claimed the teacher, "and we were planning such a fine time too," she finished

I am very sorry this has happed madam," said the boatman," but we are in no great danger, as I have a friend near here who will help me get ashore."

At this the boatman took a shining white whistle from his pocket and blew three long shrill blasts, which I suppose was some signal for a heavily built man was soon on the bank and after finding what was wanted he was soon in his boat house after his row boat.

Soon every one was safely landed on the opposite shore. and to judge by their faces enjoying themselves very much.

The boat was fixed in a short time and they all got in and had a happy time riding.

They all thought this landing place was fully as nice as the other and it fact as good as any other.

9.7

"What is the matter"? asked Miss Green the teacher of the school, to the man who was running the little launch. "I'm sorry mam," he said, "But the gasoline has given out." Some of the more timid children began to cry. "Hush," said the teacher a little sternly, "We cannot let this accident spoil our picnic." "Why can't we have our lunch right in the boat?" cried Mary, Brightly. "That is a fine idea, Mary," the teacher said gratefully. With the help of the pupils Miss Green managed to set the lunch on the floor of the boat. After lunch their spirits began to rise, and they amused themselves by telling stories.

All this while they were drifting along quietly. "There is a launch coming towards us!" exclaimed a small boy. Miss Green looked and sure enough there was a launch heading directly towards them. They were towed back home by this boat. That was

a fine picnic after all," chorused the
children as they stepped on firm
land once more.

The aim of the Breed and Frostic scale is to furnish an instrument for measuring general merit in composition for sixth-grade pupils.[7] The initial part of a selected narrative, "The Picnic," was read to the children.

THE PICNIC

It was a beautiful day in June, and the pupils were busily planning for a picnic which was to take place that afternoon in the park a mile down the river.

"Now, John, don't forget to bring your spoon and tin cup, and, Mary, be sure that you have enough sandwiches," said the teacher. After a few words to some of the other pupils who were going to the picnic, she dismissed them, all eager for the coming event, and all promising to be on hand at one o'clock, at the landing, ready for a jolly time.

One o'clock found them all assembled, with baskets packed and happy faces. The boat in which they were to start was a sturdy little gasoline launch, with plenty of room in it for all. They stowed themselves aboard, and shouted to be off. Soon they were chugging merrily down the stream.

Everything seemed to be going along smoothly, when suddenly the engine stopped running!

The pupils were then given twenty minutes in which to complete the story. The samples submitted to the judges were typewritten in such a manner as to repro-

[7] F. S. Breed and F. W. Frostic, *A Scale for Measuring the General Ability of English Composition in the Sixth Grade* (University of Chicago Press).

HOW TO MEASURE PROGRESS IN COMPOSITION

duce, as closely as possible, the form of the compositions, handwriting alone being excluded. This meant that margins, paragraphing, relative length of lines, and erasures, as well as errors in spelling, capitalization and punctuation, were reproduced. By a process similar to that followed in developing the Hillegas Scale, 481 samples were scored and a scale of nine graded steps of merit was formulated.

Many of the limitations of the scales previously discussed are apparent in this one. Once more general composition merit alone is measured, pupil products are scored but not analyzed, pupils are classified, but their language limitations not diagnosed. And finally, the fixed range augments the limitations of the scale. But, as Hudelson points out, "This is the only composition scale which attempts to reproduce, in type, the physical characteristics of the written compositions which compose it."[8]

The Willing Scale.—Willing offers a diagnostic scale for grades 4A-8A made up of eight graded specimens, all on the topic, "An Exciting Experience."[9] The total value of each composition in the scale is derived by synthesizing the ratings given to specific elements of *form* and *story*. The values ascribed to each of the constituent elements of general merit are arbitrarily

[8] *Twenty-Second Year Book* of the National Society for the Study of Education, 1923, p. 51.
[9] M. H. Willing, *Willing Scale for Measuring Written Composition* (Public School Publishing Company, Bloomington, Ill.)

set. With each specimen is an explanatory statement of its deficiencies.

The Willing Scale has been criticised because it undoes what it does. It sets out to evolve an analytical scale and then combines the ratings of its constituent elements. What if it does? Is not the final score, derived by synthesizing the scores for specific elements, likely to be more exact than the score derived by regarding merit as a gross quality? The Willing Scale errs rather in assigning arbitrary values to its samples and in not analyzing composition merit sufficiently. It stands out as a pioneer effort to achieve a valuable diagnostic scale, but it gives no real diagnosis and no set of standards.

Van Wagenen's Composition Scale.—This is a specialized diagnostic measure which offers distinct scales for description, narration and exposition, based on separate values for (a) *thought content,* (b) *mechanics* and (c) *structure.*[10]

The Van Wagenen Scale does not win favor among teachers because it is difficult to use. The scores for each of the three merits—content, mechanics, and structure—are not expressed in terms that have corresponding values. Thus score X in thought content of a composition is not equivalent to score X in mechanics of that composition, score X in content in the narration scale is equivalent to score X in content in the exposition scale. For practical school purposes, a

[10] M. J. Van Wagenen, *Van Wagenen's Minnesota English Composition Scale* (World Book Co., Yonkers-on-Hudson, N. Y.).

composite grade for a pupil's composition effort is necessary. Teachers therefore find it very confusing to work out a general composition score of separate subscores that are not expressed in equivalent values. Thus far, general merit scores obtained by this scale are, at best, no more accurate than the scores obtained by judging general merit as a single quality.

The Lewis Scales. *Aim.*—The Lewis Scales offer five scales to measure five important types of composition:[11] (1) business letters ordering goods; (2) business letters, applications for positions; (3) friendly letters of a personal and intimate type; (4) personal letters that are expository; (5) narration on the topic, "One of My Most Interesting Experiences." The first four scales are new and offer a measuring instrument for the most useful forms of written composition.

Description.—Let us see how the scale for "order letters" was developed. About 800 pupils in grades 5-12 in five school systems were asked to write these letters without any preparation. The normal-school conditions under which such letters are usually written were preserved. Children were given catalogues, magazines and newspapers advertising a variety of materials, and were asked to examine the advertisements preparatory to writing the letter. No time limit was set. Few pupils took more than twenty minutes.

Thirty-three samples were selected by competent

[11] Ervin Eugene Lewis, *The Lewis Scales for Measuring Special Types of English Compositions* (copyright, 1923, by World Book Co., Yonkers-on-Hudson, N. Y.).

judges who agreed that they were representative of the entire group. These were then submitted to 63 judges of proved competence, who rated them by the Nassau Supplement to the Hillegas Scales. After careful statistical treatment, the 33 compositions were arranged in order of merit, as is shown by the accompanying specimens.

1.53

Apr 17 Boston, Mas

Dear Sir

I wrote to ask you that you no I want want leggins or boots and bicicles. yes sir quickly.

    Evan Kimpson

2.67

April 19, 1918.
Hillcrest Ave.

Rear Vendome & Co,

Would you please send to Hillcrest Ave., N.. Y a pink screen with pictures of birds on it and also a white kimmona with pink roses on it.

  per Constance Rowell.

2.93

34 Cedar Pl.
April 19, 1918

Iveli Bros.

Please send me two pakages of radisk seeds, two pakages of lettuce seeds, a basket of pansys, two qts. of apples, and a pakage of corn seeds and rubarb seeds

    Yours Truly
     William Sims

HOW TO MEASURE PROGRESS IN COMPOSITION

3.46

16 Morris Street
Springfield, Mass

Boone & Co.
  New York City,
    New York.
Gentlemen:

Will you kindly send me a baseball mask, a baseball suit and a bat and a ball. And kindly send them as soon possible.
Yours truly
Leonard Sears

3.79

59 Hamilton Avenue
Atlantic City, N. J.
April 19, 1918

Boy Scouts of America
  200 Fifth Avenue
    New York City
Gentlemen:

Please send me the flowing: 8 tents, 1 uniform, 1 tellegraph outfit, 8 pocket size First aide outfits and 2 dozen of Binacqulors. Charge same to my account.
Yours truly,
Fred Forbes

4.37

15 Fairfield Place
Butte, Mont.
April 19, 1918

The Providence Co.
  Chicago, Illinois.
Dear Sirs:

In your catalogue I saw a search light, a body of a car, and a wire wheel. Enclosed find a check for fifty-five dollars ($55) for which please send me these things as soon as possible.
Yours truly
Arthur Dennis

august.

4.82

16 Culver Street
Albany, New York
April 19, 1918

Hudson Book Company.
New York City, New York.

Dear Sirs,

An pamplet of your books you have for sale has been sent to me, On looking through it I saw two or three looks I would like to order from you.

Please send me a copy of Skinner's Merry Tales, which you advertised at forty-eight cents a piece. Also two copies of Carpenter's Around the World with the Children at sixty cents a copy.

Please send the books as soon as possible.

I remain,
Yours truly,
Emma E. Avery.

5.86

344 Riverdale Avenue
Columbus, Ohio

B. Benson & Company
 43 Madison Avenue
  Los Angeles, Cal.

Gentlemen:

Inclosed please find twelve dollars ($12) for which please send me three yards of blue serge to match the enclosed sample at three dollars per yard ($3); one book at one dollar ($1) called "Over The Top" and one blue tie to match serge at two dollars ($2).

Yours truly
Grace Donovan

HOW TO MEASURE PROGRESS IN COMPOSITION

5.99

Keokuk, Iowa.
Apr. 19. 1918.

Central Book Co. Inc.
  New York City.
Gentlemen:

Enclosed please find money order for two dollars and twenty-four cents $2.24 for which please send me Dorrance's The Story of the Forest, Wilson's Indian Hero Tales, Baldwins Fifty Famous Rides and Riders, and McBrien's America First at fifty-six cents ($.56), sixty cents $(.60) sixty $(.60) and sixty-four cents $(.64) respectively

> Yours truly
> Fred Long.

6.76

114 State Street,
  Camden, N. J.
  January 22, 1917.

John Smith Co.
Asto Place,
New York City
Dear Sir:
  Please send to the above address the following,

1 copy "Boy Allies With the Tenor of the Seas at $.40	$.40
1 copy "Boy Allies In the Baltic at $.40	$.40
1 copy "Boy Allies With the Battleships at $.40	$.40

Enclosed find check for $1.20 in payment of above

> Yous truly
> George Doeinus

7.98

2 Morris Place
Watertown, N. Y.
Apr. 19, 1918

The Goldberg Furniture Co.
 Spokane, Wash.
Gentlemen:

I have received your answer to my letter of inquiry with descriptive catalogue enclosed, from which I have selected the following:

1 Morris Chair	No 632	$24.50	$24.50
2 Willow Porch Chairs	246	3.50	7.00
1. Willow Rocker	247	4.75	4.75

Enclosed you will find check for Thirty-six dollars and twenty-five cents in full payment of the bill.

Please send the articles, express prepaid, to the address given above.

Yours truly.
Lillian McCarthy

2.98

36 Main Street,
Yonkers, Florida,
May 2, 1918.

Dear Sir,

Since I have saw the job I learned in my school-days, I would like to take it. I will report Wednesday to this building My name is Ernest Holze.

Yours truly,
Ernest Holze

HOW TO MEASURE PROGRESS IN COMPOSITION

3.47

67 Clinton Street
Carthage, New York
May 2, 1918.

Dear Sir,

I am a girl of 16 years and would like to work in your office. When shall I come to work in the office. I am a girl who knows how to work in an office. I want to know my salary before I begin to work in your office. I must have everything I need in the office because when I need it I must have it. This is all I can write to you about my position.

Yours truly,
Mary Fabachar

3.97

186 Passaic St.
St. Louis, Mo.
April 30, 1918.

J. B. Schoenfeld.
25 Madison Ave.
City,
Dear Sir,

I have read (for) your advertisement in the paper and would like to apply for the situation.

Yours truly,
Marian Smith.

4.87

184 Buena Vista Avenue
Fairport, N. J.
May 2, 1918

Dear Mr. Overhage,

I would like to have this job as I have been experienced in this work. I have been an errand boy in a butchershop and in two other stores. One store that I worked in was a large concern in New York. I have worked in a printing place before and I know a quite deal of printing. I have forgot to tell you that I worked in a Postal Telegraph Office as a messenger. Please write me if you want me to see you.

Yours truly,
Arnold Kopper

5.57

5 Clinton Street
Nashville, Tenn.
May 2, 1918.

New York Telephone Co.
R. 251 Times, Downtown
Gentlemen:

I have read your advertisement in the New York American. I would like to apply for that position as I am experienced in domestic science.

My age is eighteen years. I have already worked in Brown and Co.'s lunchroom. If references are required, they can easily be obtained Please notify me if you are willing to accept me.

Yours truly,
Rose Lipschitz

HOW TO MEASURE PROGRESS IN COMPOSITION

6.13

67 Grove Street;
St. Levege, Ohio.
April, 30, 1918

Dear Sir:

I am applying for a position as stenographer in your concern. I am a graduate of Drake's Business College. Am accurate and have large knowledge of stenography. Am well recommended by former employers. I am twenty-five years old and expect on an average of sixty dollars per month. Have had five years experience.

Respectfully yours,
Alice C. Parker.

6.67

56 Prospect Street
Springdale, Nevada,
May 2, 1918

New York Leather Belting Co.
South 11 St. Kent Ave.
Brooklyn, N. Y.

Dear Sirs:

I read of your advertisement in the New York paper and I would like to be given a chance at this position.

I am twenty-one years old and have experience in the kind of work that you require. I have graduated from School No. 10, Yonkers and have gone four years to the Yonkers High School. I have been employed in the Overland Company in Yonkers, but due to the company leaving the city I was forced to give up the position. If references are required they may be secured at the above company on 57th St, New York and from Mr. Baker of the Yonkers High School.

Yours respectfully
Otilda Smith

THE TEACHING OF ENGLISH

6.99

264 Capron Street
January 4

Mrs. J. C. Simpson
239 May Street
Dear Madam:

I learn through your advertisement in tonight's Times that you desire a young girl to read to you and to write letters from dictation. Please consider me an applicant.

I am sixteen, a high school senior. I am not a trained reader; that is, I cannot read with elocutionary effect. Nor can I claim to be unusually good in composition. It seems to me, however, that I should be able to read ordinary prose distinctly, and write with reasonable accuracy. By permission I refer you to Principal Wilbur F. Howells, who may be addressed at the high school.

I shall be pleased to call at your home whenever it may be convenient to you.

Very truly yours,
Adele M. Peberdy

7.49

October 4, 1916

X 239
    Bulletin
        Philadelphia, Pa.
Gentlemen:

I am a stenographer of two years' experience, and am looking for a position because my present employer, an attorney, is retiring. You will find inclosed a letter of recommendation from him.

I am a graduate of the Commercial High School, can write 125 words a minute, and ready my notes easily. I am willing to go out of the city.

May I hope for an interview?

Very truly yours,
Miriam C. Norton

7.89

680 East 13th St.
Salt Lake City, Utah.
August 1, 1917.

P 19, Herald Republican,
 Salt Lake City, Utah.
Dear Sir:

In reply to your advertisement in yesterday's paper for a boy over sixteen years old, who can use a typewriter, I should like to submit my application.

I am eighteen years of age, and have just completed a course in typewriting at Henager's Business College. During the afternoons for the past two months, I have been doing special work in typewriting for several printing houses.

Should you wish references, you may write to Mr. J. J. Brown, principal of the Business College, or the F. W. Gardiner Printing Co. At present I am at liberty in the morning and, if you care to consider my application and give me a personal interview, I shall be pleased to call upon you at any time you may suggest.

Respectfully yours,
Paul Kennedy.

8.44

1331 Clay Street,
San Francisco, Califormnia
March 26, 1918.

Messrs. White, Harwood & Calkins,
 1349 Market Street,
  San Francisco, California.
Gentlemen:

My friend John C. Henry employed by you in you draughting department has told me of a new position in your shops caused by the installation of a Hartwell and March No. 9 machine. I wish to apply for the position.

While I was working in Lebanon, Ill., in 1915-18, in the

employ of William Henry Granger and Son, I ran a Hartwell and Marsh No. 8 machine almost exclusively and so became thoroughly familiar with the older model, which, I understand, is not very different from the new No. 9. My four years' training in the Cleveland (Ohio) Technical High School, where I completed in June, 1915, the prescribed general scientific course with the supplemental half-time work in the Hopkins Manufacturing Works of Cleveland, has given me practical experience, in running and repairing many machines similar to those manufactured by the Hartwell and Marsh Company.

I am enclosing recommendations from Mr. William Henry Granger, whose employ I left because of our family's moving here, and from Mr. Frank R. Carpenter, under whom I did most of my machine shop work in the Cleveland Technical High School.

>Very respectfully yours,
>Edward D. Wilson.

Evaluation of the Lewis Scales.—It is clear that these scales are a distinct advance over their predecessors. The specialized character of the scales adds to their usefulness. They are free from the artificial classification into narration, description, exposition and argumentation, characteristic of the Harvard-Newton Scales. Although the scales are not diagnostic but designed to measure general merit, their differentiation tends to facilitate the diagnosis of pupil needs in composition.

The Hudelson Scales.—Junior-high-school teachers of composition will find the Hudelson Scale useful for

HOW TO MEASURE PROGRESS IN COMPOSITION

their grade of pupils.[12] This scale refines the Hillegas Scale by producing a measure of merit that progresses by uniform or even steps. Hudelson's work is carefully planned to give teachers the practice that develops accuracy in using scientific measures.

From approximately 1,000 first-year high-school compositions written in Virginia, 100 were selected as representing all degrees of merit, from the poorest to the best. These 100 compositions were then scored by as many judges trained in the use of the Nassau County Supplement to the Hillegas Scale. As in the Lewis Scales, judges with greater average deviation than 0.5 from the true value were excluded from the final scoring. The value of each specimen in the scale is the median of 96 judgments. The subject is the same in all compositions, "The Most Exciting Ride I Ever Had." A scale of sixteen equadistant grades is thus evolved.

The scale is too recent to warrant any judgment based on extensive actual practice. It has no diagnostic value, for it measures merit as a gross quality. As can be seen from the part of the specimens here reproduced, its samples are more attractive than those in the Hillegas Scale, and, placed at equal distances, are more readily understood and more easily used. The inclusion of practice material and simple specific direc-

[12] Earl Hudelson, *The Hudelson English Composition Scales* (copyright, 1921, 1923, by World Book Co., Yonkers-on-Hudson, N. Y.).

tions for use is wise and will help popularize this very promising language scale.

2.067

THE MOST EXCITING RIDE I EVER HAD

The Most exciting ride I ever had was a Hay ride, it was early in the morning when we went out on the hay ride it was quite a injoyable trip every one seemed to be so cheerfuly the rode that we were traveling on it was very hilly on of the parties took sick and far a little while no one did not think that the Girl were as sick as she was all at once she come mence comeplaining so she arroused ones curosity we found out that the girl were verry ell thought she was going to die.

2.50

THE MOST EXCITING RIDE I EVER HAD

One dag Friends I decided to go car riding my friend and myself started.

We was going around a sharp curve and another car was coming toward us the driver did not know what to do. The road was so narrow we couldn't stop. So the other car ran into us and turned us over the bank. and it hurt three of my frimses very bad.

3.557

THE MOST EXCITING RIDE I EVER HAD

Summer before last my sister was going to see her girl friend, she lived out in the country, forty miles from here. we had a car, so my brother said he would take her out there and I could go with then, we ask daddy if he cared and he, said no,

So that night about seven thirty we left home, and went by town to get some gasoline. then we left for the country, we got out of town the roads were very bad at first, but we went on. we forgot the way out there so we ask someone how we could get there, they told us, so we kept on, the roads were gradually getting better. we got half off the way, then we ask some one else to direct us to the road to take, they did, we went on as they told us, we got out in the country on the wrong road, but we did not know it until we ask some tome. then brother got mad and jercked the car from one side of the road to the other. I didn't think we were ever going to get there or anywhere else alive. We turned around and went back, and took the right road. and got there about twelve o'clock. that night.

4.509

THE MOST EXCITING RIDE I EVER HAD

One day my brother took me to Richmond in his racer. We did not go gast zoing down. We spent two days in Richmond. We had a good time there.

When we started back my brother said he was going to run fast, which he did.

We were going along about 40 miles an hour, when, coming around a short carne we saw another car coming at about an equal rate of speed. We missed him by about six inches.

After that the road was stright and the speedometor showed that we were going seventy five mile an hour.

We arrived here just one hour and a half from the time we left Richmond.

5.062

THE MOST EXCITING RIDE I EVER HAD

It was the afternoon of a day in July that we started off in an automobile to go to a place about twenty miles away.

Before we had gotten half way something happened to the engine and we couldn't go very fast.

We had nearly gotton to the place where we were going when another car with two negroes in it got across the road and wouldn't let us pass. They pulled out their pistols, and one shot, but he did not hit anyone.

He was just coming over to our car when the sheriff happened to come along, and he took the two men and carried them away with him, and we went on our journey.

It is very exciting to have anyone to hold you up on the road and I think you will find it out if you every have anyone to hold you up.

5.933

The most exciting ride I ever had

The most exciting ride I ever had was when we first got our Pony. One day we started out, and he did very nicely for a while, until he saw a automobile and then the fun began. He tried to turn around right in the road, and when he found that he could not he started to run. There were only two of us in the cart, my brother and myself and neither were very strong. But we pulled back on him for all we were worth, but he seemed to go faster instead of stopping.

After a while the Pony seemed to be getting tired, so he slowed down and was soon alright. We then began to laugh and thought we had had a fine ride and all the excitement that we had been wishing for.

7.50

Westward Ho!

About ten years ago father bought a large ranch up in the northern part of Minnesota. We were all eager to go to this ranch, so he also bought a fine horse which we called Prince, and a double seated buggy. We were to drive up. The day of our departure drew near, and about three o'clock, one lovely morning, mother awakened me and told me to hurry as we wanted to start in an hour. I was up and dressed in a few moments, and hurried through breakfast. In half an hour we were ready to start. I had never seen so beautiful a morning. The sun was just showing its great golden face over the horizon. The birds were popping up out of their next, and all the world seemed to awaken to their thrilling songs. We rode all that day, stopping only for food and drink, and to let the horse rest. So we went on for a week, having the most delightful ride and the best time I have ever spent. One morning about ten o'clock we arrived at our destination, all tired out, but happy. And though other occurrences on the drive have been blotted out of my mind, that one morning when all the world seemed glad will forever be fresh in my memory.

9.50

Niagara Falls

Oh that I had never heard of Niagara till I beheld it! Blessed were the wanderers of old, who heard its deep roar, sounding through the woords, as the summons to an unknown wonder, and approached its awful brink, in all the freshness of native feeling. Had its own mysterious voice been the first to warn me of its existence, then, indeed, I might have knelt down and worshipped. But I had come thither, haunted with a vision of foam and fury, and dizzy cliffs, and an ocean tumbling down out of the sky—a scene, in short, which nature had too much good taste and calm simplicity to realize. My mind had struggled to adapt these false conceptions to the reality, and finding the effort vain, a wretched sense of disappointment weighed me down. I climbed the precipice, and threw myself on the earth feeling that I was unworthy to look at the Great Falls, and careless about beholding them again.

The Maximal and Typical Composition Scales.[13]—The existing scales in composition are designed to gauge

[13] By Earl Hudelson in "English Composition, Its Aim, Methods and Measurement," *Twenty-Second Year Book* of the National Society for Study of Education (Bloomington, Ill., 1923).

how well a pupil can do on an assigned topic. But the composition written under these circumstances may not be a measure of the pupil's full ability in self expression. Some topics are not as closely related to their interests, nor as much a part of their daily experience, as others. The closer the subject of a composition touches the life of a pupil, the greater are the chances that it will stir his imagination and stimulate a fuller and richer flow of language. We criticized the Hillegas Scale severely because of the formal and bookish specimen compositions that make up its successive gradations. It is necessary to know how well children *can do* in addition to knowing how well they really *do* in a given circumstance. Existing scales are designed to answer how well the child *does,* not how well the child *can do*.

Hudelson subjected a number of frequently used composition topics to a test to ascertain which topic will afford pupils the fullest opportunity for an expression of the maximum language power. After careful statistical refinement of the judgments of competent teachers, he thinks he has discovered that topic which produces for pupils an opportunity for an expression of their maximum language power, and also a topic which will produce a composition whose merit is approximately the merit of their average composition. A composition scale made up of scientifically graded specimens of composition on a topic designed to provoke all the expressional ability of pupils is called a Maximal Composition Ability Scale. A composition

HOW TO MEASURE PROGRESS IN COMPOSITION

scale made up of scientifically graded specimens of composition on a topic designed to produce a representative example of pupil ability is called a Typical Composition Ability Scale. The topic in the Maximal Scale is "How I Learned a Lesson"; in the Typical Scale, "A Snowball Fight on Slatter's Hill." The former is an inventive composition, the latter, a reproduction after the reading of a set narrative by the teacher.

The Maximal Scale measures, according to Hudelson's statistical conclusion, *how well pupils can do;* the Typical Scale, *how well pupils do.* The Maximal Scale is most useful at the beginning of the year in classifying pupils; the Typical Scale is most helpful during, or at the end of, the term when pupils must be rated for their effort and actual achievement.

No critical judgment of these two scales can be given at this time. We must content ourselves with a mere announcement of their formulation. To say that a careful analysis of all the statistical travail attending their birth leaves one unconvinced, is not necessarily to indict these Maximal and Typical Scales. The need for two such scales is apparent. The development of a composition scale, crude and experimental in character, is an accomplished fact. But the announcement that "How I Learned a Lesson" and "The Snowball Fight on Slatter's Hill" are the topic that give two scales that actually measure how well a child can do and how well he actually does, is startling. We must ever be mindful of the fact that experimentalists in education are dealing with a complex of human intelligence not yet understood; that their methods are still crude and far from scientific; and, finally, that their procedure

CLASSIFICATION OF COMPOSITION SCALES

Basis of Classification	The Scales
Those that classify according to general merit	Hillegas, Thorndike Extension, Trabue Nassau County Supplement, Harvard-Newton, Breed and Frostic, Lewis, Hudelson
Those that diagnose and analyze	Willing, Van Wagenen
Those that measure all types of writing	Hillegas, Thorndike Extension, Trabue Nassau County Supplement, Breed and Frostic, Willing, Hudelson
Those that measure special types of writing, like narration, exposition, letter writing	Harvard-Newton, Van Wagenen, Lewis
Those designed for use regardless of school grade	Hillegas, Thorndike Extension, Trabue Nassau County Supplement, Willing, Lewis, Van Wagenen, Hudelson
Those that apply to specific school grades	Harvard-Newton (8th Grade), Breed and Frostic (6th Grade)
Specially adapted for junior high schools	Trabue Nassau County Supplement, Breed and Frostic, Willing, Van Wagenen, Hudelson, Lewis Narration

HOW TO MEASURE PROGRESS IN COMPOSITION

is shot through with assumptions and personal opinions absent in experimental procedure in the physical sciences.

Classification of Composition Scales.—To classify all these serious and laborious efforts to develop scientific, objective scales for measuring composition may serve as a helpful review. The student is invited to justify the classifications on the preceding page.

Outstanding Need of Scale for Oral Composition.—The development of composition scales seems to have proceeded, thus far, on the assumption that skill in written composition is the primary need of school pupils. In the life of the average person, written composition is only incidental. Not only is his written composition confined to letter writing, but his letter writing is infrequent and simple. Nevertheless, development of skill in written composition seems to be the outstanding purpose of class instruction in composition. The composition skill that functions constantly is in oral, not written, language. We need a composition scale that measures ability to order ideas quickly and to express them orally in clear, correct and attractive form. A satisfactory oral composition scale will not only measure what is more important but will place the emphasis in composition teaching where it rightly belongs.

How to Use a Composition Scale.—Improper use of a standardized scale more than offsets the values inherent in it. It is suggested that teachers using any one of the scales study the suggestive procedure outlined below.

1. Approach your task in a spirit of open-mindedness. Do not prejudge the measuring instrument. It may be another instance of "much ado about nothing," but this characterization should come at the end of careful analysis of the scale and extensive practical use of it. Without faith in the superiority of a composite judgment over personal judgment, no teacher is ready to use a scale. It is true that the same set of papers scored by the same person using the same scale at intervals of two weeks will show variations. But the significant fact to remember is that the variations of judgment when a scale is used are decidedly less than when reliance is placed solely on personal judgment.

2. Understand the scale. Know its aims, the method by which it was formulated, the type of scale it is, its distinctive characteristics, the grade for which it was intended, and its relative value.

3. Read and reread the sample compositions in the scale. Analyze each of them and list its merits and its limitations. Make an honest effort to find why the composite judgment regards it as inferior to the one that follows it and superior to the one that precedes it.

4. Practice using the scale. A carefully elaborated scale gives teachers test specimens which are to be used in practice rating. Compare your ratings with the standard one. What is your variation? What is your average variation? How closely can you come to the standard rating?

5. Read a pupil's composition. Determine what

specimens in the scale are inferior to it. What is the first scale specimen that is superior to it? Is it more like the superior one or like the best of the inferior ones? Give it the score of the scale specimen it approximates most closely.

6. Make sure that the class wrote the composition under uniform conditions. The same topic must be given to all. The introductory remarks, the explanatory statements, the preparatory guides must be the same for all.

Cautions in Using a Standardized Scale.—(1) The scales are more reliable when used for a group than for an individual. (2) To rate a pupil, obtain more than one sample of his work, preferably not less than three, on subjects that prompt different types of writing. (3) In judging a single pupil, it is well to supplement the scale score by the information in possession of the teacher, and by the findings of a reliable intelligence test. (4) A score must not be regarded as a percentile equivalent. Score 5.5 in the Hudelson Scale *does not* mean 55 per cent or 5.5 per cent merit. It does mean that a given composition has 5.5 units of merit beyond the sample at the zero point in the scale and half the merit of the composition at the 11.0 point (if there were one). (5) And finally, a scale should be used at intervals far enough apart to permit ability to develop. Children progress, especially in habit acquisition experiences, irregularly. To use a scale each week gives results that are not helpful and may be misleading.

The Educational Significance of Standard Scales.—To describe a pupil's performance, we should know:

1. How fast he works. What can he achieve in a given time?
2. How accurate are his reactions.
3. The character of the task that is assigned.
4. The normal achievements of pupils of approximately the same age and the same preparatory training.

Does the usual test given by teachers or supervisors measure performance in relation to time, or the rate of accuracy in relation to time? Does it present a series of tasks evolved after laborious effort and checked under experimental conditions? What if a pupil's composition is rated 70 per cent by his teacher? Is this necessarily a good rating? How good a composition should a pupil of his age and his previous language training write in twenty minutes on the assigned topic? The child's composition, judged as an isolated pupil product, may be distinctly below or distinctly above what we may reasonably expect from him. What does 70 per cent mean then? A standard composition scale gives a test that meets all the conditions set forth above, and enables us to obtain a score that can be interpreted intelligently.

Instructional Values of Composition Scales. 1. *They Substitute Accuracy for Personal Judgment.*—Standard scales offer a quantitative measure for qualities that no one person can measure. A telling instance of the need of a fixed measure to replace the fluctuations inherent in personal judgment is reported in the

HOW TO MEASURE PROGRESS IN COMPOSITION

Twenty-Second Year Book of the National Society for the Study of Education (pp. 32-36). Three teachers of English, teaching different sections of the same class, and knowing that the ten anonymous compositions they were asked to arrange in order of merit were written by eighth-grade pupils, showed variations of judgment graphically set forth in the figure below.

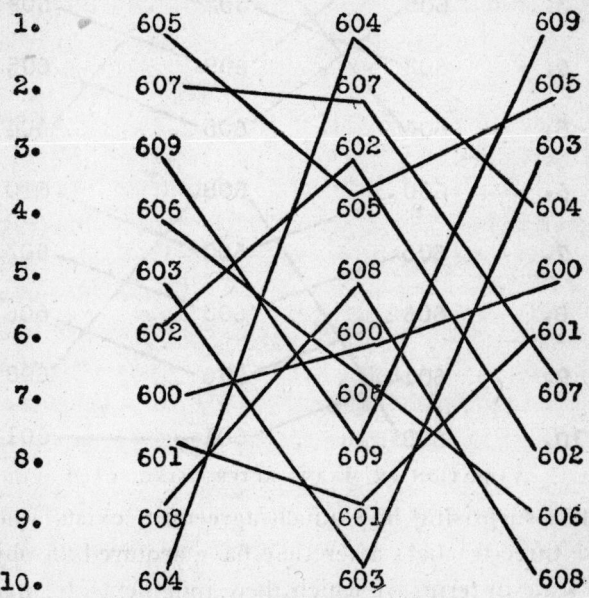

VARIATION IN MARKS BEFORE USING SCALE

Notice that composition designated as No. 604 was rated the worst by one teacher and the best by the second; specimen 609 was judged third, eighth and first by these three teachers; specimen 607 was rated second and seventh.

THE TEACHING OF ENGLISH

But after using a composition scale for one month, these three teachers rated the same composition far less erratically, as is shown in the accompanying figure.

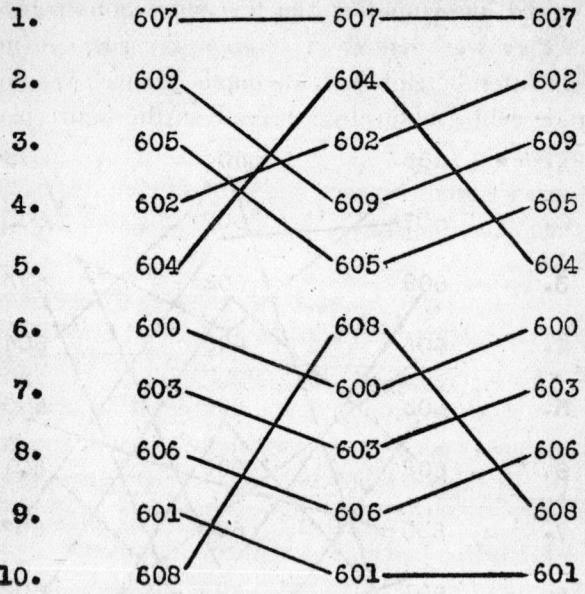

VARIATION IN MARKS AFTER USING SCALE

It is surprising how much agreement exists among these three teachers after they have acquired an objective scale in terms of which their judgments are made. Now all agree that specimen 607 is the best of the ten; specimen 604 still shows variations but these are not so startling and 609 shows practical agreement.

2. *The Elements of an Experience Are Included and Rated According to Their Importance.*—In a scientific scale, regardless of the subject, the most important

facts and skills are not only included but are given values commensurate with their significance. This fact is more clearly illustrated in such subjects as arithmetic, geography and history than in composition, for we showed that most composition scales measure general merit. But this advantage holds in composition scales in so far as they prevent teachers from exaggerating a particular failing like faulty punctuation or a specific merit like correctness of spelling. The whole composition and all its elements are rated by a scale.

3. *The Governing Conditions Under Which Ability Expresses Itself Are Considered.*—We know that the time element, the topic, the conditions under which a piece of work is produced, the degree of accuracy that is demanded and the preparatory help that is given, all govern the pupil's result. A scale makes definite provisions for each of these and to that extent gives us a basis for better and more uniform judgment.

4. *Scales Have Diagnostic Value.*—A complete scale, properly developed, reveals the degree of weakness in each of the important aspects of a subject or skill. Here, again, we saw that composition scales were essentially weak. Penmanship and arithmetic scales not only measure the pupil's habits in these subjects but indicate clearly in what particular the child is lacking, whether it be in legibility, fundamental combinations, reasoning, division, form, etc. The analytic composition scale suggested in the early part of our discussion has unmistakable diagnostic worth.

It gives the teacher a real basis for differentiating instruction and assigning specialized drills according to pupil needs.

5. *Scales Make Self Evaluation Possible.*—Most scales enable a pupil to gauge his own progress more definitely. Under prevailing conditions, a pupil is told that his composition work is satisfactory by one teacher and not satisfactory by another. But when the teacher's judgment is expressed in terms of a fixed objective scale, the pupil knows that his work at the beginning and at the end of the term had the merit of specimen 5.5. He realizes that he has made no progress and may bestir himself to greater effort.

Supervisory Values of Composition Scales. 1. *Scales Give Pupils Greater Confidence in Teachers' Judgments.*—The pupil is often the victim of the erratic judgment of a teacher. With the standardization of judgment by a scale, greater justice is done the individual pupil.

2. *Real Comparisons and Evaluations Are Possible.*—Without standardized scores, it is manifestly impossible to compare with justice the achievements of different classes and different schools. Nor can a supervisor really gauge the status of a class without definite norms of pupil achievements for each grade. Thus, the following grade norms are computed after extensive use of Trabue's Supplement to the Hillegas Scale. They indicate what may reasonably be expected in composition of pupils in the various grades.[14]

[14] Earl Hudelson, *Hudelson's English Composition Scales* (copyright, 1921, 1923, by World Book Co.), pp. 22–23.

HOW TO MEASURE PROGRESS IN COMPOSITION

NORMS FOR VARIOUS GRADES

In Grade...	IV	V	VI	VII	VIII	IX	X	XI	XII
Quality....	3.0	3.6	4.2	4.7	5.3	5.5	5.9	6.3	6.7

Let us assume that schools or school systems make the following grade scores by the Trabue Supplement to the Hillegas Scales:

GRADE SCORES BY THE TRABUE SUPPLEMENT TO THE HILLEGAS SCALES

Grade	IV	V	VI	VII	VIII	IX	X	XI	XII	Month
School A	2.15	2.24	2.85	3.15	4.0	5.2	5.8	6.2	6.6	January
School B	2.85	3.74	4.40	4.95	4.87	5.68	7.10	6.94	7.20	February
School System C	2.22	2.38	3.54	4.12	4.96	5.83	5.66	6.27	6.64	Spring
School System D	2.99	3.26	3.28	3.97	4.58	4.69	5.62	6.42	6.22	Spring

Grade scores B, C, and D are genuine, A is supposititious. School B is a private school with a carefully selected clientele. The language ability is unusually high and home influence is a significant factor. School A, let us assume, is a parochial school in a foreign neighborhood. The scores are below normal and reflect the lack of English in the environment of the pupils. Those who stay in school and continue are not only more serious minded but are also fortunate in the teacher selected for them. What significant facts are revealed by the grade scores for C, a small city in New Jersey, and for D, a highly industrialized town in the Middle West?

A superintendent complains that a school in a foreign section is not doing all that it can in written composition. What is the principal's answer if the grade scores are as follows:

Grade..............	IV	V	VI	VII	VIII	Month
Score..............	2.50	2.8	3.4	3.8	4.2	February
	2.74	3.2	3.7	4	4.6	June

3. *Scales Give a Basis for Classification.*—Although reliable intelligence tests help materially in grouping children, it is obvious that pupil performance must play a major part in classifying pupils. No further discussion is necessary to justify the assertion that standardized composition scales give us a tentative basis for grouping children for language study.

4. *Scales Help Us Measure Teacher Achievement.*— How can a supervisor determine how much a teacher did for her class in any given subject? The teacher insists she did all that was humanly possible, and that the children have made gratifying progress in one semester. The principal, relying on personal judgment based on what he saw in his occasional visits, or on his estimate of a test composition, holds no such laudatory opinion of the teacher's achievement. Is the principal's personal judgment necessarily better than the teacher's? Whose judgment should prevail?

Although a standardized scale used intelligently does not guarantee a perfect measure, there is, however, greater chance that justice will prevail.

5. *Standard Scales Help Determine the Value of Teaching Methods.*—There is a divergence of opinion as to the relative value of various teaching methods among teachers and supervisors. Some hold tenaciously that freedom of expression will ultimately produce the greatest development in expression. Others insist that language follows arbitrary forms and therefore composition must be formal and severe. Many experienced and highly esteemed teachers of English urge that only in written composition does the child develop respect for language form, and that oral composition, so ardently advocated, is essentially ineffective. This view is stoutly contested by teachers equally experienced and esteemed. Whose judgment should prevail? But, with an objective measuring instrument, we can give the contesting systems a full trial and then determine which produces better results.

Conclusions.—Scientific scales for measuring school achievement, like most intelligence and vocational scales, are still imperfect instruments. Composition scales, because of the nature of the subject matter and the skill they attempt to measure, are, on the whole, not among the most satisfactory standardized scales yet developed. They still presuppose much technical information, and are not designed for indiscriminate use by the novice. They give promise that is far-reaching and must command the respect and critical attention of all earnest students of educational methods.

PART II

THE FORMAL ASPECT OF COMPOSITION

CHAPTER X

THE TEACHING OF SPELLING

Expressional vs. Formal Aspect of Composition.—It is obvious that the teaching of composition presents two phases: The first deals with the problem of ordering ideas and giving expression to them so that the meaning is conveyed, clearly and convincingly, to another mind. This expressional aspect of composition was treated in the first part of the book. But ideas must be expressed in commonly accepted forms of spelling, capitalization and punctuation, and in accordance with grammatical standards. This second phase of composition, the purely formal or technical aspect, must now be treated. The second part of this book will therefore concern itself with the teaching of spelling, meaning and use, dictation, memory gems and grammar.

Spelling Usually Tested, not Taught.—To children and teachers alike, the spelling lesson is usually a dull period and a hard memory grind. Despite the vigorous drills in spelling, the results are poor. The writer's visits to classes led him to the conclusion that in most instances spelling is tested, not taught. Lists of varying lengths are assigned in various ways for memorization. The succeeding spelling lesson is occupied with a test to discover those children who know the words and those who do not. Problems and devices in the methodology of spelling have received more than passing attention, for spelling is rich in fads. The spelling matches, word analyses, and diacritical markings which were the boast of the teachers of the last generation have given way to contextual spelling, multiple sense appeal, exclusive muscular appeal, and phonogrammic grouping which are the methods of the teacher of to-day.

Objects of the Teaching of Spelling.—We shall be in a better position to estimate the relative worth of all these devices and to evolve a method of teaching spelling if we formulate in definite terms the ultimate ends which must be achieved in spelling lessons. (1) The dominant aim is *to inculcate the habit of writing the commonly used words correctly in context* while consciousness is intent on thought. The child who writes correctly a word that his teacher dictates with exaggerated clearness while the mind focalizes on the form of the word in question has not attained the highest end in spelling. Can the child write this word correctly while he is lost in the thought that he is expressing? This is the standard by which good spelling must be judged. (2) A second aim is *to develop the ability of self-correction*. The spelling lessons must teach children simple rules of spelling, the use of the dictionary, and a method of word comparison so that they can correct the spelling in all their written work. (3) A third aim is *to make correct spelling a matter of deep concern* to the children so that they will gladly suffer the inconvenience of going to the dictionary, or make inquiries rather than put down incorrect forms of spelling. This "word conscience" can be developed in the higher grades through proper motivation in spelling lessons, in which teachers lead children to feel the social need of correct spelling.

Principles Guiding the Selection of Spelling Words.— How shall words be chosen for the spelling exercises of a grade? This is a matter of importance when we note the wide divergences among the lists suggested in standard spelling books.

1. *Spelling Words to be Taken from Expressional Rather than Interpretational Vocabularies.* — Each person is the possessor of two vocabularies. The first, the expressional vocabulary, is the sum total of the words he uses in all his writings and oral intercourse. But each one of us knows a greater stock of words than he employs. In listening to others and in reading, we meet words, the meanings of which are known to us but which we would nevertheless not use in our own speech. This is the interpretational vocabulary. Thus, a child in the eighth grade may know the meaning of *rectitude, mien, consecrate,* but only the unusual child would·use them. These words are evidently part of the child's interpretational vocabulary. But every eighth-grade child uses *receive,*

believe, judgment, prejudice, guarantee, repetition, and *separate* in his expressional exercises. Since the need for spelling is felt only in written intercourse, and since only those words which are in the expressional vocabulary will be used in writing, it follows that spelling words must be taken out of the expressional rather than the interpretational vocabulary.

Teachers complain that so much of the fifteen-or twenty-minute spelling lesson goes to explaining the meaning of words that there is no time left to teach the spelling. The inference is obvious. The spelling words are unwisely selected; they come from the children's interpretational, not expressional, vocabulary.

2. *Words Previously Tested.*—All words selected for a class or grade list should be dictated to the children in natural context and then corrected. Only such words as are missed by a majority of the class ought to become part of the class list. Those that are misspelled by a few or even by a minority should be incorporated in the individual spelling list kept by each child. A test will readily reveal the fact that many words in the grade or class list can be spelled by a large part of the class and must therefore be transferred to the individual lists.

3. *Words to Be Selected with a View to Class Subjects.*—In assigning spelling words for any grade, it should be the practice to assign them in that class in which they will correlate with the other subjects. Words like *attribute, modify, dependent,* should be taught in the grade that begins formal grammar; *borough, county,* etc., in the grade that studies local ge-

ography. In the teaching of spelling, correlation becomes a means of motivation.

Source of Spelling Words.—Assumed that spelling words will be selected in accordance with rational principles, the next problem concerns itself with the possible sources of these words. Chief among them we must mention:

1. *All Expressional Exercises.*—Teachers must be ever mindful of the fact that spelling tends to become highly formalized, because it lacks content and is taught without motive. But when all the children's written exercises—compositions, dictations, notebooks, test papers, etc.—are regarded as the first source of the spelling list, the spelling lessons become possessed, at once, of both content and motive. In reading any written work of the pupils, teachers will find those words that must become part of the spelling list.

2. *Terms Found Necessary in Class Subjects.*—All the subjects taught contain words and expressions that the children must use in their oral and written recitations. Words like *premium, commission, insurance, brokerage, remittance,* etc., will be contributed by the term's work in arithmetic. In the same way every subject will present its addition to the child's expressional vocabulary and, therefore, in the last analysis, to the spelling list.

3. *The Teacher's Experience.*—Every teacher has found that, regardless of the grade, certain words are generally misspelled by the children. Such words must, therefore, be incorporated in the spelling list

without reference to the grade of the children. A teacher in a seventh-year class may find it necessary to submit words like *too, their, wear, awkward, believe, receive, proceed, procedure, judgment,* and *guarantee* to the regular spelling drill.

4. *Good Spelling Books.*—The disadvantages of spelling books are many; they will be discussed in another connection in this chapter. But it is evident that a good spelling book may be a helpful guide and a suggestive standard in terms of which one's own list may be judged. After a tentative list has been collected and arranged, it should be compared with the lists for the same grade found in standard spellers. This comparison will reveal at once many weaknesses and omissions which must be rectified. To make the spelling book the sole source of spelling words is obviously wrong, but to ignore it is an unjustifiable neglect of a valuable aid.

5. *Standard Spelling Lists.*—In recent years, careful investigations have been made to discover the probable spelling needs of mature people. In each of these studies every effort was made to secure scientific data and to put aside preconceived notions of spelling needs. Each investigator sought his spelling list in actual correspondence.

(a) Ayres[1] made a study of 2,000 short business and professional letters and found 2,001 different words. A further refinement resulted in a list of the 1,000 most commonly used words. Surely, all spelling lists should contain these words.

[1] See Bibliography at the end of this chapter.

(b) Jones[1] made a list of 4,532 different words selected from 7,500 compositions of 1,050 children in the elementary grades of four states.

(c) Cook and O'Shea[1] formulated a list of 3,200 different words from the writings of thirteen intelligent adults.

(d) Chancellor, W. E.,[1] tabulated 1,000 words from letters he received.

(e) Tidyman[1] made a spelling list of the words occurring in at least two of the lists that were formulated by the above investigators.

(f) Anderson[1] analyzed the correspondence of adults in Iowa and formulated 2,977 different words that were commonly used.

Results of These Studies of Word Lists.—These investigations serve many useful purposes. They show us how unreliable is the spelling list selected on the basis of personal opinion. Elementary schools have taught approximately 8,000 spelling words. We know now that an elementary-school graduate has an expressional vocabulary of about 2,500 words, and that of a high-school graduate is about 4,000 words. About 50 words and their repetitions constitute 50 per cent of all the words the average person uses in writing. In order to formulate a list of the 1,000 most common words, it was necessary to include words that occurred only 44 times in 368,000 words. Surely, we found teaching difficulties in spelling because we made them. We formulated spelling lists not by a study of actual

[1] See Bibliography at the end of this chapter.

needs but by relying on vague impressions of probable needs.

We must also remember that most spelling books, "spellers," are compiled on the same unreliable basis, personal opinion. Thirteen common spellers were examined: four-fifths of the words prescribed for Grade VII and two-thirds of those for Grade IV were not found in a list of 3,324 words common to two or more of the lists enumerated above. A carefully selected list of 3,000 to 3,500 words and a good grounding in phonetics will meet the spelling needs of a school graduate.

Grading Spelling Lists.—In the concluding part of the chapter, scientific grading of words will be considered in greater detail. At this point, it is necessary to note that *frequency of use* rather than the length or the phonic character determines whether a word should be taught early or later in the school course. In spelling, children progress more rapidly in the lower than in the upper grades. We must therefore make every effort to teach the most common words as early as possible. Words that give most trouble in the highest grades are often in the lists for second, third and fourth years. This can be seen from the list of 100 demons tabulated by Jones and given on the page following. These words are most frequently misspelled in 4,500 different words used by pupils.

These demons are useful in measuring spelling ability of pupils below the seventh year. They serve also to emphasize the most difficult of the most frequently

THE TEACHING OF ENGLISH

The One Hundred Spelling Demons

making	writing	having	used
some	tired	just	wrote
much	don't	dear	friend
very	Tuesday	break	forty
shoes	knew	here	instead
blue	through	every	none
read	raise	said	can't
color	enough	where	truly
would	whole	could	which
two	since	hour	women
any	does	coming	answer
easy	trouble	they	though
week	their	tonight	laid
many	tear	done	choose
once	cough	country	ache
know	lose	early	believe
half	busy	buy	piece
seems	won't	ready	business
says	too	again	guess
grammar	often	sugar	meant
there	hoarse	been	straight
always	Wednesday	hear	wear
write	minute	heard	loose
sure	whether	among	beginning
built	separate	doctor	February

used words. We labor to secure correct spelling by our pupils of such words as *pneumonia*, *aqueous* and *phthisis*, whereas they misspell *beginning*, *February*, *buy*, *Wednesdays*, *enough* and *coming*. College seniors misspell such words as *principal*, *receive*, *judgment*, *guarantee*, *seize*, *counsel*, *coming* in their essays and in writing their answers to examination questions.

THE TEACHING OF SPELLING

The Grouping of Spelling Words.—Various ways have been evolved for grouping spelling words:

(a) *By Associated Meaning.*—Words related in meaning are often grouped under an appropriate title. Thus, under the heading *Foods,* we find such words as *vegetables, sirloin, wheat, asparagus, tomato,* etc. It is obvious that this method has little value for spelling.

(b) *By Common Phonetic Elements.*—This method teaches *could, would,* and *should* together; so, too, with *niece, piece,* or with *extreme* and *supreme.* In a strictly phonetic language like German or Spanish, this grouping is exceedingly helpful. But a language like ours that has so many different sounds for *ea* and so many different ways of representing the sound of ē, this practice is helpful only when the pupil keeps the words in their proper phonetic family. Too often, this grouping is the source of numerous and serious errors for children are tempted to spell greeting with *ea* and to put *taught* with the *ought* family.

(c) *By Common Difficulty.*—Words that have the same difficulty are taught together. Thus, *swimming, running, beginning; always, also, altogether, always.* It is estimated by some teachers that this grouping holds for 90 per cent of all the words that present distinctive difficulty. But teaching according to this grouping is not free from the danger noted in the second method.

All three methods may be used, but it must be borne in mind that, contrary to the claims set up by "spellers" that follow one or the other, these grouping devices give neither a solution of spelling problems nor a real system of grading spelling words.

Whatever the system of grouping may be, it is well to repeat in successive grades the words that experience shows are misspelled by children. Words from the 100 demons should be found in the seventh grade as well as in the third. Spelling lists of higher grades must not hesitate to include words like *their, too, truly, busy, answer* and *always*. It is also helpful to group enough words to make up the work of a week. Such a group should include about twenty new ones and ten old ones, making a maximum of thirty words for a week of five days.

The Preliminary Testing of Words. *Causes of Misspelling.*—Careful studies have been made of the causes of misspelling and their comparative frequency. These are:

1. Carelessness or mere "slip of the pen": remai*m*, free-do*n*.
2. Mispronunciation: lib(*r*)ary; chim*ley*; gove*r*ment.
3. Confusion of phonetic elements:
    (a) doubling wrong letters and non-doublings: *weel* for *well, felow* for *fellow*
    (b) attraction to a familiar form—*bair* for *bare* or *bear*
    (c) similar sounds: *ei, ie; sion, tion; ar, or, er, ir; ent, ant.*
4. Omissions:
    (a) of silent letter: of*t*en, com*b*
    (b) of sounded letters: couse for co*u*rse
5. Additions:
    (a) of finals: picnic*k;* most*e;* wolf*e*

THE TEACHING OF SPELLING

  (b) of intermediates: mak*e*ing, mis*s*take
6. Unclassified anomalies: *judgment, awful, precede, proceed, guarantee, separate, truly.*
7. Indifference of the pupil towards correct spelling.
8. Physical or mental defect: low intelligence; speech de-defect; eye or ear defect

From causes 2, 3, 4, 5, and 6, it is obvious that there is a crucial part in the more difficult spelling words. These crucial spelling parts must be discovered before the words are taught. Most pupils misspell *nervous,* thus *nerveous.* Investigation has repeatedly shown that very few teachers anticipate that the crucial part lies in the succession of letters, *v, o*. A test establishes the fact.

Value of the Preliminary Test.—Too frequently one hears the complaint that necessary subject matter cannot be reduced to habit because there is not enough time to drill. Critical analysis of classroom procedure soon shows that, not more, but less, time should be given to drill. The time given to drill must be adjusted to the difficulty of the experience and the needs of the individual pupil. Great waste is involved in drilling on all words and on all parts of any one word equally. Time devoted to drill must be distributed so that the more difficult words and their crucial parts will receive greater emphasis. In teaching the word *nervous,* why drill on *ner* and *ous*—parts of the word rarely misspelled? Therefore, let the pupil associate $\left. \begin{array}{l} nerve \\ nervous \end{array} \right\}$ and focalize attention on the dropping of the final *e* of *nerve* before adding the suffix *ous*. In this way, the time spent on the word is used to its maximum value.

How to Make the Preliminary Test.—Set aside a period once a week, or, in higher grades, once in two weeks. Dictate the words and have the children write them in ink. Dictate the spelling of each word and require pupils to check their work in pencil or colored crayon. Now tabulate (1) the number of times each word was misspelled and (2) the prevailing type of error in the misspelled form of each word. These preliminary tests will give at once (1) the crucial part of each word; (2) a definite and more scientific basis for method of teaching; and (3) two distinct spelling lists,—the class list of words misspelled by a considerable number of pupils and an individual list of words misspelled only by a few.

Media of Presenting Spelling Words.—The teacher who has selected her spelling list correctly and has had recourse to all useful sources is now confronted by the problem of the medium by means of which the words are to be presented to the class. The various media that are suggested must now be analyzed and their relative worth noted.

1. *Incidental Presentation.*—Many writers would abolish all formal presentation of spelling and rely upon the repeated but incidental and informal meeting of these words in the course of reading and studying. Chubb tells us, "Do not be fussy about it (spelling). Good reading, clear enunciation and the ear

THE TEACHING OF SPELLING

training that goes with it will do more for spelling than the routine of the spelling book. Write on the blackboard words that are generally misspelled, and let them be listed in the notebooks, by way of providing for the eye-minded and the motor-minded child, as well as for the ear-minded."[1]

The teacher, accustomed to the grind of the formal spelling drill and disheartened by the persistence of spelling errors, may be somewhat startled by this complete elimination of formal spelling. Experience teaches that incidental spelling in the average class in the ordinary public school is out of the question. Most children read little and write less. Their incidental experience with symbols will not suffice to give them a mastery of words. A psychological analysis of the problems of reading and spelling will reënforce this objection against incidental teaching of spelling. Words and phrases are read as wholes, and not by the synthesis of their component elements. Spelling is an analytical process that focalizes attention on constituent symbols in a given word. Reading is a process of thought acquisition. Spelling is a process of mastery of symbols in sequence, and is, therefore, no function in reading. When introduced in reading it develops habits that militate against rapid, thoughtful reading and make for slow word reading and lip movements.

2. *The Spelling Book.*—A medium of presenting spelling words that is now being revived is the spelling book. Its use is a moot question. Those in favor

[1] Chubb, *The Teaching of English*, p. 170.

of a spelling book urge that it saves time and gives the teacher a rich list graded by a specialist. But assuming that the spelling book is the best on the market, we must remember that there is no agreement, thus far, on a common list of spelling words. A list suitable for one school may not be appropriate for another. Gradation in spelling is almost impossible, as neither length nor phonetic characteristics are the basis of classification; *mien,* although shorter than *freedom,* is considered more difficult, and *once,* although highly unphonetic, is regarded as simpler than *independent.* In addition to these limitations we must add that the spelling book makes the spelling list a series of words unrelated to other subjects, for it is not an outgrowth of difficulties encountered in written expressional exercises and motive is, therefore, lacking. The spelling book must be used, as was previously suggested, as a standard by means of which a teacher may judge the worth of her own list.

3. *The Teacher's List.*—A means of overcoming most of the limitations of a spelling book is the practice of requiring each teacher to collect and systematize her own list. In this way words selected are more appropriate to the grade and related to the written exercises of the children. Where a teacher's list is used it must be mimeographed so that time will not be lost in needless copying and words will not be miscopied by the children.

But a list, culled by teachers or textbook writers, is open to the serious criticism that mastery of any

THE TEACHING OF SPELLING

elements in a list is no guarantee of even approximate proficiency in using the same elements in natural context. As has been said before, children who spell correctly words that are dictated in lists by the teacher in a spelling test misspell these very words when they use them in their own compositions. It is essential that words be taught in the same associations in which they will be used later in life.

4. *The Teacher's List in Natural Context.*—It is evident from the objections to formal lists, that the list which is selected by the teacher and then incorporated into a natural text will overcome the limitations of the media previously suggested. After the teacher has decided on the spelling list, the words should be grouped and a context supplied for them. The first twelve words in a list selected by a fourth-year teacher were:

1. brought √	5. continent	9. success √
2. discover √	6. weave	10. enemy √
3. thankful	7. receive	11. courage
4. prison √	8. jealous √	12. Columbus √

Those words that can be related in any way are checked as noted above and a sentence is then woven about them. Thus, "*Jealous* of his *success,* the *enemies* of *Columbus brought* the *discoverer* of the New World back to Spain as a *prisoner,*" affords a context for seven words, which form the first day's spelling lesson. Very often it will be necessary to write as many as four sentences to include the words for a lesson. But if the selection is made, not from twelve words but from a larger part of the list, the text will follow more naturally. At times a stanza of a familiar poem or an extract from a selection in the reader will give this context. Thus an interesting context was afforded for two days' spelling work in a third-year class, by Stevenson's stanza:

> In *winter* I get up at *night*
> And *dress* by *yellow candle-light.*
> In *summer, quite* the other *way,*
> I have to go to bed by *day.*

These four lines suggest that a phonic basis may be selected for grouping the words in the formal list. Thus the word *night* suggests *light, way* suggests *day,* etc. Upon examining her list a teacher may find the words *would, could,* and *should,* or *extreme* and *supreme,* or *valleys, keys, toys, days, ladies, babies,* and *enemies* scattered through the term's work. It is advisable, therefore, to gather all phonic similarities together and teach them in the same lesson, thus supplanting a mechanical association by one that is logical. The old gradation of spelling based on the number of syllables is therefore giving way to gradation based on related meaning or phonic similarities. At regular intervals each child receives a mimeographed sheet giving in sentences, paragraphs, and stanzas the spelling words in proper context.

5. *Supplementary Lists.*—Spelling lists should be as flexible as possible, so that every teacher may feel

free to modify the assignment in accordance with the dictates of personal judgment and experience with a particular class. It follows also that in large schools there must be some uniformity in requirements for the sake of the children as well as for convenience of supervision. For these reasons supplementary lists are advocated so that there may be three lists used by a teacher, the *grade list,* the *class list,* and the *individual list.*

The *grade list* is that list which is uniform for each grade in a school or in a school district. These words may be taught parallel with, or in advance of, the subjects from which they are taken, the aim being to prepare children for difficulties that must inevitably arise in their paths and thus prevent misspelling.

The *class list* is composed of those words which are misspelled by the majority of the class in all written exercises. The aim of this list is to eliminate inaccuracies that children have already acquired. This list varies with the class and with each term.

The *individual list* is kept by each child and varies necessarily with each child. Children must be required to list all words that they misspell in written exercises but which are not taught in class. These lists should be subject to regular inspections, and spelling periods should be set aside when each child tests his neighbor on the words in the individual list. Children may be told to write all the words they can recall in a limited time. These words are corrected and the incorrect ones are then added to the individual list. In this way a child is learning not only those words which the majority of his classmates cannot spell, but also those that sum up his personal weaknesses in spelling.

Method of Teaching Spelling.—We must pass on to the consideration of the method of teaching spelling. The complete method has three distinct parts: 1. *the teaching,* in which the child learns under the teacher's supervision the phonic peculiarities of the words. 2. *the independent study,* in which the child tries to master the words taught in class. 3. *the test,* in which the teacher seeks to ascertain the child's mastery of the words taught and studied. Fifteen minutes a day will suffice. Spelling should be taught four days and tested one day each week.

Procedure in Teaching Words.—1. *Meaning.*—The first step must be the reading of the text that contains the words to be taught and the attempt to explain their meaning. Since proper spelling lists come from the children's expressional rather than interpretational vocabularies, little or no time will be consumed in making clear the meaning of the words.

2. *Accurate Pronunciation.*—Unusual care must be taken to guarantee accurate pronunciation of each word. The teacher should offer the pronunciation and should then call upon children individually to sound the word. Concert recitation should be used with caution and only after a sufficient number of children have individually pronounced the word correctly. Mispronunciation or slovenly pronunciation lies at the root of most faults in spelling. A foreign child wrote in his composition, *He vent vid me,* but

later in the day, when his teacher dictated the same sentence, he wrote, *He went with me.* The cause for the change is obvious: in the first case, the child sounded these words to himself and spelled accordingly; in the second case, the child's ear heard the correct sound and reproduced it accurately. What is true in this case is true of all children—incorrect auditory images prompt incorrect spelling.

In teaching correct pronunciation, the method of imitating the teacher should not be the sole procedure. Words should be marked diacritically and the children should be called upon to sound them. Other words should be syllabicated as a cue to proper pronunciation. In later classes the words should be found in the dictionary and the pronunciation evolved. Time spent on careful pronunciation is time saved in teaching spelling.

3. *Syllabication and Division into Phonogrammic Units.*—The difficulties in most words are removed in the next step, the syllabication of the word or its division into known phonic units. Words like *emancipation, nationality, modification, comparative,* etc., are purely phonic; the child that can syllabicate them and recognize the known phonograms of *tion, man,* etc., has no difficulty in spelling these words.

4. *When Necessary, Focalize Attention on the Difficulty in a Word.*—Many words are purely phonic in all but one respect. It is much better to have the child's attention directed to this difficulty exclusively than to drill on the whole word. Thus, if the word is *supreme,* it is related to *extreme* and the *eme* of each

is underlined in colored chalk on the board. In the case of the word *altogether*, the rule is taught and the child now knows the spelling of *always, also,* etc. If the word is *separate,* we elicit that it means "cut into parts." Since *part* is spelled with an *a*, *separate* is spelled sep*a*, not sep*e*, as children repeatedly do. In the case of phonic anomalies like *comb, pneumonia,* etc., the peculiarity is singled out and attention called to it by encircling it with colored chalk or by writing it in different forms and in exaggerated sizes. Every means must be taken to focalize attention on the phonetic anomaly.

5. *The Class Drills.*—Rigorous drills should follow the instruction step in spelling. These drills must be spirited, planned to stir maximum self-activity, and designed to appeal to children of different sense gifts. Among the important forms of drill in spelling we may mention the following:

a. Individual Oral Spelling. Various children are called upon in promiscuous order to spell the word as the rest of the class listens to the spelling and sees the forms on the board.

b. Light Concert Spelling. The class as a whole may be asked to spell the word orally in concert as each child follows visually the teacher's pointer going from letter to letter.

c. Flash Method. The word is written on a card or on the blackboard and is exposed to the view of the class for only two or three seconds. At the end of that time various children are called upon to spell the word as they saw it. If the class is warned of the limited time that will be allowed and the concentration necessary, the results are usually gratifying.

d. Motor Appeal. The word is written *at first slowly* and *then more rapidly* by the children with their fingers in the air or on the desk or with pencil on paper. For most, this proves to be the strongest sense appeal.

e. Visualization. A popular means of drill is through strong visual appeal. The visualization drills may be given in many forms. The simplest of these drills is to have the children look steadily at the word written in unusually large size on the board. At the end of a limited time the children are asked to shut their eyes and "see" the word. Those who cannot "see" the word with eyes shut are permitted to look at the word again and then try to visualize it with eyes shut. When all children can "see" the word, they are asked to spell it as they "see" it.

Another method of conducting visualization drills is especially applicable to higher classes. Three or four words are selected for simultaneous drill and are written on the blackboard either in one line or in a column. A word is erased and then a child is called upon to spell the word that must be replaced. This procedure is repeated with each of the words. Later in the term two words are erased, e. g., the second and the fourth, and children are called upon to spell "the word that was in the second place," or "the word that was in the fourth place." This spirited drill is known as the method of immediate corrected recall.

f. Dictionary. Another means of drill on words

is to have the class locate the word in the dictionary. The effort in finding the proper page and column, in comparing the word on the board with the word in the dictionary, in noting the mode of syllabication, arouses enough self-activity and forms enough associations to give permanence to the impression that the word makes.

g. Drill Through Games. In the lower grades, effective drill can be given through games. Spelling tag, spelling relay races, catching the spelling word—these are a few adaptions of games, and they suggest many others that might be devised. Some teachers prefer to make a "yell," like a school "yell," of these demons. The following is an illustration of one type:

soft	*loud*	*soft*	
R - E - C - E - I - V - E			................very slow
R - E - C - E - I - V - E			................faster
REC-E-I-VE			................very fast
Receive EI.	Receive EI.	Receive EI.	

These drills are designed to give variety, speed, and interest to the spelling periods. It must be remembered, however, that no one word is to be subjected to all these forms of drill. The method of drill should change with each succeeding word so that the elements of variety and novelty give spirit and enthusiasm to the lesson.

In the past the visual appeal was thought to make the most vital contribution to the general image of the word. But recent psychological investigations tend to prove that it is the motor appeal that makes permanent the graphic character of a word and habituates its writing. Experiments with patients suffering from aphasia and agraphia show that although the visual center must make its contributions if we are to write words easily, writing can be accomplished without these contributions. Adults and children were taught the Greek alphabet in two ways. One group was blindfolded and learned the letters by tracing them with their fingers; the other group learned them through visual experience. When the results were tabulated they bore out Professor O'Shea's contentions, "The visual image is not the all controlling factor. . . . As development occurs, the visual imagery takes on even more the simple function of mere suggestion. . . . It (visual imagery) does not appear to be essential to the graphic reproduction of auditory words."

The practical estimate of the relative importance of the contributions made by the various senses reenforces the conclusion of psychological investigations as to the vital importance of the motor appeal. The primary object in spelling is to reduce the *writing* of the word to habit. Oral spelling and visual appeals are used only as aids toward permanent fixation, but neither has worth in social intercourse. The child who wins the oral spelling match but who hesitates in writing these words is a poor speller, while his neighbor who is utterly confused in oral spelling but who writes the words automatically has reached a high level of proficiency. Since spelling is made necessary by written intercourse the written appeal must be considered the most important form of spelling drill.

Independent Study of Spelling.—Many children need no further drill than was outlined in the discussion of the procedure in the teaching of spelling. But in every class there are pupils whose impressionability and retention are weak and further memory appeals are necessary. Only these latter children require additional drill, *e. g.*, writing spelling words in and out of context. The practice of excusing from further drill those children for whom the class spelling lesson is sufficient will tend to intensify attention during the period of instruction.

Teaching Children to Study Spelling.—In later grades children should be taught how to study spelling without the teacher's aid and direction. A paragraph in one of the textbooks should be assigned for this purpose. Elicit from the class that the first task must be a selective one in which they eliminate such words as offer no difficulties either because they are known or because they are purely phonetic in their spelling. The words that merit attention are then looked up in the dictionary for meaning, if necessary, and for pronunciation and syllabication. Children in a seventh-year grade when asked to do this with such words as *appreciate, surety, patiently, siphon,* etc., showed very clearly that they lacked an elementary knowledge of the alphabetic sequence in the dictionary and of diacritical marks. After the dictionary work is accomplished children must be led to detect that phonic element in each word that renders it difficult. That done, they can now follow any of the forms of drill used in the class.

Study lessons in spelling may take other forms. A list of words like *consider, companion, tax, pleasure, value, adapt, measure, favor,* etc., is written on the board. The children are told to add *able* to each and then look up the spelling in the dictionary to see if any changes are necessary. This task completed, each child must try to formulate a rule in spelling to govern such cases or must try to find the suitable rule in the "Rules for Spelling" given in his dictionary. Such study lessons are means of developing judgment, initiative, power of organization, and self-reliance, and afford a natural method of teaching children those mechanical elements in the use of the dictionary that every school graduate should know.

The Test in Spelling.—In current methods of testing children's ability to spell, the teacher dictates the list of words taught and the children write these in a column. The correct form is then shown or recited and each child checks his neighbor's inaccuracies. When the papers are returned to their owners, all words misspelled are written correctly a given number of times. This writing degenerates into careless penmanship, in which the child is hardly conscious of the phonic elements and especially of those that gave him trouble.

Test Ability to Use Word in Context.—We have need for a method that is personal and constructive and that tests the child's ability to use the words in a natural context of his own. In the test period the teacher should dictate the word and the child should be required to write a sentence for it. Oral spelling is not a test; it is a means of further drill and an aid toward retention. Only when the child, intent on a sentence, writes the dictated word correctly from force of habit, is he giving evidence of his mastery of the word.

Spelling Record in Books.—The tests in spelling should be written in notebooks rather than on loose sheets of paper. A notebook record of such work is cumulative; it shows teacher and pupil, at a glance, the curve of progress. A convenient arrangement, shown in the accompanying diagram, divides the page into two columns, the wider one for the sentences containing the words dictated, and the narrower for the insertion of correct forms for all misspelled words. Each teacher must decide on the best means of correct-

Date	Rating	Jan. 5, 1913	95%
Sentences containing words dictated by the teacher	Correct form of words misspelled	1. The friends were very sad when the time came for t h e m to *seperate*. 2.	*separate*

ing spelling, whether by neighbors, by children themselves, by monitors or by herself. But in writing the misspelled word correctly the child should be required

THE TEACHING OF SPELLING

to mark in some way that phonic element which is a source of trouble to him.

Record of Misspelled Words.—Teachers will do well to devise some means by which a record can be kept which would show the number of children who misspelled each word and the prevailing errors made in these words. Such a record would be an excellent index of the amount of drill that should be given on various words in the following terms and the phonic elements that should be emphasized in teaching them. In upper grades the teacher can easily be relieved, by a reliable pupil, of most of the mechanical work entailed by such a record.

Enriching the Spelling List.—There should be included in the spelling list useful homonyms, abbreviations, rules of spelling, and proper names. These are part of the expressional stock necessary in all correspondence. Experimental data seem to indicate that best results will be obtained if, at first, homonyms are taught separately and on different days. A week later they should be presented in contrasting sentences, such as, "*There* they stand holding *their* hats in *their* hands," for the association which gives them permanence is the contrast. In presenting them we should lead children to infer from the text (a) the elements of similarity, and (b) the elements of difference. This should be followed by a drill that seeks to make their proper use habitual. Rules of spelling are best taught inductively in study lessons, as was outlined in the topic "Study Lessons in Spelling" in this chapter.

Supervising Auxiliary Lists.—Spelling lists cannot be enriched as was suggested unless supervising officers take the initiative in the matter of allotting proper names, abbreviations, homonyms, and rules of spelling to the various grades. In most schools visited by the author teachers are held responsible for "useful rules of spelling" or "necessary proper names." It is evident that this general assignment to all teachers means either total neglect of these lists or an attempt to teach all in each grade. The supervisor must collect all useful homonyms, rules of spelling, proper names and abbreviations and then, in conference with teachers, decide on a gradation of these lists and an apportionment of each list among the various grades. Each teacher having a certain number of the facts to teach can give them the attention and the drill that will make them part of the permanent expressional stock of each child.

Spelling Projects.—The significance of the project in teaching was set forth in an earlier chapter. It is obvious that we may introduce project teaching in spelling. In connection with certain types of business letters, we may formulate the project, "to master the spelling of the most commonly used words in correspondence," for example, *acknowledge, truly, sincerely, answer,* etc. If a series of compositions is to be written on a civic project, "A Campaign to Keep the Parks Clean," it is a simple matter to set up the spelling project, "to master the spelling of the words that will occur in the slogans and posters we shall make." A list of 100 words may be reviewed through a diction-

THE TEACHING OF SPELLING

ary project in which these words are alphabetized, syllabicated, marked diacritically, accents indicated and suitable definitions given.

Evaluating a Spelling Book.—What shall guide us in the selection of a speller? We offer below a tabular summary of the ten most essential qualities that determine the worth of a book. Whether each quality shall be given equal value, or shall be rated relatively, should be decided by supervisors and principals.

1. The Spelling List: Are the most common words given? Are the lists in harmony with the results of investigations? Are words repeated to insure their functioning of habit? Are more words given than the necessary minimum? Is the list enriched by suffixes, prefixes, roots, proper names, abbreviations, and homonyms?
2. Context: Are the words introduced in agreeable and varied content? Can the context be used for dictation lessons so that rules of punctuation and capitalization will be learned incidentally?
3. Phonetic Families: Are words so grouped as to give an effective grounding in phonetics?
4. Does the book give graded and systematic dictionary exercises?
5. Is the material set off in convenient lesson units?
6. Does the book reduce the work of the teacher by teaching children how to study spelling?
7. Does the book include a measuring scale in spelling?
8. Does the book develop spelling intelligence and a concern for correct spelling?
9. Are the books attractively illustrated?
10. Is the book standard in size of type, quality of paper, binding?

THE TEACHING OF ENGLISH

Instead of relying on general impression, use this analysis of a good speller. Personal opinion is not supplanted but supplemented by an inclusive and critical judgment.

SCALES FOR MEASURING SPELLING ABILITY

Need for a Scale.—In spelling as in other subjects we frequently ask, How does my class compare with other classes? Is a pupil doing as well as he should? What is the final value of a particular device that is emphasized in this school? How are we to answer these questions without falling back on vague opinion?

The Ayres Scale and Buckingham's Extension.[2]—Ayres arranged the 1,000 most commonly used words in 26 groups so that the words in any one group are of equal difficulty. A section of the Ayres Scale with the Buckingham Extension is reproduced on pages 264-265.

Buckingham extended the scale by adding 505 words that are common to two or more of the five spelling books he analyzed. These words are easy enough to test third-grade pupils and difficult enough for the eighth grade. At the head of each column is given the percentage of correct spelling that may be expected from pupils in each grade. Thus, for Column L, second-grade pupils should average 50 per cent, third-grade, 73 per cent, fourth-grade, 88 per cent, and eighth-grade, 100 per cent.

[2] See Bibliography at the end of this chapter.

The Ayres Scale with the Buckingham Extension is not a test but rather a list of words from which a test can be made. All the words for a test should be chosen from a single column. Twenty words are sufficient to give a reasonably correct measure of the spelling ability of a class. Fifty to one hundred words will give a more reliable measure. To be sure that the list is well adjusted to a given class, select that column in which the average for a given grade is between 50 and 66.

Ashbaugh's Iowa Scales.[3]—With the 2,977 most commonly used words as compiled by Anderson, Ashbaugh tested pupils to discover (1) the order of difficulty of these words; (2) how to group them; (3) the average score for the different grades for each group of words. For each grade, say the fifth, there is a group of words on which these children should score 100 per cent, a second group on which they should score 99 per cent, a third 98 per cent, etc., to 4 per cent. The study is most detailed and gives material to which supervisors should constantly refer in planning grade work and grade tests in spelling.

Monroe's Timed Sentence Spelling Test.[3]—This test presents for each grade fifty words "embedded in sentences which have been arranged so that pupils will write at their normal rate" as determined by measuring the handwriting rate of over 6,000 school children. The words are taken from the Ayres list. On page 266 are specimen sentences from some grades.

[3] See Bibliography at the end of this chapter.

SECTION OF AYRES SCALE WITH THE BUCKINGHAM EXTENSION

	H	I	J	K	L	M	N	O	P
Second Grade..	79	73	66	58	50	42	34	27	21
Third Grade..	92	88	84	79	73	66	58	50	42
Fourth Grade..	98	96	94	92	88	84	79	73	66
Fifth Grade...	100	99	93	96	94	92	88	84	79
Sixth Grade...			100	99	98	96	94	92	88
Seventh Grade					100	99	98	96	94
Eighth Grade..							100	99	98
Ninth Grade..									100
	day	nine	seven	became	catch	trust	except	eight	spend
	eat	face	forget	brother	black	extra	aunt	afraid	enjoy
	sit	miss	happy	rain	warm	dress	capture	uncle	awful
	lot	ride	noon	keep	unless	beside	wrote	rather	usual
	box	tree	think	start	clothing	teach	else	comfort	complaint
	belong	sick	sister	mail	began	happen	bridge	elect	auto
	door	got	cast	eye	able	begun	offer	aboard	vacation
	yes	north	card	glass	gone	collect	suffer	jail	beautiful
	low	white	south	party	suit	file	built	shed	flight
	soft	spent	deep	upon	track	provide	center	retire	travel
	stand	foot	inside	two	watch	sight	front	refuse	rapid
	yard	blow	blue	they	dash	stood	rule	district	repair
	bring	block	post	would	fell	fix	carry	restrain	trouble
	tell	spring	town	any	fight	born	chain	royal	entrance
	five	river	stay	could	buy	goes	death	objection	importance
	ball	plant	grand	should	stop	hold	learn	pleasure	carried
	law	cut	outside	city	walk	drill	wonder	navy	loss
	ask	song	dark	only	grant	army	tire	fourth	fortune
	just	winter	band	where	soap	pretty	pair	population	empire
	way	stone	game	week	news	stole	check	proper	mayor
	get	free	boat	first	small	income	prove	judge	wait

264

THE TEACHING OF SPELLING

home	lake	rest	sent	war	bought	heard	weather	beg
much	page	east	mile	summer	paid	inspect	worth	degree
call	nice	son	seem	above	enter	itself	contain	prison
long	end	help	even	express	railroad	something	figure	engine
love	fall	hard	without	turn	unable	always	sudden	visit
then	feet	race	afternoon	lesson	ticket	write	forty	guest
house	went	cover	Friday	half	account	expect	instead	department
year	back	fire	hour	father	driven	need	throw	obtain
to	away	age	wife	anything	real	thus	personal	family
I	paper	gold	state	table	recover	woman	everything	favor
as	each	read	July	high	mountain	young	rate	Mrs.
send	put	fine	head	talk	steamer	fair	chief	husband
one	soon	cannot	story	right	speak	dollar	perfect	amount
has	came	May	open	date	past	evening	second	human
some	Sunday	line	short	June	might	plan	slide	view
if	show	left	lady	road	begin	broke	farther	election
how	Monday	ship	reach	March	contract	feel	duty	clerk
her	yet	train	better	next	deal	sure	intend	though
them	find	saw	water	indeed	almost	least	company	o'clock
other	give	pay	round	four	brought	sorry	quite	support
baby	new	large	cost	herself	less	press	none	does
well	letter	near	price	power	event	God	knew	regard
about	take	down	become	wish	off	teacher	remain	escape
men	after	why	class	because	true	November	direct	since
for	thing	bill	horse	world	took	subject	appear	which
ran	what	want	care	country	again	April	liberty	length
was	than	girl	try	meet	inform	history	enough	destroy
that	its	part	move	another	both	cause	fact	newspaper
his	very	still	delay	trip	heart	study	board	daughter
led	or	place	pound	list	month	himself	September	answer
lay	thank	report	behind	people	children	matter	station	reply
	dear	never	around	ever	build	thought	attend	oblige
	west	found	burn	held	understand	use	between	sail
	sold	side	camp	church	follow	person	public	cities
	told	kind	bear	once	charge	nor	friend	known
	best	life	clear	before	says	January	during	several
	form	here	clean	know	case	mean	through	desire
	far	car	spell	were	member	vote	police	nearly
	gave	word	poor	dead	while	court	until	*animal*
		every	finish		also	copy	madam	*basin*
	etc.	*etc.*	*etc.*	*etc.*	*etc.*	*etc.*	*etc.*	*etc.*

THE TEACHING OF ENGLISH

SPECIMENS FROM MONROE'S TIMED SPELLING TEST

Grade	Time, seconds	Specimen Sentences	Norms — Number of words spelled correctly out of a total of 50	Per Cent
III	60	He *bought* a *railroad ticket* to the city.	28	56
	24	Please *omit both* names.		
	54	*Again,* he *took* the car		
IV	60	He *bought* a *railroad ticket* to the city.	39	78
	19	Please *omit both* names.		
	24	*Again* he *took* the car.		
V	48	The *women* were *present* at the time.	33	66
	30	*Suppose* a *special attempt* is made.		
	55	The *addition* to the *property* was begun.		
VI	44	The *women* were *present* at the time.	40	80
	19	*Suppose* a *special attempt* is made.		
	29	The *addition* to the *property* was begun.		

The number immediately before each sentence indicates the number of seconds allowed for writing that sentence. The test words are in italics. Note that no

THE TEACHING OF SPELLING

test word is placed at the end of the sentence so that slow writers may not be penalized.

Morrison-McCall Spelling Scales.[4]—This scale consists of eight lists of fifty words each, each list or group being of equal difficulty. The scale is more elaborately worked out so that one can not only compare class or pupil achievements with others, but also ascertain a pupil's grade status in spelling. The tabulations in this scale are designed to tell how a pupil compares in spelling ability with pupils of the same age and for what age a pupil's spelling ability is normal.

The fifty words in List I are typical. For each word a sentence is given.

run	shut	written	reference
top	done	search	character
red	body	popular	separate
book	anyway	interest	committee
sea	omit	career	annual
play	fifth	pleasant	principle
lay	reason	therefore	immense
led	perfect	folks	judgment
add	friend	celebration	acquaintance
alike	getting	minute	discipline
nine	nearly	divide	lieutenant
with	desire	necessary	
easy	arrange	height	

What may reasonably be expected from each grade? The table below gives the answer.

[4] J. C. Morrison and W. A. McCall, *Spelling Scale* (copyright, 1923, by World Book Co., Yonkers-on-Hudson, N. Y.).

Grade Norms in Terms of Average Number of Words Spelled Correctly

Grade	II	III	IV	V	VI	VII	VIII	IX
Average number of words spelled correctly	11	18	24	30	35	39	42	44

Values of Standard Spelling Lists.—These standard spelling lists have many values. (1) They give us the best index of how frequently a word is used. Varying opinion of teachers and authors of spellers must give way to results obtained by tabulating words of actual correspondence. The standard spelling lists really tell us how common a word is. They do more; (2) they tell us the relative difficulty of words usually found in the expressional vocabularies of elementary and high-school graduates.

(3) Standard spelling lists and tests offer a fixed measure of ability. With them we can measure the spelling progress of a pupil, a class, a school or even a school system. But, they must never be used to measure the teaching ability of a single teacher, for these tests are based on the words that were taught the pupils before the current term. (4) It is, therefore, possible to make comparative studies of spelling efficiency of class and schools.

(5) With standard lists and tests, we can judge the worth of a particular set of teaching devices used in one school and not in another. There are those who insist that spelling in context gives no greater

spelling efficiency than spelling in list. Let each of two schools follow each of these two methods respectively. At the end of every half semester, test pupils and tabulate the results for a year or two. The relative worth of the two methods will then be demonstrated.

(6) Standard spelling lists and tests are significant aids in teaching. They serve as excellent checks on teachers' lists and by revealing the comparative difficulty of words, indicate the relative emphasis to be given to each word in the drill. (7) It follows, therefore, that these lists make for economy in teaching. Only words of demonstrated frequency are taught and overdrill is greatly minimized. We must not rest content with the old class average of 80 per cent in spelling. We must strive to come as close to maximum as possible. The spelling score of a class should at least equal the standard achievement for a grade.

SUGGESTED READING

ANDERSON, W. N. The Determination of a Spelling Ability. University of Iowa. Iowa City, Iowa.

ASHBAUGH, E. J. Iowa Spelling Scale. University of Iowa.

AYRES, LEONARD P. Spelling Vocabularies of Personal and Business Letters. A Measuring Scale for Spelling Ability. Division of Education, Russell Sage Foundation.

BUCKINGHAM, B. R. Spelling Ability: Its Measurement and Distribution. Teachers' College, Columbia University, Contributions to Education, No. 59.

Cook, W. A., and O'Shea, M. V. The Child and His Spelling. Bobbs-Merrill Co.

Courtis, S. A. Teaching Spelling by Plays and Games. Detroit, Mich.

Horn, E. Principles and Methods of Teaching Spelling as Determined by Scientific Investigations. Eighteenth Year Book of the National Society for the Study of Education. Public School Publishing Co., Bloomington, Ill.

Jones, W. F. Concrete Investigation of the Materials of English Spelling. University of South Dakota, Vermilion, S. D.

Monroe, W. S. Timed Sentence Spelling Tests. Bureau of Educational Research, University of Illinois, Urbana, Ill.

Morrison, J. C., and McCall, W. A. Spelling Scale. World Book Co., Yonkers, N. Y.

Nifenecker, E. A. Pamphlets 3, 4, 5. Bureau of Reference and Research, Board of Education, City of New York.

Parker, S. C. Types of Elementary Teaching and Learning, chap. IV. Ginn & Co.

Rice, J. M. Futility of the Spelling Grind. Forum, Vol. 23.

Spalding, F. E. Measuring Text Books. Part IV. Newson & Co.

Suzzallo, Henry. The Teaching of Spelling. Houghton-Mifflin Co.

Tidyman, W. F. The Teaching of Spelling. World Book Co., Yonkers, N. Y.

CHAPTER XI

THE MEANING AND USE OF NEW WORDS

THE ENRICHMENT OF VOCABULARY

Shall There Be Formal Instruction in the Meaning and Use of New Words?—Many teachers of elementary grades have characterized formal lessons on the meaning of unfamiliar words and expressions as sheer waste of time and effort. It is their opinion that growth of vocabulary must be informal and incidental in the course of reading and social intercourse. In support of their conclusions they cite their own experiences: children remember the meaning of very few of the new words taught; their sentences are always artificial; the "meaning and use" list is usually unrelated to other subjects; the need for the meaning of these new words is not felt in their own lives; those children who have a language sense and who read have a vocabulary that is rich and varied, and those who lack this sense do not develop it in formal lessons in "meaning and use." A cursory investigation will undoubtedly bear out these contentions but an analysis of these indictments reveals them to be the results of poor methods of instruction. If the "meaning and use" list is properly selected, if each word arises in a need felt by the class, if natural drills are provided, the serious limitations of the current "meaning and use" lesson will disappear, for they are limitations that are not inherent in this form of language exercise. It is the aim of this chapter to evolve a method that possesses these corrective influences.

Selection of the "Meaning and Use" List.—The proper selection of the new words whose meanings are to be taught often determines the final efficiency of the lessons. We must omit, therefore, (a) most technical words; (b) common words used in an unusual sense, as, "This was a happy *conceit* of the author"; (c) such words as can be really understood only by a mature mind; (d) subtle distinctions in synonyms. At the beginning of the term the teacher should not have a single word in the list. In the course of the day's work words will arise which the children do not know and upon which the meaning of the text depends. When such a situation arises in the teaching of any subject, whether it be arithmetic or reading, the teacher has an opportunity to add to the "meaning and use" list. But not all new words become part of the formal lesson. As a new word arises the teacher must decide whether it is reasonable to expect children of her grade to have it in their expressional vocabularies. If she decides in the negative, the meaning of the word should be told to the class and the lesson should continue without further attention to it. Should the decision be affirmative, the word is written on a large cardboard or on an unused part of the blackboard after the meaning is given. The children thus see the source of these words and ample motive for a formal lesson is given. It is essential that most of the new words be eliminated and that attention be confined to those that are of greatest worth for the children.

Methods of Teaching Meaning of New Words.—There is no fixed method of teaching the meaning of new words. Each type of word necessitates a different mode of treatment. Chief among the many methods we have the following:

1. *Deductive or Direct Telling.*—When it is necessary that technical words be taught or when words have a meaning that cannot readily be inferred from the text, the method of direct telling must be used. In modern methodology the inductive or development method has become a fetish. We must realize that there are teaching situations in which deductive teaching may be used without apology. Words like *mythology, sprite, aqueduct* must often be taught in this deductive method to young children. Then, too, when new words arise in a literature or a history lesson it shows lack of judgment of relative values to halt the lesson in question in order to develop the new word by inductive treatment. In all such cases the meaning of the word should be given and the forward movement of the lesson should not be sacrificed.

2. *Objective Method.*—When clear imaging must be attained with children whose apperceptive stock lacks that experience which will enable them to construct the mental picture from verbal expression, a

picture or the object itself is of greatest service. The child who has never seen a *wigwam*, a *tomahawk*, a *mariner's compass*, etc., must be taught what these terms represent by means of some graphic appeal.

3. *Inductive or Context Method.*—When the new word is one whose meaning is always made clear by the context, the inductive method is to be preferred. If the word *chagrin* is to be taught, the teacher uses it in a number of sentences, each of which tends to bring out its meaning. The teacher then asks the class to substitute appropriate synonymous expressions for *chagrin*, and the meaning is thus elicited. Although it is a method which costs dearly in time, it nevertheless has its compensating advantages—maximum self-activity is aroused, each child is put in the position of discoverer rather than recipient, the impressions are more lasting, the meaning is clearer, and the child learns a method which he can use in post-school days.

4. *Dramatization.*—A method very similar to the objective method but one which is characterized by its exclusive motor appeal is dramatization. When the pupils' vocabularies are so meager that they can obtain meaning from neither the context nor the teacher's explanation, the word should be acted out if it lends itself to such treatment. This is the device used almost exclusively with foreigners who know no English. Expressions like *with arms akimbo, he strutted about, a frowning face,* etc., when dramatized, convey meaning clearly and with economy of

THE MEANING AND USE OF NEW WORDS

time to children whose language possessions are very limited.

5. *Using the Dictionary.*—Most words are so poorly defined in the abridged editions of the dictionaries used by schools that the child finds a synonym as new to him as the word which he looked up. But despite this handicap the habit of using the dictionary should be inculcated in children as soon as their capabilities will allow. Carefully graded lessons throughout the school course must be given our pupils, in order to develop not only ability to use the dictionary but also the *habit* of using it. It must be emphasized and reëmphasized that the legitimate time for the use of the dictionary is the formal "meaning and use" period, in home work, or in seat work. It should rarely be used during any lesson in geography, history, nature study, arithmetic, or reading.

6. *Etymological Analysis.*—In the second half of the school course children must begin to study the most common prefixes, suffixes and roots used in the English language. Carefully compiled lists for school use give about thirty prefixes, twenty suffixes, and about thirty-five roots. If these were apportioned among the grades, beginning with the fifth year, each grade would average about five prefixes, three suffixes, and five roots per term. It is obvious, therefore, that with a little drill children can be taught those necessary language elements which would enable them to evolve the meaning of such words as *depose, supersede, descent, circumspect, transparent, transmit, su-*

perstructure, etc., by a process of etymological analysis. Lessons in etymology should be thoroughly inductive. If a prefix is to be taught, a number of words beginning with it should be placed on the board. Children should then be required to give or find the meaning of each word. The class must then be led to perceive that all these words have similar beginnings. Through a series of questions we must elicit that these words also have a similar element in their meanings. It then becomes evident that the common prefix produces the common thought in each word and the function of the prefix is discovered by each child. The lesson concludes with an application of this knowledge to new words having the same prefix. Spelling books and elementary English books are replete with exercises and drills which seek to apply these etymological elements and make their meaning a permanent possession of the children.

How Make the Use of New Words Habitual.—The vital aim in the "meaning and use" lesson is evidently to make each new word learned a part of the child's active expressional vocabulary. To achieve this end we must teach the use of new words by a method which duplicates the method of learning new words outside the classroom. It is for this reason that no "meaning and use" list should be organized in advance. The teacher should wait until the class sees the need for the meaning of certain words. After the meaning is taught by one of the methods explained, the teacher must use the word in a number of sentences to show the children its value. Volunteers are now called

THE MEANING AND USE OF NEW WORDS

upon. It is not wise to force children to use the word too early in the lesson. After a number of voluntary answers have been accepted the teacher may insist on having the word used by any child designated. If a pupil cannot think of an original sentence in which the word in question applies, the child may be allowed either to paraphrase or modify a sentence already given or to formulate a sentence around an incident suggested by the teacher. Thus, if, for the word *venture,* one child offered the sentence "Washington did not *venture* to fight the English army on Long Island," another child who cannot give an original sentence should be allowed to give, "In the retreat through Manhattan Island Washington did not *venture* to fight the enemy"; or the teacher might suggest, "Columbus—earth round—unknown seas," and the child might reasonably be expected to say, "Columbus *ventured* across unknown seas." Every means must be taken to lead the child to *feel the value* of the word and then to *desire to use* it.

But this mere formal use will not make the word part of the child's expressional vocabulary. There must be spontaneous use in answer to a definite need. The "meaning and use" chart must, therefore, be constantly before the class. On every occasion, in every explanation, and in every command the teacher must use as many of these words as she can. Children should be encouraged to use them in all recitations and in answer to every question; if necessary, rewards in the form of praise and even marks should be used to stimulate an interest and a desire to use these words in all communications. When children write their compositions they should have the chart before them and should attempt to use as many in the list as possible. This insistence on the use of the word will make it imperative that the same chart be kept many days and that few words be taught. It is probable that in this procedure only half or even a third of the number of words usually taught will be taken up, but we may rest unconcerned, for every means has been taken to make these words part of the natural and spontaneous expressional vocabulary.

Definitions.—Much time and useful energy are dissipated in teaching definitions in all subjects. The notion persists that ability to formulate or reproduce set definitions measures proficiency in a branch of knowledge. This standard fails absolutely when applied to life. Few people can define that which is part of their lives. The electrician, unable to define electricity, proceeds with his work intelligently and achieves the end he seeks; the judge, unable, perhaps, to define justice satisfactorily, nevertheless metes it out daily; the teacher of ethics, unable to define morality, nevertheless inspires in his pupils a love for right conduct. In school, especially in grammar and "meaning and use" lessons, the definition is elevated to a place that almost glorifies it. We must insist that formal definitions be relegated in teaching to the same plane of relative unimportance that they occupy in practical life, for function, not definition, determines use and therefore importance in life.

In recitation of "meaning and use" lessons teachers

THE MEANING AND USE OF NEW WORDS

should require pupils to give a sentence for the given word before stating the definition. If the sentence is both original and correct, the child knows the function of the word; its definition will add little to its comprehension. Let the reader select from the page a few words that are constantly used by him and then attempt to formulate satisfactory definitions, and he will realize the relative worth of function and definition. If, therefore, a notebook record must be made of these words, the page should be divided into three columns, the word should be written in the first, the sentence in the second, and the definition, if deemed necessary, in the third. The notebook arrangement would take the following form:

Word	*Original Sentence*	*Definition*
1. observation	1. The astronomer makes his observations of the heavens with a telescope.	1. A careful noting.
2.	2.	2.

Sentences that are isolated and so worded that they do not indicate the meaning of the word should be discouraged from the very beginning. Sentences must be taken from the reading, the geography, and the history that are taught as well as from the round of experiences that form the child's life. "The man is *courageous*," has no relation to any of the subjects taught in the grade and does not indicate the characteristics possessed by a courageous person.

The Supplementary Means of Increasing Vocabulary.—The formal "meaning and use" drills are not the only means of increasing the child's vocabulary. Although the other agents are often less direct, they are nevertheless not less effective in many cases. Among these, we must include the following:

1. *Study of Synonyms.*—A formal drill on a list of synonyms, e. g., *discover* and *invent, bring* and *fetch, content* and *satisfied,* etc., usually resolves itself into subtle analysis but does little to add vital elements to the child's vocabulary. Unless these pairs of synonyms arise naturally in the child's experience, they had better be neglected. Much can be done through drills on synonymous expressions. The teacher selects an expression used too frequently by the children and subjects that to a process of variations. For some reason which the teacher could not explain a class was using the expression "mad with," as in "He was mad with joy, excitement, anger," etc. This was put on the board and by questions and suggestions the teacher elicited that the general idea of the sentence "He was mad with joy" could be expressed by "He was overjoyed," "He was beside himself with joy," "His joy knew no bounds," etc. Thus the expression that had become stereotyped through overuse gave way to more varied sentence structure. Such a drill takes stock of each child's verbal possessions and brings words known but not used into active expression. The *variation method* suggested

in the study of composition is the most elaborated form of these drills on synonymous expressions.

2. *The Library and Reading Circles.*—Every effort must be made to interest children in the library so that they will be eager to avail themselves of every privilege that it offers. Very often much can be done through the organization of reading circles that meet regularly for discussion of books read since the last meeting. The child that contracts the reading habit soon gives evidence of new language possessions. He knows more words in the reading lesson, his sentences are better in form and in content, and his general knowledge grows beyond the confining limits of personal experience.

3. *Oral Composition in Reading Lessons.*—The selection that is read in class should be subdivided into its logical parts. After the first division is read it should be subjected to a series of questions which call for a reproduction and a discussion on the text. Children should be encouraged to appropriate words and expressions of the author. If the child, in formulating his answer, should look at the page and elect to incorporate almost an entire sentence, he should be encouraged, for he sees the value and experiences the need of this phraseology. He has taken the first step toward adding a good expression to his meager vocabulary.

4. *Etymology and the Habit of Using the Dictionary.*—In the discussion of the various methods of teaching the meaning of new words, we noted that a knowledge of the common etymological elements and

a habit of using the dictionary are of vital importance to the child because they give permanent means of enlarging vocabulary.

5. *The Subjects in the Curriculum.*—Every subject that is taught adds to the child's stock of expressions. In grammar *modify* and *dependent* are only two of many useful words that are learned. In like manner arithmetic, geography, history, and nature study make their permanent contributions to vocabulary.

6. *Memorization and Recitation.*—When children memorize what they understand and appreciate and then recite, not to prove to the teacher that a given text was memorized in obedience to a command, but because of a rational motive, they are incorporating many necessary words and expressions in their own vocabularies. The details of the method that must govern these memorization lessons will be discussed in the chapter on "Memory Gems."

7. *Participation in Social Intercourse.*—Vocabularies grow, usually, in response to conscious needs. When, therefore, the social life of the child necessitates ready and frequent speech, the mind acquires an ever-increasing stock of words to meet this need. Children who belong to social clubs and participate in the discussion of the business before the group, or who take active part in the administration of the pupils' self-government scheme in the school, usually give evidence of growing vocabularies. Children should, therefore, be encouraged to affiliate themselves with some group and to become active participants in its social affairs.

THE MEANING AND USE OF NEW WORDS

Developing Mastery of the Dictionary and the Dictionary Habit.—In an early part of the chapter it was suggested that throughout the grades, beginning with the fourth year, pupils should be given graded lessons that will develop *ability to use* the dictionary as well as *the habit to use* it. It is frequently assumed that consulting a dictionary is a simple process. But list the facts one must know to use a dictionary intelligently and expeditiously, and it becomes apparent that the process requires experience and even formal training. It is therefore suggested that dictionary lessons be developed around the following centers:

1. Alphabetizing words, cards, letters, etc. Use twenty-six divisions.
2. The subalphabet. Practice in alphabetizing, using 52 to 78 classes. A, *ag, ak, as,* etc.
3. Alphabetical order within each letter. Locating words in the dictionary, names in the telephone directory, etc. Include key words at top and bottom of page in the dictionary.
4. Finding meaning of words.
5. Finding syllabication. Correlate with spelling, and dividing words at end of line.
6. Finding accent. Drill using such words as *positively; abdomen; permit,* as noun and verb, etc.
7. Finding pronunciation; the common diacritical marks. Real spelling vs. phonetic spelling.
8. Further drill in finding meaning appropriate to the text.
9. Finding parts of speech from the dictionary. The common abbreviations used in the dictionary.
10. Finding plurals of nouns.
11. Finding principal parts of verbs.
12. Finding comparison of adjectives and adverbs.

13. Finding meaning of expressions of more than one word.
14. Finding whether an expression is slang, colloquial or standard.

Little added time is necessary to give this dictionary practice if teachers will remember that many of these lessons can be made part of a real project and that most of them can be made part of an effective drill in spelling, in "meaning and use" and in grammar.

Language Power and Intelligence.—Many standard tests have been devised to measure vocabularies of children. Trabue's *Language Completion Test* and Holley's *Sentence Vocabulary Test* are examples of this type of scale. Teachers who are eager to ascertain how the vocabularies of their pupils compare with others in the same grade will find these scales very helpful. It is significant that the score obtained in a vocabulary test such as the two mentioned above shows a high correlation with general intelligence. Of course, language limitation may be due to causes other than limited intelligence, and great care must be used in employing a language scale as a measure of intelligence.

CHAPTER XII

DICTATION: TEACHING THE FORMAL ASPECT OF COMPOSITION

There is lack of unanimity of opinion among teachers as to the function of the dictation lesson. To many it is merely an opportunity to test pupils' knowledge of the formal phase of language. It is evident that dictation for such a purpose is of little importance, unless we add a preceding function—to teach the laws governing the purely formal elements of written speech. We must posit, definitely, the aims of dictation before we proceed with the method of class instruction.

Objects of Dictation Lessons.—We will now consider the several objects of dictation lessons. (1) *They teach the technicalities of written composition.* All written composition has two aspects, we noted: the expressional and the formal aspect. Ideas cannot group themselves logically, clear and forceful sentences cannot form, when the mind is troubled with matters of punctuation, capitalization, spelling, and penmanship. It is the function of the dictation lesson to teach these technical elements and thus set free the mind to give itself exclusively to the expressional elements in written composition.

Among the other aims of the dictation lesson we may mention the following: (2) *It teaches spelling in a natural form.* In the spelling lesson the child learns those words that present some difficulty to a majority of his class; but in the dictation lesson there is revealed to the child his own shortcomings. (3) *It makes the ear sensitive* to spoken language and thus trains for better auditory perception of the spoken tongue. (4) *Rapid as well as neat penmanship is developed.* There is great danger in penmanship teaching, that neatness and accuracy of form will be acquired at the cost of speed. Teachers used to put a premium on the slow, painful drawing of letters, failing to realize that speed as well as legibility must be attained. In the dictation lesson the penmanship must necessarily be more rapid. (5) In a correct method, *concentration is developed* in the process of dictation. (6) *Habits of self-criticism and self-correction are acquired* by the children, for every dictation lesson ends with a correction by the children of their products.

The Choice of the Selection to Be Dictated.—The ends to be attained in a dictation lesson are often defeated by poor selection of the text that is dictated. It is necessary, first, that *each selection should illustrate only one point* in the technicalities of language. Thus, one paragraph is chosen because it shows how to write social titles; another because it illustrates the use of commas in a series, or the use of quotation marks; still another because some rule of capitalization is applied. That selection which can be used to teach any one of a half-dozen facts of language usually teaches nothing.

A second requisite insists that *the successive texts to be dictated be graded and so organized that they repeat a law until its application becomes habitual.* An examination of the dictation exercises to-day discloses the fact that teachers in every class are trying to teach all the rules of spelling, punctuation, and capitalization in one term. Not until these rules are graded and allotted in limited numbers to each grade will their use become habit. When each teacher knows that she is responsible for only three definite rules of punctuation, four in capitalization, and two in spelling, she can so grade her dictation selections that the repetition will make them permanent possessions of the children.

Third, it is necessary that the selection be *suitable in theme and language.* Why dictate anything as insipid as "John bought paper, pens, ink, blotters, and blank books. Coming home he traveled by car, train, bus, and bicycle. On his way he saw Mary, James, William, and Henry." The language of the text ought to be above the children's literary level, although on their plane of comprehension. In current articles on dictation found in pedagogical journals, fervid pleas are made for selections that inculcate lessons of ethics and patriotism. This is evidently sentimentalism gone astray. No practical teacher reserves part of the lesson on the use of the semicolon for an appeal to an ideal of conduct. Ethics and patriotism must be taught in content lessons, in history, in literature—subjects with human backgrounds and vibrant with the emotions and impulses of life.

Procedure in the Dictation Lesson.—A complete dictation lesson requires a minimum of two periods and has three distinct parts. The first period is occupied with the problem of teaching the new formal element of language; the second period covers the second part of the lesson in which the fact taught is tested, and the third part deals with the correction of the children's results. We must follow the procedure through these successive parts.

1. *The Teaching Period.*—Let us assume that the aim is to give a first lesson on the use of quotation marks. The teacher dictates pairs of sentences which follow the type form of, *Lawrence said that his sailors should not give up the ship,* and, *Lawrence said to his sailors, "Don't give up the ship."* Children are called upon to write these on the board, putting one under the other. Through questions the teacher then elicits, first, the difference in thought in each pair of sentences, viz., the narration of an incident as opposed to the repetition of the words of another, and second, the need of indicating this difference by some form of punctuation. The teacher then shows children the correct form of direct quotations and leads them to conclude that in using the words of another we must have (a) comma, (b) quotation marks, and (c) capitalization. Sentences which have been written incorrectly on the blackboard are now corrected in the light of the rule of punctuation that was evolved.

More sentences may be written and incorrect punctuation may be corrected until the end of the first period. This ends the teaching part of the dictation lesson.

2. *Testing for Mastery of Language Fact Taught.* —In the following period a selection that illustrates the use of the rule for direct quotations is dictated to the class. In all classes below the seventh year it is advisable to show the children the selection the day preceding the dictation. True, this is not the mode of dictation in after life, but the child in the fourth or fifth school year is not ready for the direct dictation of the commercial world. It is unwise to force the child to commit errors, even though they are all corrected, for the mind may carry away wrong forms. We must constantly guard against the commission of errors by forestalling them. Hence in the early classes children are shown the selection and attention is directed to certain spellings, punctuations, capitalizations, and arrangements. On the following day the selection is dictated. For the lesson taught above an appropriate text would be the following:

The Death of Wolfe at Quebec

Wolfe, weary and sick, kept constant watch during the battle. Suddenly, he fell, fatally wounded. He realized that his end was near. As he lay waiting for the last moment, he heard, "They fly." He weakly asked, "Who fly?" His bodyguard replied, "The enemy, sir." His face seemed to brighten as he mumbled, "Then thank God, I die in peace." The Angel of Death then claimed him for his own.

The selection is first read as a whole to the class and then is dictated by pausing regularly at the end of each logical or grammatical subdivision in each sentence. No greater error can be committed in dictation than to make pauses after each eighth or tenth word. Such a procedure, although commonly seen in classrooms, reduces the selection to an arbitrary succession of words and phrases and makes rational punctuation impossible.

A second important caution is never to repeat after the signal has been given for the class to write. The teacher should therefore insist upon absolute attention while the children listen to the dictation of the first logical part. The signal is then given and all children pick up pens and write. No hand is allowed to be raised and no questions should be permitted. When a reasonable period has elapsed a signal is given for work to stop, the class comes to attention and the next portion is dictated. Under no circumstance should the teacher dictate while some children are writing, or repeat after the class has begun to write. The violation of this simple dictum courts inattention or confuses those who are trying to write. Ability to concentrate, it was shown, is one of the important ends of dictation exercises. When the entire selection has been dictated it may be reread as a whole, but this is not always necessary or advisable. Throughout the dictation, children should be required to write at the rate set as the standard of penmanship speed for their grade.

3. *The Correction of the Children's Work.*—The

children should now be required to put all pens and ink away. The perfect copy is shown and each pupil corrects his own product with ruler and pencil. Every error is underlined and the correction is written above it. As in the correction of composition, it is not necessary to have every type of error marked by proofreaders' marks; a mere underline is sufficient to call attention to an error that needs correction. To discourage efforts at spurious corrections and to encourage exclusive attention to correct form, a different writing medium is advocated for the correction period. If dictations, written in ink, are corrected in ink, children spend their best energies in devising ingenious ways of changing a *t* to *p*, a small *s* to a capital *S*, etc., thus losing the benefit inherent in all honest self-correction. Every incentive for thorough correction should be given. Children should exchange papers with their neighbors, who will help them to discover errors that were passed over. It should be explained that errors neatly corrected will be counted only half a mark, but errors overlooked will count doubly against a pupil. By these means—of course, petty devices—children are made to feel that careful correction is worth their best endeavors.

The rewriting of the dictation in absolutely correct form is a disputed procedure. The arguments offered by the disputants are precisely those listed in the debate for the rewriting of compositions and need not be repeated here. Most supervisors agree that if errors are carefully and intelligently corrected, the child will learn more from additional dictation lessons than from mere rewriting of selections already dictated.

Further Test and Drill.—It is evident that no new fact need be taught for weeks. Each succeeding dictation lesson may consist of further test and correction, until the law of punctuation is applied by the children automatically. In teaching the correct use of quotation marks it is necessary to grade the topic by successive steps of difficulty. The child who can write the selection, "The Death of Wolfe at Quebec," may not be able to punctuate a sentence of the type, "Then I die in peace," he said, "for I have captured Quebec." The "broken quotation" must then be in a separate lesson. But thus far we have not considered long quotations extending over two or three paragraphs; here the punctuation and the arrangement are different and must be taught at a later time. In lessons on the comma, the semicolon, capitalization, the need for gradation is even more urgent because the topics are wider in scope.

The Unprepared Dictation.—The procedure for dictation lessons has thus far neglected the drill in unprepared dictation necessary in commercial life. Beginning with the sixth year occasional periods should be set aside for the dictation of text not seen by the class before the lesson and dictated without the nicety of logical pauses and successive signals for attention and writing. With the advancing grades this unprepared dictation should be given with greater frequency until the children become accustomed to the form of dictation heard in the business world.

DICTATION

Types of Unprepared Dictation.—In upper grades, this unprepared dictation may take many interesting forms. To illustrate: writing from dictation and making the necessary rearrangements in form,

1. A bill of goods, a receipt, a check, a note.
2. A telephone message.
3. A short business letter.
4. Names, addresses and telephone numbers.
5. An advertisement as received by telephone.

This list can readily be enlarged by bringing into class the dictation of actual business.

SUGGESTED READING

BRIGGS, T. H. English Form Tests. Public School Publishing Co., Bloomington, Ill.

CRONSON, B. Graded Dictation and Spelling Lessons. The Macmillan Co.

GOLDWASSER, I. E. Method and Methods in the Teaching of English, chap. XIII. D. C. Heath & Co.

STARCH, DANIEL. Punctuation Scale. Public School Publishing Co.

CHAPTER XIII

MEMORY GEMS: MEMORIZATION AND RECITATION

Value of Memory Gems.—Memorization and recitation of standard prose and poetical selections have always been an essential part of every child's linguistic education. They are the means that are used in all stages of the child's development, from the "School of the Mother's Knee" through the high-school course. Their values are many and far-reaching, and can be summed up as follows:

1. Memorizing the gems of literature is a means of enriching the child's limited expressional stock. New words, strong phrases, traditional allusions, and classical expressions are acquired through a context that helps to give them both richer meaning and greater retention.

2. The mere knowledge of the literary gems that are memorized is an acquisition that is worth while for its own sake. We must acquaint the child in an informal way with his literary heritage.

3. Memorization of literary gems gives children a permanent possession of sentiments deep in ethical significance and rich in poetic charm, which grow in meaning and beauty with the ever-widening experi-

ence of life. "The Chambered Nautilus" which attracted us in youth by its rich imagery is now a symbol of the moral urge that is prompted by a growing soul. "As the swift seasons roll" the poem glows richer and more beautiful in its symbolism.

4. But aside from the content aspect of these literary possessions, the child is becoming familiar with language structure that serves as a model for his own modes of expression. The child may not consciously set himself to imitate the selections he memorizes, but they nevertheless have a deep and subtle influence on his linguistic development.

5. The recitation of the memorized literary gems affords the teacher an excellent means of training his pupils in correct enunciation, clear articulation, correct voice control and modulation.

6. Another important gain that follows in the wake of dramatized recitation of memorized selections is increased confidence and more graceful self-expression. These values give the memory gem lesson a definite and undisputed place in every curriculum of English.

The Selection of the Memory Gem.—The standard of selection must be determined to a great extent by the child's conception of delightful literature. What is artistic and literary to us may awake no response from the child. Not the mature conception of the teacher, but the growing, aspiring conception of the child should determine what will be selected from our vast literary storehouse. The poem, "I Live for Those Who Love Me," expresses the basic tenet of Christianity. But to require children in the third year of the elementary school course to mouth it and to pledge themselves to "live for the cause that needs assistance" and "for the wrongs that lack resistance," is a procedure that borders on the ludicrous. Gray's "Elegy in a Country Church Yard" highly merits its place of honor in most carefully selected anthologies, but its recognized literary merit does not necessarily make it appropriate for an elementary school child. A forced study of what is above the child's artistic power of appreciation may undermine the child's interest in all literary form. But, it has been asked, will not this standard lead to the memorization of the commonplace in our language? There is no cause for alarm because it is not proposed to invite immature and unread children to select the content of their literary course. The standard formulated merely suggests that mature and widely read teachers and supervisors select from the rich literary sources those gems whose emotional and artistic appeals are so universal that even the developing child can respond to them, can feel their thrill and grow under their influence.

Motivating the Memory Gems.—The memorization of a literary gem should proceed from the children's desire to count it among their possessions. The discussion of the values of memorizing literary selections sums up the teacher's reasons for making this type of language exercise a vital part of the English course. But they do not necessarily evoke in the child a desire to memorize any selection. The problem that confronts the teacher in teaching the memory gem is how to motivate it for the children.

The problem of motivation may be solved by using the selection as the text for an intensive, appreciative reading lesson. Through the entire period the teacher must aim to bring within the children's sphere of appreciation all the elements that make the literary gem beautiful and rich in poetic imagery. At the end of the lesson the teacher must try to ascertain whether the selection was a source of pleasure to the pupils. If they caught the message and feel its spirit, the memorization can be based on real motive; if, for some reason, the selection proved uninspiring, it should not be forced upon them.

Let us assume that the class responded to the appeal of the literary gem. Children are called upon to dramatize it. The most enthusiastic volunteers are called upon. They eagerly come before the class, and with eyes on the page proceed with the dramatization. When it becomes apparent that the dramatization is a failure, the teacher asks the children to account for the result and elicits that unless the selection is known "by heart" its proper rendition is impossible. Here, then, is the motive for the memorization. The desire to recite the selection to the assembled school, an eagerness to possess what is beautiful and inspiring, and the preparation for a recitation contest may serve as added motives which reduce the tedium involved in memorization exercises.

Procedure in Memorizing Literary Gems.—1. *Sympathetic Comprehension of the Selection.*—It was suggested that the literary selection that is to be memorized should first be used as a text for an intensive reading lesson. In this appreciative reading the children feel the message of the selection, become familiar with the development of the central theme, and learn the meaning of new words, phrases, and allusions. With this basis of literary appreciation, the teacher is assured of a sympathetic comprehension by the class and a motive for memorization.

2. *Tracing the Sequence of Ideas.*—The second step preparatory to the memory appeal is to lead the children to trace the sequence of ideas in the selection studied. Let us assume that Kingsley's "Three Fishers" is to be memorized.

THE THREE FISHERS

Three fishers went sailing away to the West,
  Away to the West as the sun went down;
Each thought of the woman who loved him the best,
  And the children stood watching them out of town;
  For men must work, and women must weep,
  And there's little to earn, and many to keep,
    Though the harbour bar be moaning.

Three wives sat up in the lighthouse tower,
  And they trimmed the lamps as the sun went down;
They looked at the squall, and they looked at the shower,
  And the night-rack came rolling up ragged and brown.
  But men must work, and women must weep,
  Though storms be sudden, and waters deep,
    And the harbour bar be moaning.

Three corpses lay out on the shining sands
  In the morning gleam as the tide went down,

MEMORY GEMS: MEMORY AND RECITATION

And the women are weeping and wringing their hands
  For those who will never come home to the town;
For men must work, and women must weep,
And the sooner it's over, the sooner to sleep;
  And good-bye to the bar and its moaning.

The successive thoughts of the first stanza analyzed by a sixth-year pupil were listed as follows: Three fishermen sail away; they sail to the west as the sun goes down; each thinks of his wife; their children watch them; men must work, women must be sad when little is earned and many must be supported; poor fishermen must go even if it looks dangerous. These ideas are now committed to memory with little effort because the entire thought is evolved most naturally and logically.

The values of memorizing the sequence of ideas in their natural order are many. First, it simplifies the memorization of the poet's words; each thought prompts its appropriate expression, and with little effort a verbatim reproduction is achieved. Second, it tends to make recall rational rather than verbal. Study the strained face of the child who recites a memorized selection; the steady stare and the nervous anxiety give evidence of the fact that the child is focalizing all conscious effort on the next line or the next word. The recitation is a verbal reproduction, not a reconstruction, thought by thought, of a real situation. When these children err, they say what is absolutely devoid of meaning. But when the child learns first the sequence of the ideas and then the poet's phraseology, he recites a series of thoughts, he thinks constantly of the next idea, and when he errs he substitutes his own clumsy wording which expresses the idea in mind in a less elegant form. A third value of such a procedure is that it trains children in systematic and sustained thinking.

3. *Thought Questions Answered in the Words of the Author.*—When the children have acquired the "thought-skeleton," each idea should be subjected to a thought question, which should be answered by the children in the words of the text to be memorized. As illustrative of this phase of the lesson, we may submit the following reproduction of questions and answers, the part of the answer in italics recited with emphasis by the children:

Teacher: How many fishers left for the trip?

Pupil: Three; *three* fishers went sailing away to the west.

Teacher: In what direction did they sail?

Pupil: Toward the west; three fishers went sailing away *to the west*.

Teacher: What time of day was it?

Pupil: Twilight; away to the west *as the sun went down*.

Teacher: Who was in the thoughts of these men?

Pupil: Their wives; *each thought of the woman* who loved him the best.

Teacher: What did these women feel toward these men?

Pupil: They loved them; each thought of the woman *who loved him the best*.

Teacher: Who were interested spectators?

Pupil: Their children; *and the children stood watching* them out of town, etc.

After these specific questions are asked, a series of general problems is formulated which necessitates the reading of that portion of the selection which is to be memorized. The teacher now requests: "Read the line that gives the saddest picture; the happiest picture. Read the line that tells most about the dangerous character of the work of these men. What line is most beautiful; least beautiful? Read these. What line gives a hint of the end of the trip? Read the line that is hardest to remember; easiest to remember. What line tells most about the homes of these men?" These are only a few or many questions that can be formulated to serve as a pretext for making children read and reread the stanza that is to be committed to memory. Let the teacher now call for volunteers and note how large a part of her class is ready to recite the stanza that was studied.

Retention Through Thought Rather than Through Memory Appeal.—Throughout this lesson the aim was to avoid an appeal to verbal memory. In "memory-gem" lessons one hears the teacher's commands, "Recite the first sentence. Say it five times. Recite the second sentence. Say it five times. Recite the first and the second sentences three times, etc." At times the sentence is not made the unit of reiteration, for the teacher requires the children to repeat the first line, the second line, the first two lines, the third line, the first three lines, etc. What wonder that most children feel that the term *gem* is a misnomer in these lessons, for the adjective *memory* overshadows its noun. The procedure that was suggested aims to produce permanent retention through thought rather than through mechanical repetition, through a method that stimulates self-activity rather than one that dulls the mind by its monotony, through devices that set problems before the class rather than incessant drill.

Aids to Memorization.—But not all children can memorize by a method that makes an exclusive thought appeal. Minds that are unimpressionable must have auxiliary appeals that are more mechanical in their nature. Among these aids to memorization are: (1) Verbal repetition; (2) singing the music that may have been composed for the selection; (3) pointing out the rhymes supplies additional auditory associations; (4) emphasizing the rhythm or the lilt is, at times, almost as effective as the music accompanying a poem; (5) multiple sense appeal, in which an effort is made to have the selection heard, seen, acted, and written by way of providing for auditory-, visual-, and motor-minded children.

The Recitation.—Few lessons are as uninspirational and devoid of social spirit as the recitations of memorized selections that one hears in a round of visits to schools. Child after child is called upon to recite in rapid succession to prove to the teacher that he has perfect mastery of the correct sequence of words. The auditors listen listlessly and hold themselves in readiness to correct the child who recites, or to continue, should the poor victim become confused and unable to proceed to the end. These recitations must

CHAPTER XIV

THE VALUES OF FORMAL GRAMMAR

The Disputed Place of Grammar in the Modern Curriculum.—Progressive teachers of English hold divergent and almost irreconcilable views on the place, the functions, and the ultimate worth of grammar as a subject in the elementary school curriculum. The camp is divided into three factions. The first justifies the traditional emphasis on formal grammar with its terminology, classifications, rules of syntax and analysis —all to be taught in separate periods with as much correlation as can naturally be introduced. The second group insists that formal grammar must be eliminated and the necessary laws of language be taught through the correction of errors that children make in their written and oral speech. The third view on the teaching of grammar is a compromise: it admits the futility of formal grammar that is taught as the scientific analysis of speech, but it has faith in the teaching of those facts of grammar that can be related to the child's needs. This last school would teach grammar as part of the course in composition; would have every lesson in grammar arise in errors committed by members of the class; would eliminate all those elements of formal grammar that cannot be applied directly by the child in the process of improving speech; and would teach grammar incidentally, not in set periods. The reaction to formal grammar is not a temporary attitude accompanying changing conceptions in teaching; it is a vigorous protest against abuses that have characterized most of the teaching of grammar.

Grammar a Discredited Subject.—The indictments brought against current procedures in the teaching of grammar are many and grave.

1. The old boast, "Grammar teaches how to write and speak a language correctly," has been disproven, not only by practical results observed in actual teaching but by a deeper analysis of the relation that exists between speech and grammar. Every teacher can bring evidence to prove that proficiency in grammar is no guarantee of equal or approximate proficiency in composition, and vice versa. A child, whose compositions leave little to be desired, may score a failure in grammar, while his neighbor, well versed in the intricacies of verbal forms and the rules of agreement in grammar, may write English that is devoid of all application of this technical knowledge. Exercises in grammar are essentially analytic; exercises in composition are creative and essentially synthetic; therefore, ability in one of these forms of language study is not necessarily carried over to the other.

2. In most classrooms, there is little or no relation between the courses in grammar and in composition for a given term. In schools organized on a departmental schedule in the last two or three years

it is usual to assign the teaching of grammar to one teacher and the teaching of composition to another. These teachers proceed independently, the one teaching children the nominative absolute, the other struggling with the class in the hope of breaking the habit of using dependent clauses for complete sentences. It is advisable to assign to one teacher all the subjects that are grouped under the head of English, so that every natural correlation will be introduced and thus the work will be given a unity of aim which it will otherwise lack.

3. Grammar as outlined in many courses of study and in textbooks written for elementary schools abounds in sterile verbal subtleties. Thus, the child is taught to keep gerund and gerundive apart. The word *sailing* in the sentence, "Sailing a boat is great sport," must be distinguished from the word *sailing* in, "The sailing of the ship was scheduled for midnight." True, the one word has an element of action in it, while the other has not; the one word cannot be introduced by the article *the,* while the other can; but when all these distinctions are noted and the proper names applied, in what vital way has the child's speech been affected? The dative object and the direct object are now taught in many schools. This terminology is absolutely essential in language like German and Latin, but in English it serves only to multiply unnecessary classification. What is gained by calling *hat* the direct object and *me* the dative object in the sentence, "John gave me the hat"? The old form, "objective case," answers the purpose because in Eng-

THE TEACHING OF ENGLISH

lish there is no difference in the form of words in the accusative or in the dative case. Such an unwarranted increase in terminology reduces grammar to a sterile study of formalism in language.

4. The prevailing method of teaching grammar is another cause of the discredit which has been cast upon the subject. In the teacher's endeavors to have children master an ever-increasing terminology and ever-growing classification, memory drills are greatly emphasized. Recitations are given over exclusively to reciting set classifications, stereotyped definitions, formal rules and memorized lists. Grammar is still a memory subject rather than a rational study, for the din of monotonous repetitions of *I, my* or *mine, me, we, our* or *ours, us,* or of *I love, you love, he* or *she loves, we love, you love, they love,* etc., is still to be heard in most schools. It seems that we have not yet learned that mastery of elements, isolated in an arbitrary list, is no guarantee of ability to use these very forms in natural context.

5. Another very serious criticism that must be urged against current courses in grammar is the undue variety of terminology. The market is flooded with a variety of books that find their way into the school. Most of these books repeat the same limitations and abuses, but each one of them justifies its appearance by a new system of names for the various elements in grammar. No attempt is made to reach any degree of uniformity in the terminology; each book insists on its own system, and each author is a law unto himself. What is the inevitable result? Different schools

use different books, and even the various classes in one school frequently do not use the same series of books. The pupils become hopelessly confused by the array of imposing terms. As the children pass from one school to another and from one class to another, they find the new teacher using a terminology unknown to them. What wonder that children leave school ignorant of the basic terms in grammar!

We have seen that these indictments against the teaching of grammar are serious and true, but they do not disclose weaknesses inherent in the subject itself, or any defects that cannot be remedied. Proper organization of the course of study and a more pedagogical teaching procedure will remove these abuses in the teaching of grammar. We must turn therefore to a consideration of the values of grammar as an elementary school study and the principles governing the methods of teaching the subject.

Values of Grammar.—A definite formulation of the values of grammar will set up for us definite aims that must be achieved in the teaching of the subject. The aims become standards, in terms of which we judge the efficiency of our methods of teaching and the wisdom of the course of study that is to be taught. The values of grammar can be grouped under five heads, viz., the *practical,* the *disciplinary,* the *literary,* the *cultural,* and the *preparatory* values.

1. *The Practical Value of Grammar: A Guide to Correct Speech.*—An investigation into the reasons why teachers and principals believe that grammar

should be taught showed that the first justification was that "grammar is a guide to correct speech." But we must not read too much into this function of grammar. It was pointed out in a previous connection that a knowledge of grammar does not guarantee correct speech. Grammar is the science of language, and serves as an aid in correct speech in the same way as the knowledge of the science of any medium of expression serves the art of expression. A knowledge of logic does not guarantee logical thought, but it does give the student a means of detecting logical fallacies and a standard in terms of which he can judge the results of his own thinking. So, too, grammar teaches us not to speak English correctly, but to understand it.

The teaching of grammar is justified only when children learn to use it for purposes of self-criticism and correction. Thus, the child who learns the functions of verbs and participles may still write in his composition "When he seen what I done," but in the period of correction he underlines *seen* and *done* and uses verb forms. The wise teaching of grammar seeks to make correction of all speech, not arbitrary changes according to the dictates of the teacher, but an intelligent process of self-criticism.

2. *The Disciplinary Values of Grammar.*—Properly taught, grammar is a means of developing powers of concentration, reason, abstraction, and analysis in verbal relationships. Grammar has been called the logic of elementary education. Laurie tells us, "Grammar is logic in the concrete and language in the abstract. . . . The boy who is intelligently ana-

lyzing in grammar is intelligently analyzing the process of thought, and is a logician without knowing it." Max Müller expresses the disciplinary value of grammar as follows: "Grammar is logic of speech even as logic is the grammar of reason."

A few illustrations will readily show that the disciplinary value of grammar is not overstated. The reason, the concentration, and the analysis required of a school child in perceiving the differences between "He was gone an hour" and "He has been gone an hour," "I want him" and "I want him to be a soldier," are as intense as the mental activity of the college student who distinguishes *extension* from *intension* in logic or *perception* from *conception* in psychology.

Cautions in Seeking the Disciplinary Value of Grammar.—Potent as the disciplinary value of grammar is, we must nevertheless remember that the mental power developed in this subject can be applied only to verbal relations. The powers of analysis and discrimination developed in grammar will undoubtedly be of service to the student in his study of rhetoric or the grammar of foreign languages, but of little or no direct help in studies and experience markedly different from the verbal relations of grammar. This is true of all mental habits, for a mode of mental activity developed in one experience is transferred to other experiences in direct proportion to their similarity. The limited value of the mental power developed in grammar proves conclusively that no topic in grammar must be taught for its disciplinary value alone. Teachers and textbook writers often teach in grammar what has no practical worth and justify themselves on purely disciplinary grounds. If the fact of grammar has no social use, it merits no place in class studies. A fact, aside from its use, has no value. Hair-splitting differences and nice verbal distinctions develop thought for more verbal puzzles. The disciplinary values of grammar must be achieved through the teaching of topics that can be used by the child in the correction of his speech and that have, therefore, social worth.

3. *Grammar as an Aid in Literary Interpretation.*—It has often been asserted by the sponsors for formal grammar that a knowledge of grammatical elements and functions is of great aid in literary interpretation and expressive reading. In the sentence, "That book that you saw belongs to me," the relative emphasis on each *that* and the correct phrasing may prove perplexing to the young mind. But the recognition of the grammatical function of each "that" indicates clearly that the demonstrative adjective and not the relative pronoun should be stressed in reading; the feeling for the clause which comes from a study of grammar prompts correct phrasing. Similarly, passages are encountered in all reading where thought is not clear because the grammatical relations or functions of certain phrases and clauses are not perceived.

This belief, firmly rooted in many minds, that a knowledge of grammar is a direct aid in literary interpretation, was subjected to a test by F. S. Hoyt. The results of examinations given in composition, grammar, and literary interpretation were tabulated in comparative lists. They prove that proficiency in any one of these three branches of the study of English is no index of the proficiency that will be attained in the other two. A cursory and superficial analysis of the marks of any class in grammar and in literary interpretation will serve to reënforce the conclusions based on this experimental evidence. Hoyt's findings are precisely what one would naturally anticipate, for the mental attitudes and activities in grammar and in literary interpretation are so different that the excellence developed in one subject need not necessarily influence the proficiency attained in the other. Only when awkward or unusual construction of sentences hinders acquisition of meaning will a knowledge of grammatical functions aid in literary interpretation. But in the elementary schools such situations are not the rule, and the child's grasp of grammatical function is so meager that it is of little service in tracing the relationship among clauses and phrases in sentences whose construction is not lucid.

4. *Cultural or Conventional Value of Grammar.*—
The teaching of grammar may be justified on the ground of social expediency. Many facts are taught, not because they have intrinsic worth but because they form part of that knowledge stock that society expects its citizen of culture to possess. The terminology of grammar adds useful words like *modify, independent, dependent, mode, tense, imperative, superlative, clause*—words that enrich vocabulary and add to expressional powers.

But while the conventional demands must be considered they must not become the sole governing factors. The merest superficial knowledge of grammar will satisfy the conventional demands. In the teaching of those elements of grammar that can be applied by the child in his endeavors at self-criticism and correction, these cultural values of the subject can be attained. This conventional justification need not guide either in teaching the subject or in organizing a course of study, for it is a result of the teaching of grammar by any method and through any course.

5. *Preparatory Value of Grammar.*—The final value of grammar lies in the fact that it is a necessary preparation for future studies. Ignorance of grammar makes work in rhetoric very difficult. Teachers of foreign languages in secondary schools complain that progress is impeded by the children's lack of basic knowledge of English grammar. If we take Goethe's dictum seriously, "He who knows only one tongue, does not know that well," the preparatory value of grammar must be regarded seriously. But when we recall the high rate of elimination in the elementary schools, it is obvious that this preparatory value justifies the teaching of grammar only to ten per cent. of the school population—those who reach the high school and pursue the study of rhetoric or foreign languages.

What to Emphasize in Language Teaching. Scientific Investigation.—The language needs of pupils must determine, in a large measure, our attitude towards grammar as a school subject. But there is no general agreement on this language need. Teachers rely on

THE VALUES OF FORMAL GRAMMAR

their experience which is too frequently not representative. To some, therefore, grammar can serve no purpose; to others, it is a vital agent in correcting speech and giving children new and higher language standards. We shall stop to analyze two language studies that were made to ascertain the actual language needs of elementary and junior high-school pupils.

Charters' Diagnostic Language Test.[1]—Charters made a careful analysis of the type and the number of language errors in children's composition. These are summed up below.

CHARTERS' ANALYSIS OF TYPE AND NUMBER OF CHILDREN'S LANGUAGE ERRORS

Error	Number of Times Found	Error	Number of Times Found
was for *were*	1,555	*ain't got*	443
seen for *saw*	1,513	*have got*	439
ain't	1,361	*ain't got no*	435
can for *may*	1,150	*come* for *came*	350
done for *did*	895	*it was (is, ain't) me*	340
is for *are*	777	*why, there was*	330
don't for *doesn't*	721	*didn't do nothing*	302
this here	684	*lay* for *lie*	280
John, he went	671	*off* for *from*	276
didn't want no	531	*went* for *gone*	245
them things	479	*give* for *gave*	202
that there	472		

On the basis of the errors actually found, Charters

[1] See Bibliography at end of Chapter XV.

formulated two sets of standard tests, the first in language and the second in grammar. Each set of tests is composed of separate tests on pronouns, verbs, and miscellaneous errors. In the language tests the pupil is required to point out the error by writing the correct form. In the grammar test, the pupil must point out the error and indicate from a list of rules that rule which governs the correction he indicates. Standard scores are given for each test so that teachers can measure the language ability and knowledge of grammar of her class and of each pupil. The test is diagnostic and shows clearly where emphasis must be placed in the language and grammar lessons.

Wilson's Language Error Test.[2]—The aim of the Wilson test is not merely to measure language ability but also:

1. to detect the most common language errors;
2. to ascertain the prevalence of each type of error;
3. to discover the language needs of each pupil;
4. to determine how to apportion class drill on the various types of errors;
5. to indicate to each pupil the type of drill that he needs most.

The children are asked to correct three compositions, each of equal difficulty and each containing twenty-eight common errors of the type caused by (a) double negatives; (b) wrong preposition; (c) wrong word, *are* for *our;* (d) objective for the nominative; (e) paste tense for the past participle and vice verse; (f)

[2] G. M. Wilson, *Language Error Test* (Copyright, 1923, by World Book Co., Yonkers-on-Hudson, N. Y.).

THE VALUES OF FORMAL GRAMMAR

double nominative, *John, he saw;* (g) *to* for *two;* etc. A sample of the first composition, as corrected by a pupil and properly scored is here given.

STORY A
Saturday Morning

✓✓ Saturday morning is a busy time ~~in~~ *at* *are* house.   A *feller* has a good chance to work. ✓
Dorothy and I
~~Me and Dorothy~~ divide the tasks between us. Then we race to see who will finish ✓✓
✓ first. Last Saturday I ~~taken~~ *took* the breakfast dishes as one of my tasks. I am *especial* ✓
✓ fond of washing dishes. You should have *saw* me work. I wanted to get through
✓ so *as* I could play.
 ✓ John *he* called up at eleven o'clock to see if I might play with him. I had ~~too~~ *two* ✓
✓ rooms to dust before I could go. John saw that I *couldn't hardly* leave my work
    until I had ~~did~~ *done* all of it. He brought over some doughnuts and gave them to me. ✓
✓✓ I *sure* appreciated the doughnuts. Then John helped me. It was *real* good of
    him. When we had finished, I suggested playing marbles until time for dinner.
✓✓ "I ~~ain't~~ *haven't* got no marbles," said John. "They ~~comes~~ *come* very handy," I replied. Then ✓✓
✓ I ~~gave~~ *give* him some of mine. I had *to* many for my bag. John and I enjoy marbles. ✓
 ✓ When dinner was ready, mother invited John to stay. "If I *was* sure my mother
    wouldn't care, I should like to stay," he replied. John *seen* ^*saw* that he was really wanted ✓
    so he telephoned to his mother. He enjoyed the dinner, and ~~et~~ *ate* heartily. When ✓
✓✓ ~~them~~ *The* apples *was* passed, John wanted one, but he couldn't eat *no more*. After dinner ✓
✓ we had another game of marbles. I *hopes* John may come over again.

Number of errors corrected ..12.. (Score)
Number of errors not corrected ..10..

CORRECTED COMPOSITION

The accompanying table gives "the best estimate of the author as to the median scores which would be

MEDIAN SCORES IN THE VARIOUS GRADES

Grade	III	IV	V	VI	VII	VIII	IX	X	XI	XII
Median Score	7	11	14	17	20	22	23	24	25	25

obtained for the several grades from 100,000 children." Each error corrected counts 1; the maximum score for each test is therefore 28.

Teachers and supervisors using these tests will soon find that they have a clearer perception of the language limitations and the language needs of their pupils. Without a reliable instrument for comparative study we may either remain satisfied with pupil results below normal achievement or suffer discouragement because our pupils do not attain an impossible standard that we have unfortunately set up for them. Then, too, such tests show us clearly that our children need that knowledge of grammar which can readily be translated into language power.

SUGGESTED READING

The suggested reading for this chapter will be found at the end of the succeeding chapter.

CHAPTER XV

PRINCIPLES GOVERNING THE TEACHING OF GRAMMAR

The discussion has thus far concerned itself with abuses that mark prevailing methods of teaching grammar and with a survey of the legitimate aims and scope of the subject. We must now turn to a consideration of the principles which may lead pupils to attain these values so that grammar may become an intelligent subject to them, intimately related to the needs of their lives.

Begin with the Sentence.—This is the first of these basic principles. In grammar, as in most subjects, an analytic-synthetic method is the rational procedure in teaching, but a cursory examination of most of our elementary books on the subject shows the reverse form of instruction. The noun, the verb, the pronoun, the subject, the predicate, are the topics emphasized in the initial pages. The mastery of these elements prepares the child for the comprehension of the sentence. But logical though this procedure may be, it is hardly psychological. If we are to make grammar rational and necessary in the eyes of the child, we must begin with that part of grammar which is related to the child's needs. The "point of contact" is the sentence. Since the child strives constantly to express thought, the sentence, the unit of thought expression, must be mastered first. It is true that when the child first begins to speak, "he is a word utterer"; but if the word is spoken spontaneously and not as an imitated sound for the edification of the proud parents, it is, in intent, a sentence. "Papa," "hat," "doll," usually symbolize "Take me, papa!" "Give me the hat!" "I want the doll." The accompanying gestures and pantomimes are evidences of the thought which governs these utterances, which are called in psychology "word-sentences."

The application of this simple dictum is obvious. There must be an emphasis on sentence structure before the parts of speech are taught. Sentences in great number should introduce lessons on participles, prepositions, conjunctions, or any specific technical element of grammar. In the course of an analysis of the structure of these sentences and the function of all their elements, the new lesson should be evolved. An illustration of this principle will be found in the lesson on subject and predicate which is outlined in the discussion of the third principle in the teaching of grammar.

Make the Work as Concrete and Practical as Possible.—This is the second guiding suggestion that we must keep in mind. Grammar finds few friends among the children in those classes where it is introduced. The reason is not far to seek. These children find it an unnecessary and arbitrary classification of the speech they think they know. As the grades ad-

THE TEACHING OF GRAMMAR

vance, children like grammar better, for the thoughtful ones now see its influence on speech. The most flagrant waste of time and energy in grammar can be traced to the absence of any intimate relation between the lessons in this subject and those in oral and written composition. There must be such a correlation between these subjects, between the art and the science phase of language, that every grammar lesson begins in the expressional errors of the children. If the rule of agreement is to be taught, select for the children's compositions sentences that violate this law; if the relative pronoun is to be presented, select for their written work sentences that are too simple. Lead them to see how the weak construction: "The poor sailor then stepped into the royal chamber. He was destined to discover a new world for Spain," can be strengthened by turning it into, "The poor sailor, who was destined to discover a new world for Spain, now stepped into the royal chamber." Add instance after instance, and let the children discover that the word *who* in one case, *which* in another, *that* in still another enable one to give the suspense and the strength to the two sentences. Ask the class what the next lesson in grammar ought to be and they will state their own aim, thus motivating the lesson. After the topic is taught, this knowledge acquired in the lesson must be applied in the correction of the past written work. Errors of agreement, like *One of the men were,* can now be changed by the children themselves; simple, isolated sentences are now fused into one suspended sentence, and the practical aspect of grammar is thus emphasized. To neglect this simple principle of motivation is to neglect the final justification for the teaching of grammar.

Shall the Method in Grammar Be Inductive or Deductive?—Teachers frequently ask this question today. To emphasize the disciplinary value of grammar, teachers adopted the long inductive method of discovery. This led to extravagant expenditure of time and very often did not eliminate the drill in the end. To save time and effort, and at the same time guarantee a mastery of the facts, other teachers reverted to the old didactic method, the deductive procedure. The teacher explains the new lesson, the children memorize the necessary information, and proceed with the application. Observation of class teaching seems to indicate that the current method in grammar is deductive rather than inductive. Extremes must be avoided, and one method must not be adopted throughout the school course to the exclusion of the other. Each method has its distinct and legitimate province. In those grades in which formal grammar is introduced the lessons may safely follow an intensely inductive procedure. It is a longer method and is more costly in time, but it is justified by the fact that a permanent foundation is being laid. In this grade the teacher is anxious to give clear and accurate concepts. The method which leads children to the conclusion rather than gives it to them, and which insists that children discover information after studying specific details, is best designed to achieve this end. But in the upper grades the development method is not necessary. Children know the basic facts, hence they can reason by analogy and arrive at new conclusions. Knowing an adjective and an adjective phrase, it becomes unnecessary to learn inductively the adjective clause. In these upper grades the book can be used as a basis; the deductive method, therefore, becomes the more natural one. It is also found that much of the advanced grammar is only an added application or a review of the simpler forms. Thus, the child who knows a substantive phrase and an infinitive, can be spared the tedium of a development lesson on the infinitive as a subject. It must also be remembered that there is much in grammar that is arbitrary; a deductive lesson is therefore more appropriate. No explanation can account for four genders in grammar and only two in life, three cases in English grammar and many more in actual speech. And finally it is evident that a deductive lesson is not synonymous with arbitrary memory drill. There can be as much thought and concentration in the deductive lesson as in the inductive. The special province of each of these modes of procedure can be made clearer by concrete illustrations through appropriate lessons.

Inductive Lesson: Subject and Predicate

Introduction.—The best means of establishing a point of contact between this topic in grammar and the child's experience is to begin with the pupil's errors of sentence structure due to omission of subject or predicate, or both. The following are typical mistakes: *"Hoping to hear soon," "Standing in the doorway," "Received your letter of last Thursday."* A few well-chosen questions will elicit from the children that in these expressions we do not know who hopes or stands in the doorway or received the letter. Proper subjects are then supplied, *I* for the first, *My brother* for the second, and *The teacher* for the third. The first expression then becomes *I hoping to hear soon*. This the children readily change to *I hope to hear soon*. After the same changes are made in the second and the third expressions the teacher announces the aim of the lesson—to learn a mode of testing whether sentences have their necessary parts.

Presentation of the Lesson.—The teacher now calls for a sentence about Columbus telling what he did, another telling what was done to him, and a third, what he was. The following sentences were obtained from a sixth-year class:

Columbus discovered the continent of America.
Columbus was imprisoned on board his ship.
Columbus was a bold navigator.

In the same manner the following series of sentences was elicited from the class:

The sun shines upon the earth.
The sun is hidden by the clouds.
The sun is a large fireball.

The teacher's questions then brought from the children that Columbus is "the person talked about" in the first group of sentences and the sun is "the thing talked about" in the second. The children were also led to conclude that the second part of each sentence in the first group "tells about" Columbus and the second part of each sentence in the second group "tells about" the sun.

The second part of the presentation required the children to substitute some other name or word for *Columbus* or *the sun* in the sentences above. "Columbus was a bold navigator" became

- Captain Drake
- Robinson Crusoe
- Paul Jones
- Magellan

} was a bold navigator.

"The sun is hidden by the clouds" was turned into

- The moon
- The bright star
- The blue sky
- The mountain top

} is hidden by the clouds.

In the same way children were required to retain *Columbus* and *the sun* and "tell other things about them." The results obtained from the class were:

Columbus {
- was a poor Italian lad.
- appeared before the Court of Spain.
- was not easily discouraged.
- did not fear his angry sailors.
}

The sun {
- warms the earth.
- gives us bright days.
- is very far from the earth.
- hurts some people's eyes.
- makes people happy.
}

The teacher then asked, "How many parts has each sentence?" "What does each part do?"

Comparison.—The next step in the development of the concept subject and predicate was a contrast between sentences and phrases or incomplete sentences. The children were led to compare each of the following pairs and tell which expression was a sentence:

To the circus.	William went to the circus.
I hope the day will be bright.	Hoping the day will be bright.
The hungry bird flew into the room.	Into the room.
Received the gift.	The poor lady received the gift.

Generalization.—The teacher then told the class that the part of a sentence that tells "what we talk about" is called *subject,* and that part that tells "what we say of the subject" is called *predicate.* The children were then required to formulate their definitions of these two new terms.

Application.—Many exercises which applied this knowledge were now introduced. Children were required to find the subject and predicate of given sentences; to supply a variety of subjects for a given predicate; to supply many predicates for a set subject; to turn phrases into sentences; to make sentences out of participial constructions; to indicate the sentences in a paragraph in which there were no capitals and no periods. The final form of application consisted in having the children reread their old compositions in their endeavor to change every faulty or incomplete sentence so that it would have both subject and predicate.

THE TEACHING OF GRAMMAR

Deductive Lesson: Infinitives

In contrast with this lesson for a sixth-year class, let us turn to a seventh-year group that must study infinitives.

Preparation.—The children were given a talk on the desirability of variety of expression, with plenty of illustrations to make the point clear. The teacher concluded this short discourse by stating the aim of the lesson, "To learn a new and more attractive form of expressing our ideas."

Presentation.—The children were told to find the chapter on infinitives in their textbook, and their attention was directed to the very first sentence—"An infinitive is a verb form, introduced by to, and used as a noun, adjective, or adverb." After the sentence was read, the children were asked to write a list of verbs on their papers; *go, see, exercise, work, do,* etc., were among those given; each verb was then introduced by *to* and the infinitives *to go, to see, to exercise,* etc., were formed.

To make the concept clearer, a few minutes were spent on such pairs of contrasting sentences as:

Go *to the store. To go to the store* when told is a boy's duty.

Write carefully *to the end. To write carefully to the end* should be our aim,

and the class was led to see clearly the differences between infinitives and prepositional phrases.

The class then turned to the first function of an infinitive, "used as a noun." The children were required to tell the functions of a noun. They reviewed their knowledge of this topic in grammar, and the class formulated the following composite result: "A noun can be used (1) as subject, (2) as object, (3) as predicate noun." The teacher then put on the board:

He likes ———.

He desires ———.

and the children supplied appropriate infinitive forms. They were led to realize that in these sentences the infinitives function as objects. The children then constructed original sentences.

In the same way, the teacher put on the board:

——— *is beneficial for the body.*

——— *pays in the end.*

and the children supplied *"To exercise"* for the first and *"To work faithfully"* for the second. An analysis of the sentences showed that the infinitives were now functioning as subjects. In similar exercises the children verified the fact that infinitives can be used as nouns.

The adjective function of infinitives was taken up in the same manner. *"He is an honorable man"* was changed to *"He is a man to honor."* The syntax of *honorable* and *to honor* was compared, and the children saw clearly that infinitives can perform the office of adjectives.

The third and final important function of the infinitive, the adverb, was taught very easily. The teacher presented, *"He came," "He wanted to see Brutus,"* and asked the children to join these two weak sentences into one strong sentence, using the fewest number of words. After a few trials and failures he obtained *"He came to see Brutus."* An analysis of this simple sentence made the adverbial function of the infinitive phrase, *to see Brutus,* apparent. Original constructions by the children were called for to emphasize this function of infinitives.

The deductive lesson as here outlined, although requiring more than a single period, saved considerable time and labor, and gave, as a result, a conception of infinitives as clear and as convincing as most inductive lessons on this topic. In addition, the class was given a very effective lesson on how to study grammar. It is obvious that to lay down a general law in favor of one method is shortsighted because the method must be determined by conditions obtaining in a given class.

By Avoiding Stereotyped Definitions and Set Formulæ We Are Saved from Another Erroneous Form of Teaching Grammar.—To many, definitions must play an important rôle in grammar which is a subject of classification and systematization. But no matter how essential they may be, we must guard against a parrot-like repetition of scientifically accurate definitions. They should always be the result of the children's own activity and should come at the end of the lesson after each child has seen the function of those elements which he defines. The wording, too, should, in the main, be the child's own; only inaccuracies of expression should be changed by the teacher. Definitions like "A preposition is a word used to show the relation between a noun or a pronoun and some other word—a verb, an adjective, another noun or a pronoun," or "A participle is a word derived from a verb, participating in the properties of a noun or adjective," are set forms that have their place in textbooks but should never be heard coming from children in the classroom, for their scientific precision presupposes a mature mind and a rich knowledge of language on the part of the pupil. Teachers are learning that ability to define is no index of comprehension. Most of the concepts which are vital parts of life and which are perceived with rare clearness are most difficult to define, for the individual lacks the necessary verbal ability. Clear perception of function, not verbal formulation, marks thoroughness of comprehension.

The safest procedure in the matter of definitions is not to demand the memorization of the phraseology but only of the basic and component ideas. These the child should state in his own words. Hence the child should be required to remember that a preposition (1) connects, (2) shows relation; a participle is (1) a verbal, (2) can be used as adjective or noun. In reciting, the child should give, first, an original illustration, then follow this by a statement expressing the ideas memorized. Hence, the child answering the teacher's question, "What is a preposition?" says: "The boy stood *on* the burning deck—*on;* a preposition is a word used to connect and show the relation of deck to stood." In similar manner the child recites the definition of a participle by saying, "*Seeing* the enemy, he ordered a retreat—*seeing;* a participle coming from the verb see, used as an adjective, relating to the subject." If no two children are allowed to give the same illustration, we have a guarantee that such recitations show rational memory of ideas grasped, rather than

THE TEACHING OF GRAMMAR

verbal memory of concepts vaguely comprehended. The recitation of a definition must be a process of rational reconstruction rather than mere verbal reproduction.

The Application Step Is the Final Justification of Grammar and Must Be Accorded the Most Important Place in the Lesson.—Attention to the application of the laws learned in grammar is a means of emphasizing the utilitarian value of the subject and of clarifying the concepts that the child has acquired. The application step is also a means of bringing out the disciplinary value of grammar for, as the type is varied, the child's ingenuity, thought, and concentration are stimulated.

Application of any topic learned is not complete unless the children have had two types of exercises. The first form of application is one of analysis. Let us assume that the first lesson on participles, the present participle, has just been completed. Selections containing present participles are taken up and the children must analyze each sentence, point out the participles and justify their answers by explaining the function of each participle. The second and more important form of application is through synthetic exercises in which children are required to originate context which shows the use of the participle. Lists of verbs are given out and the pupils must now use the present participial form in a sentence. Pairs of simple related sentences are written on the board, and each child must combine each pair into a long, suspended sentence through the use of a present participle. Such synthetic exercises test not the verbal memory of definitions, classifications, names or forms, but measure efficiency in the correct use of language elements.

A further illustration may serve to clinch the point. The adjective and the adverb were taught to a sixth-year class. The method of application by analysis contained exercises which asked: "In the following paragraph, which are adjectives? Which adverbs? Why?" The method of application by synthesis gave the children sentences like, "The swift eagle flew through the air." The child called upon was required to tell the syntax of *swift* and to change it to the opposite form. The pupil's answer was: "*Swift* talks about eagle, therefore it is an adjective. The opposite form is, 'The eagle flew *swiftly* through the air.'" The sentence, "He writes well," was given to another member of the class. She recited: "*Well* tells in what manner he recites, therefore it is an adverb. The opposite is 'He is a good writer.'" A more difficult application by synthesis, suitable for seventh-year work, asks the child to tell which form he would use in the following sentence and why: "He ground the knife sharp or sharply"; "The flower smells sweetly or sweet"; "He looks stern or sternly"; "The food tastes well or good." These synthetic exercises concern themselves with testing the final aim of grammar, *ability to use*. The method of application by analysis is not even a guarantee of comprehension. Children often recognize grammatical forms by accidental endings like *ly* or *ing* and rarely by the perception of their function.

THE TEACHING OF GRAMMAR

Function Should Be Made Focal in All Grammatical Analysis.—This vital suggestion often determines the progress of all future work. It is obvious that no element in language, whether word, or phrase, or clause, has a fixed grammatical classification, for, as the function varies, the classification changes. Children must be taught the absurdity of calling *milk* a noun or *who* a relative pronoun. They must be taught from the very beginning to seek the function that a given element discharges in the sentence. They will soon realize that *milk* may be a noun or a verb. Since function determines grammatical classification, courses of study and textbooks insist that all terms be defined in terms of use. The usual form is therefore, A noun is a word *used* as the name of a person, place, or thing; milk is a noun *because* it is *used* to name a thing.

The suggestion is helpful, but it does not go far enough. Since the function not only determines classification but also lies at the very basis of efficiency of grammar, why not give the function first? Hence, the child should recite, "*Milk* shows action; *therefore* it is a verb." In the sentence, "Who was it who came into the room?" the first *who* asks the question, *therefore* it is an interrogative pronoun; but the second *who* connects the clauses and stands for the person, *therefore* it is a relative pronoun. At first glance the objection may appear petty, but practical experience soon shows how helpful is the use of *therefore* in place of *because,* for the word *therefore* forces the child to determine the function of the element in question. Very often children state the correct function of the word but err in the classification; such pupils show ability to think correctly and consistently, for the incorrect answer is due to faulty memory rather than lack of ability to reason. This form of parsing develops a useful attitude in all advanced work. When the child in his later work meets the sentence, "The Lorelei on the rock sat combing her golden hair," he says, " 'On the rock' tells me about the Lorelei, *therefore* it is an adjective phrase." It has been part of the exasperating experience of all teachers of grammar to have a child give a wrong classification, and when asked for the reason to find him inventing a justification more stupid than his original error merely to seem consistent. Such absurd procedures are guarded against and even undermined when children are taught from their very earliest lessons in grammar to state the function first and then the classification.

Do Not Analyze for the Sake of Analysis.—This principle saves much time and useless effort. Exercises in analysis of sentences give helpful insight into language structure, teach how to apply grammar to derive obscured meaning and train in logical thought.

But not all sentences are worthy of analysis. We should analyze only those sentences which (1) are doubtful of comprehension and hence need analysis, or, (2) present constructions that allow for useful synthetic drills. Thus, in the two sentences, *The snow, falling thickly, blinded the soldiers* and *The snow falling thickly, the soldiers were blinded,* the use of the commas, and the change from the active to the passive voice, give practice in variety of sentence structure.

THE TEACHING OF GRAMMAR

So, too, analysis of sentences like, *One of the soldiers were captured* and *A committee of upper class pupils were appointed monitors*, reveals faulty agreement and affords opportunity for rich language drill.

"False Syntax" Must Be Emphasized, for It Is an Effective Means of Applying the Facts of Grammar.— Many teachers of English and textbook writers are bitter opponents of the traditional exercises in "false syntax," for they hold that these language drills are both unpedagogical and fraught with grave danger. Their argument reduces itself to the oft-quoted dictum that language is learned through imitation; they argue that the child must be surrounded with models of correct speech, which become unconscious sources of suggestion and imitation. But in "false syntax" the method is opposite in spirit and in aim, for the incorrect forms are presented and it becomes a source of either imitation or confusion with correct speech. The protest would be well founded if the facts implied were true. In all "false syntax" we present those errors that the children make in their own speech or that they constantly hear from those about them. These errors are analyzed, the reason for the incorrectness is noted, and the justification for the corrections is given. The very mistakes in English that constantly assail the children's ears are so thoroughly undermined that they are avoided by the pupils. Judging from the position taken by those who protest against "false syntax," one would infer that children either hear only the correct forms or, as would be the case in a foreign language, know neither correct nor incorrect forms. If this were true, "false syntax" would indeed be a gross pedagogical error.

The next question concerns itself with the time when the correction of "false syntax" should be emphasized. In the earlier textbooks of grammar, it was customary to study first the laws of grammar, and then to apply them in the correction of common errors. But the current method is more logical, for it applies every law of grammar to correction of errors directly it is understood. After the child learns that every sentence has a subject and a predicate, his attention should be directed to such errors of incomplete sentences as *"Hoping to hear from you,"* or *"Awaiting your reply,"* or *"Am delighted to hear of your success"*; after the rule of agreement has been learned, correction of such typical mistakes as *"William or John are the guilty person"* should be taken up; a knowledge of the possessive case should lead to the correction of such errors as *childrens', mens'*, etc. To postpone such constructive work means to continue grammar as an arbitrary subject despite the fact that we can interpret it in terms of social need and social value for the child.

Great Care Must Be Exercised in the Organization of Tests.—The nature of examination questions often indicates wrong conceptions of the aims in teaching any subject. All test questions must be designed to test the child's progress along those lines that mark the guiding values of the subject. With this standard of judging test questions, the weakness of the following questions becomes apparent. "What is an interrogative pronoun?", "What is a relative pronoun?", "Give three examples of each," "State the rule for the formation of the possessives in nouns," "Decline the first personal pronoun," are typical of those found in school examinations, and must be condemned, for they test verbal memory, not ability to apply the lessons of grammar to the needs of speech.

Proper test questions in grammar always reveal knowledge of function and ability to apply it to speech correction, for these are the ultimate ends of the subject. In contrast to the questions mentioned, the following show a marked superiority: "Correct the following." "Which form is correct? Why?" "Combine each pair of sentences through the use of a relative pronoun," "Combine them through the use of a participle," "Give sentences using *who* in three different cases," "Expand the following phrases into clauses," "Reduce the clauses in the following sentences into phrases," "Change the number of each noun in the following sentence and indicate the changes that must be made in verbs and pronouns." In answering these questions, neither mere memory of form nor glib recital of textbook definitions will be of service, for they test ability to use grammatical elements in original context.

An eighth-year class was given the following test after a complete study of relative pronouns and relative clauses:

Part I

1. Analyze the following sentences and state the syntax of each clause:

THE TEACHING OF ENGLISH

    (a) The man, whom all the world honors, was once a poor farmer boy.

    (b) The house, which we bought recently, we sold again to the man who called yesterday.

2. Parse all the relative pronouns in the following:
   (a) To him who hath, much shall be given.
   (b) They have rights who dare maintain them.
   (c) Such of his songs as were sung were much applauded.
   (d) I know the man of whom you speak.

3. Expand the adjectives in the following sentences into clauses:
   (a) "A soft answer turneth away wrath."
   (b) My kind friends helped me to obtain an excellent position.
   (c) The past summer has brought me a pleasant friendship.

4. Contract the relative clauses in the following into adjective phrases or adjective words:
   (a) I was expected to accomplish a task that is impossible.
   (b) I do not wish to do work that is unnecessary.
   (c) The man who is blind was injured in the street
   (d) In the tree that had lost its leaves, were three nests.

5. Insert the proper relative pronoun in the following and give reasons for your choice:
   (a) Man is the only animal ——— can talk.
   (b) There are many persons ———, though they be starving, will not beg.
   (c) This is the malt ——— lay in the house ——— Jack built.
   (d) There are many ——— saw him fall.
   (e) He ——— does all ——— he can, does all ——— can be expected.

THE TEACHING OF GRAMMAR

Part II

1. Correct the following, giving reasons for each change:
    (a) Whom did you think that it was?
    (b) I saw the person who you described.
    (c) This is the man which I saw.
2. Combine the following pairs of sentences through the use of a relative pronoun and show why the single sentence is better:
    (a) The poor Italian lad stood before the queen. He was destined to discover a new world.
    (b) Lafayette was a French nobleman. He came to America to help Washington.
3. Use *who* or its forms as relatives in three different sentences showing three different cases. Do the same with *which*.
4. Rewrite the following sentences, selecting the form you think correct:
    (a) The man (who, whom) I took to be your brother, has enlisted in the army.
    (b) Is he the man (who, whom) I am supposed to resemble?
    (c) I suggested those (who, whom) should be invited.

An analysis of this test shows at once that all questions test thoroughness of comprehension and ability at application. Part I, given one day, contains questions that follow type forms and that can therefore be answered by any child who is attentive and makes an honest effort at mastering his class work. Part II, given the succeeding day, emphasizes versatility in the use of relative forms. The exercises are more difficult in character and require originality and deeper insight into grammatical functions. The pupil who secures a satisfactory rating in such a test gives evidence of comprehension and ability to apply his knowledge in his attempts at self-correction.

But the teacher must not suppose that a test of such a practical nature cannot be given in the lower grades where only elementary facts are taught. The following is a reproduction of an examination given to a fourth-year class in one of our city schools:

Grade 4B

1. Change these to mean more than **one**:
    (a) The boy is tired.
    (b) That man works hard.
    (c) The dish is broken.
    (d) The calf is gentle.
    (e) The city is large.
2. Underline the subject and the predicate in the following:
    (a) Nathan Hale was hanged.
    (b) The spider spins his web.
    (c) Near the stream stood a house.
    (d) Down flew the eagle.
    (e) The Dutch traded with the Indians.
3. Put the right word in the blank space:
    (do) I have ——— my lessons.
    (is) There ——— two apples.
    (break) The pencil is ———.
    (come) Yesterday he ——— to see me.
    (run) He has ——— his last race.
4. Rewrite the following sentences changing the underlined words to the singular or plural:
    (a) The mouse ate the cheese.
    (b) The oxen drew the plow across the field.
    (c) The children went home.

THE VALUES OF FORMAL GRAMMAR

    (d) John took the box.
    (e) The knife is sharp.
5. If you have studied a stanza about a flower or a tree, write it; if not, write any stanza of poetry studied this term.
6. Write correctly:
    (a) I seen your brother yesterday.
    (b) Jack done it.
    (c) You was there.
    (d) I broke me pencil.
    (e) I stood up early.
7. Write five sentences about the flag flying above our school. Make the sentences tell:
    (a) What things do. (Two sentences.)
    (b) What is done to things.
    (c) What things are.
    (d) What the quality of things is.
8. Underline subjects and predicates in the following sentences—put a single line for subject, double line for predicate:
    (a) Is Jack coming?
    (b) Down came the snow.
    (c) The boy won the medal.
    (d) The games were fine.
    (e) Ex-President Roosevelt was in England.
9. Dictate:
    "We're going to have a new maple tree in the park," said Sam to his teacher.
    "How do you know?" said the teacher.
    "Well," replied the boy, "I stuck a seed in the ground."
   Points covered:
    (a) Quotation marks, (b) capitals, (c) punctuation, (d) spelling, (e) paragraph.
10. Rewrite the following, putting in abbreviations wherever possible:

Mary went to the store to buy a pound of tea, two dozen eggs, a peck of onions, a pint of cream, and an ounce of pepper.

Proper Reviews Are Essential for Successful Work in Grammar.—Grammar makes an unusual demand on retentive power because of its extensive subject-matter, rich in terminology, laws, and classifications. To make all this necessary information permanent, frequent reviews are essential. But there is no need of setting aside definite periods given over exclusively to set reviews on a limited portion of the subject. The most successful reviews can be incidental in the course of ordinary application exercises that are part of daily teaching. Let us illustrate such a review. In a seventh-year class, the sentence for analysis was taken from Lincoln's Gettysburg Address, "We have come to dedicate a portion of that field as a resting-place for those who here gave their lives that that nation might live." Among the questions were the following:

1. Analyze the sentence and give the syntax of each clause.
2. What is there the same in the use of *to dedicate* and *that that nation might live?*
3. Change the phrase to a clause and the clause to a phrase.
4. What is the difference between the two words *that?*
5. How would that difference help you in correct reading?
6. What is the word *those?* Apply the test and prove that you are right.
7. The word *lives* is what part of speech? Change it to a verb without changing its spelling.

Such a spirited lesson demands keen thought and insures a good review, for old knowledge is called up incidentally and is seen from a new aspect. A set review lesson on a definite topic in grammar often lacks the effectiveness of the informal review.

The Textbook Must Be Used Frequently in the Teaching of Grammar.—Proper methods of teaching in grammar give the textbook a prominent place. It must be used for purposes of comparison and verification in all inductive lessons. At the end of the lesson on subject and predicate, it was shown that the children are led to formulate their own definitions. The children's result should be compared with the definition in the book and the elements in the two statements should be noted carefully. The teacher must elicit from the class the reason for the discrepancy, if any exists, and then lead them to decide whether the definition in the book, or their own, is worthy of memorization. Often the statement in the book is voted too difficult or too long and it must give way to the simpler formulation by the class.

A second invaluable aid rendered by the book is in the application step. A good textbook in grammar must be replete with a host of well-graded and varied exercises which give the children drill in the use of the facts that were taught and thus relieve the teacher of the burden of seeking satisfactory forms of application. This is the most important single factor which determines the value of a textbook in grammar in elementary schools. A third use of the book is to give a logically arranged summary of the facts taught in the class and thus make unnecessary the keeping of notes by children in anticipation of tests. And, finally, a good textbook in grammar gives suitable text for deductive lessons and thus serves as a means of teaching children how to study the subject. In the lesson on *infinitives,* the reader will find an illustration and an amplification of this function of the book. In the upper grades the emphasis must shift from *the teaching of grammar* to *teaching how to study grammar.* In discharging this function, the textbook is of greatest service.

Careful Gradation Is a Potent Factor in Removing Difficulties of Comprehension in Grammar.—In grammar, as in arithmetic, undue difficulties are introduced in the course of teaching, by a lack of careful gradation. Teachers take the objective view of a topic and plan it by subdividing it into its logical parts, teaching them in successive periods. It is absolutely essential that the teacher take the child's place, imagine himself on the child's plane of ignorance of the basic facts of grammar, and then try to foresee the successive difficulties that will beset the path of the immature mind as the entire topic is unfolded. Failure to do this, whether due to lack of preparation or of sympathetic insight, undermines successful teaching, for a new difficulty is introduced before a preceding one is solved and cumulative confusion results. An analysis of the sequence of topics in the following lessons will give a conception of the kind of gradation often absolutely necessary in grammar.

THE TEACHING OF GRAMMAR

Topic: Predicate Adjective and Predicate Noun or Pronoun

1. Exercises in which constructions like *The happy birds, The beautiful flowers, The green grass,* etc., are changed to *The birds are happy, The flowers are beautiful, The grass is green.* Repeat, changing *The French people are artistic, The Japanese are shrewd,* etc., to *The artistic French people, The shrewd Japanese.*

Elicit: *happy, beautiful, green, artistic, shrewd,* as used in the full sentences are (a) adjectives and (b) in the predicate, hence (c) called predicate adjectives.

2. Pick out predicate adjectives in the following and apply the test to each:
   The weather is mild—*mild*—The *mild* weather.
3. Complete the following by using predicate adjectives to make complete sentences:
   The Indians ———— ————.
   Rabbits ———— ————.

Care must be taken not to supply the verbs in this form of drill for then most children answer correctly though they may not understand the function of the predicate adjective.

4. Which of the following are objects and which predicate adjectives? I saw John. He is studious. He studies grammar. Grammar is useful, etc.
5. Enriched conception, the predicate noun taught through the idea of identity by a method similar to that used for the predicate adjective. The test: can subject and predicate noun be interchanged?
6. Exercises like those under 2, 3, 4, adapted to predicate noun.
7. The introduction of the pronoun.
8. Exercise like 2, 3, 4, adapted to the pronoun.
9. Compound predicate adjectives and nouns.
   He is keen, conscientious and just. He is commander of the army and leader of the people.

10. False syntax. Exercises in which errors like *It is me, It was her*, etc., are corrected.

11. Distinction between adjective and adverb in following constructions: *The flowers smell sweet, The child writes well,* etc. This is the most advanced phase of the topic and must be postponed for work in later grades. The teacher who tries to save time in the average class by omitting some steps in this gradation invariably loses time and effort for a confusion is introduced which almost defies later attempts at clarification.

All Grammatical Forms and Functions Must Be Taught in the Same Association in Which They Will Be Used in Natural Speech.—The bulk of the subject-matter of grammar deals with modification of important parts of speech. In nouns and pronouns, much time is taken up in teaching person, number, gender and case; in adjectives and adverbs, comparisons with the three degrees of positive, comparative, and superlative, in regular and irregular forms; in verbs, person, number, mood, tense, and voice. The teaching problems that arise in these modifications are simple enough, for the difficulties involved can be solved readily by the application of the principles discussed in this chapter.

In teaching the forms and the functions that constitute the modifications of English grammar, it is general to find teachers presenting them in lists devoid of all natural context. But mastery of forms without content does not develop ability to use these forms in content. Children recite rules for the formation of plurals or of opposite genders until every detail is known beyond doubt. In classes, one hears the monotonous babble of *child, children; ox, oxen; sheep, sheep; scissors, scissors; actor, actress; gander, goose; hero, heroine;* etc. But despite this glib recital in list form, one finds the compositions of these children replete with "She was an *actor*," "Five *oxes* pulled the wagon," "In this picture I see many *sheeps*." Such results after tedious drills in lists come with unfailing regularity, for the language forms were not taught in those associations in which they will be used later in life. The changing forms of gender and number must be taught in context, the teacher giving one form and the children the opposite one in a sentence, e. g.:

Teacher	*Pupil*
I	*We* all intend to study.
oxen	An *ox* is a strong animal.
actor	She is a great *actress*.

Such recitations and drills take longer than those in list forms, but they produce gratifying results in oral and written composition.

In teaching case forms, the teacher's problem is simplified by beginning with a context that shows the child clearly that this new phase of grammar is essential. "Case" must therefore be taught through pronouns, for, aside from the possessive form, it plays no important rôle in nouns. In teaching cases of pronouns, the law which insists on natural context must be obeyed rigidly. To make children repeat incessantly *I, my* or *mine, me, we, our* or *ours, us,* is no guarantee that they will use these forms correctly.

The declension of the first personal pronoun should take the following form:

I have a book.	*We* have many books.
The book is *mine*.	They are *ours*.
It is *my* book.	They are *our* books.
Give the book to *me*.	Give the books to *us*.

A later drill should require children to read the following sentences and insert the correct form of the first personal pronoun:

My brother, James, and .... took a walk.

We passed .... school.

Jane Smith was just coming out. She saw ..., but did not know it was ....

The same procedure applies to drills on positive, comparative, and superlative degrees of adjectives and adverbs and to all modifications of verbs. The principal parts of commonly used irregular verbs form one of the most important topics in teaching verbs, because they are constantly misused by children. One hears with disturbing frequency, "We *brang* our lunch"; "Yesterday we *come* into the class"; "We *done* our lesson in a book that *costed* five cents"; "I *hurted* myself." Realizing the need of vigorous effort in improving this type of error, teachers subject the principal parts of verbs to incessant drill in tabular form. The din of *go, went, going, gone; come, came, coming, come; hurt, hurt, hurting, hurt;* etc., is heard through transoms and open doors, but when compositions of the succeeding weeks are examined, it becomes manifest, again, that recitation of grammatical forms in isolated lists is a pedagogical practice made reverent by age rather than by results. Let the teacher insist on having the parts of the verbs in context. The child's successful recitation of "I *come* into this room every morning; yesterday I *came* into the room; you *are coming* into the room now; the boy *has come* into the room to-day," gives the teacher good cause to hope that part of the grammatical forms and functions may pass over into the expressional stock of her children.

Summary: Place of Grammar in the Elementary Curriculum.—We saw in the course of this discussion that grammar has been attacked most vigorously by many progressive teachers, and the indictments found against it are just. But most of the objections are remedial, for they are due not to the inherent limitations of grammar as an elementary school subject, but rather to poorly organized courses of study and faulty methods of teaching. We must look, therefore, to a liberal reduction in the requirements of courses in formal grammar, to a simplification and standardization of its terminology, and to the introduction of methods of teaching which emphasize the function rather than the form. Then, and only then, will grammar come into its own in the pedagogical sphere of elementary education.

SUGGESTED READING

CARPENTER, BAKER and SCOTT. The Teaching of English, pp. 144-152. Longmans, Green & Co.

CHARTERS, W. W. Diagnostic Language and Grammar Test. Public School Publishing Co., Bloomington, Ill.

CHUBB, P. The Teaching of English, chap. XII. The Macmillan Co.

GOLDWASSER, I. E. Method and Methods in the Teaching of English, chaps. XXIII, XXV. D. C. Heath & Co.

HOSIC, JAMES F. The Elementary Course in English, pp. 31-34. University of Chicago Press.

HOYT, F. S. Studies in the Teaching of English Grammar. *Teachers' College Record,* Nov., 1906.

LEONARD, MARY H. Grammar and Its Reasons. A. S. Barnes & Co.

O'SHEA, M. V. Linguistic Development and Education, chaps. III-V.

Report of Committee of Fifteen, on Teaching of Grammar.

WILSON, G. M. Language Error Test. World Book Co., Yonkers, N. Y.

See also texts suggested in Chapter VIII by Bolenius; Driggs; Kirchwey and Pearson; Klapper and London; Simons, Orr and Given; Wohlfarth and Mahoney.

INDEX

Abuses in teaching grammar, 305-308

Aids in memorization, 302

Analysis in grammar, 334

Analytic applications in grammar, 331

Anderson, W. N., 238, 269

Applications of grammar, 331

Argumentation, 106-108

Ashbaugh, E. J., 263, 269

Association by meaning for spelling, 241

Ayres, L. P., 237, 269

Ayres Spelling Scale, 262, 264, 269

Ballou Composition Scale, 189-190

Biographical narratives, 165

Bolenius, E. M., 43, 172

Breed and Frostic Composition Scale, 190-199

Briggs, T. H., 293

Buckingham Spelling Scale, 262, 264, 269

Carpenter, Baker and Scott, 9, 43, 172, 350

Causes of misspelling, 242-243

Chancellor, W. E., 238

Charters, W. W., 315, 350

Chubb, P., 43, 172, 244, 350

Class correction of composition, 136; *see also* Correction

Class journal, 144

Classification of composition scales, 220

Climax, how to write, 108-109

Committee of Fifteen, Report of, 350

Common difficulties in spelling, 241

Composition defined, 1

Composition and reading, 281

Composition scales, how to use them, 221-223; evaluation of, 223-231; enumeration and description, 181-221; need for, 174-181

Composition kept as cumulative product, 138

Content vs. formal correction, 138

Contextual method, in grammar, 319, 346-349; in teaching new words, 274; in spelling, 247, 257

Conversation, 12

Cook and O'Shea, 238, 270

Correct speech through grammar, 309

Correction of composition, 129-140

Correction of dictation exercises, 290-291

Correction of typical errors, 32-36

Correlation of grammar and composition, 306

Correlations in composition, 55-58

Correlations in spelling, 235

Courtis, S. A., 270

Cultural values of grammar, 313

351

INDEX

Debate, 145, 156; see also Argumentation

Deductive teaching of grammar, 322, 327-329; of new words, 273

Definitions, in grammar, 329; of new words, 278

Demons in spelling, 239-240

Description, 110, 149-152

Diagnostic scoring of compositions, 176, 184, 200, 227

Dialogue, 156-160, 164; see also Conversation and Dramatization

Diaries as compositions, 165

Dictation, 285-293

Dictionary, 275, 281, 283-284

Direct source in composition, 47-54

Disciplinary values of composition, 3; of grammar, 310-312

Dramatization, 15, 18, 274; see also Dialogue

Driggs, H. L., 172

Drills, in language, 26-32; on new words, 276; on outlines, 75-78; in spelling, 251, 252-254; see also Habit

Ear training, 286

Ethical values of poetry, 294-295

Etymological analysis of words, 275, 281

Exposition, 152-156

Expressional vs. formal English, 232

Expressional vs. interpretational vocabulary, 234

Fables, imitation of, 18, 161

False syntax, 335

Formal language drills, 23-24

Formal vs. expressional composition, 285; see also Expressional composition and Self-expression

Formalism, 20

Functional grammar, 333

Games, in language forms, 36; in spelling, 254

General merit in composition, 184-185

General subjects, dangers of, 85-86

Goldwasser, I. E., 172, 293, 303, 350

Gradation, of dictation exercises, 283; of dictionary exercises, 287; of grammar, 344-346; of spelling, 239

Grammar, 305-349

Grammar correlated with composition, 90

Grammar and literary appreciation, 312

Group teaching in composition, 89

Group spelling, 241-242

Habits developed, in composition, 8; by outlines, 82-84; in spelling, 233

Habitual use of new words, 276

Haliburton and Smith, 304

Harvard-Newton Composition Scale, 189-190

Hillegas, M. B., 181-185

Homonyms, 259

Horn, E., 270

Hosic, James F., 9, 43, 172, 304, 350

Hoyt, F. S., 312-313, 350

Hudelson Composition Scale, 212-217

Humor, 18

352

INDEX

Imitation, 295; as a principle of method, 93, 114

Incidental teaching of spelling, 244

Increasing vocabulary, 280-284

Individual errors corrected, 134

Individual spelling list, 248-249

Inductive teaching of grammar, 322-326; of new words, 274

Intelligence and language, 284

Inventive compositions, 156-165

Jones, W. F., 283, 270

Kingsley, Charles, 298

Kirkpatrick, E. A., 172

Lack of standardized judgment in composition, 174, 224

Language and intelligence, 284

Language errors, 315

Leonard, Mary H., 350

Leonard, S. A., 9, 173

Letters, 141-144, 168, 202-212

Lewis Composition Scales, 201

Library, 281

Limitations, of organization, 71; of expression, 88

Literary appreciation and grammar, 312

McCall, W. A., 267

McMurry, C. A., 173

Mahoney, J. J., 304

Maximal Composition Scale, 217

Measurement of composition ability, 174

Media of presenting spelling, 244

Memorization, and recitation, 24, 282, 294-304; values of, 294; selection of text for, 295; motivation of, 296; methods in, 297; aids in, 302; recitation, 302

Method, in conversation lessons, 13-16; in dictation, 288; in teaching grammar, 319-349; in language lesson, 25; in memorizing, 297-302; in spelling, 250-260

Minimum course in language, 25-32

Models in composition, 92-124; governing principle, 92; how to select, 93-101; how to teach, 101-113; degrees of imitation, 113-114; precede or follow pupil expression, 114-116; how prevent repressive influence, 116-124

Monroe Spelling Scale, 263-270

Morrison-McCall Spelling Scale, 267-268

Motivating composition, 141-169

Motivation, 96; *see also* Subjects for Composition; in grammar, 320; in letter writing, 141, 143; in memorization, 296; in recitation of memory gems, 302

Narration, 108, 147-149

Nifenecker, E. A., 270

Norms in composition, 228-230

Objective method with new words, 273

Objectives in memorization, 294-295; *see also* Values

Objects of dictation, 285-286

Objects in teaching spelling, 233-234

Oral composition, 65-70; in primary grades, 10-22

Oral composition scale, 221

Organization, in composition, 71-85; lack of, 71-72; taught

INDEX

by outlining, 72-82; drills on outlines, 75-80; cautions in outlining, 78-79; habits inculcated through outlines, 82-84; through pictures, 84; through specific subjects, 85; through other means, 86-87; aids in self-expression, 90

O'Shea, M. V., 43, 90, 238, 255, 270, 350

Outlines, 72-82, 90; as aids in study, 86

Parker, S. C., 9, 270

Pearson and Kirchwey, 43, 173

Penmanship, 127-128, 286

Personal judgment in measurement, 174-175

Personification in composition, 162-165; *see also* Dramatization

Phonetic grouping in spelling, 241

Pictures in language teaching, 36; as aids in organizing data, 84-85

Poetry in composition, 17

Preliminary tests in spelling, 242

Preparatory period in composition, 46

Preparatory values of grammar, 314

Problems, in composition teaching, 6; in primary composition, 10-11

Progressive imitation, 113-114

Projects, in composition, 168-171; in spelling, 260-261

Pronunciation in relation to spelling, 250

Pupil correction of composition, 134-135

Pupil spelling book, 258

Qualities of effective composition subjects, 47, 54-59

Rambling in composition, **71-72**

Rapeer, L. W., 9

Reading circles, 281

Reading and composition, 281

Recitation of memorized selections, 282, 302

Refinements in formal grammar, 307

Repression, 38

Reproduction lessons, 12-20

Reviews in grammar, 342

Rewriting dictation lessons, 291

Rewriting of compositions, 139

Rice, J. M., 270

Riddles in oral composition, 17

Rules of spelling, 259

Savitz, Bates and Starry, 68, 173

Scales, in composition, 174-231; in language, 314-318; in punctuation, 293; in spelling, 262-269

Scientific study of language needs, 315-318

Selection, of composition models, 93-101; of dictation material, 286-287; of memory gems, 295; of new words, 272; of spelling words, 234-239

Self-confidence, 295; *see also* Self-expression

Self-correction, in composition, 134-135, 286; in dictation, 290-291; through grammar, 310; in spelling, 233

Self-expression, and the composition models, 116-124; and outlines, 81

Sentence sense, 27-32, 319

Simons, Orr, and Given, 173

INDEX

Social participation and language growth, 282

Sources of spelling words, 236

Spalding, F. E., 270

Speech and native endowment, 38

Speech training, 295

Spelling, 232-269, 286; teaching vs. testing, 232; objects of teaching, 233; selection of words, 234; source of words, 236; standard spelling lists, 237; grading, 239; grouping of words, 241; preliminary testing, 242; media of presenting words, 244; individual vs. class lists, 249; methods of teaching, 250-260; scales for measuring, 262-269

Spelling books, 237, 245, 261

Spelling vocabulary, 238

Standard spelling lists, 237-239

Starch, Daniel, 293

Study of spelling, 256-257

Study of grammar, 327-329

Subjects suitable for composition, 12, 16-17, 47-54, 69, 142, 168

Suzzallo, H., 270

Syllabication and spelling, 251

Synonyms, 104, 117, 259, 272, 280; *see also* Variation method

Synthetic applications in grammar, 331

Taylor, J. S., 173

Teacher achievement measured in composition, 230

Teacher correction of composition, 137

Teacher-made spelling lists, 246

Terminology in grammar, 308

Testing words for spelling, 235

Tests, in grammar, 336-341; in spelling, 257; *see also* Scales

Textbook, in grammar, 343; in spelling, 237, 245, 261

Thinking in composition, 74; *see also* Disciplinary values

Thorndike Extension Composition Scale, 185-186

Thought value, 3; *see also* Disciplinary values

"Three Fishers, The," 298

Tidyman, W. F., 238, 270

Trabue Composition Scale, 186-189

Transition to written composition, 41

Typical Composition Scale, 217

Typical errors corrected, 129-134

Unprepared dictation, 292

Values of formal grammar, 305-318; *see also* Objects and Objectives

Van Wagenen Composition Scale, 200

Variation Method, 118

Variety, of introductions, 67-69, 81-82; of endings, 81-82; of organization, 67-70, 80, 79-82, 116; of composition subjects, 67, 120, 146-169

Viewpoints changed in composition subjects, 67

Vocabulary, 234-235, 271-284, 294

Willing Composition Scale, 199

Wilson, G. M., 316-317, 350

Wohlfarth and Mahoney, 173

Written composition, in primary grades, 40; in upper grades, 125-129

Young and Memmott, 173

F 2407